John Wanamaker

Living Hymns

for use in the Sabbath school, Christian Endeavor meetings, the church and home

John Wanamaker

Living Hymns

for use in the Sabbath school, Christian Endeavor meetings, the church and home

ISBN/EAN: 9783337089849

Printed in Europe, USA, Canada, Australia, Japan

Cover: Foto ©Lupo / pixelio.de

More available books at **www.hansebooks.com**

FOR USE IN

The Sabbath School,
Christian Endeavor Meetings,
The Church and Home.

COMPILED BY

JOHN WANAMAKER,

ASSISTED BY

JOHN R. SWENEY, Mus. Doc.

Philadelphia: JOHN J. HOOD, 1024 Arch St.

PREFACE.

HUNDREDS of letters and personal inquiries come to us asking, "What hymns do you use in your Sunday-schools and night meetings?" *This book is the answer.*

To the good old hymns of our mothers we add some of the newer songs that have been blest. With ministers, superintendents and teachers it is a burning question, Which of our sermons, books—hymns and helpers—is it that God blesses? When we have made this discovery it is wise to take heed to it. But one thought has led us in making this compilation, to wit, to get together as many as possible of the hymns that have been marked, in a long course of varied work, as used of God. We would like to have included other good hymns scattered through many books, here one and there another, but the right to use them was denied us for love or money. We obtained all we could, and we are informed that in no other one book can so many of the best hymns be found for such work as ours.

The LIVING HYMNS are good hymns to live by. We expect the scholars to buy them, bring them to every meeting, and use them at home and in Church. This is all the singing book we shall need for a life-time.

Jno. Wanamaker
J. Wilbur Chapman
J. R. Miller

PUBLISHER'S NOTICE.

TO PRINT, for sale or otherwise, any copyright hymn of this collection, unless written permission shall have been obtained, is an infringement of copyright.

Seeking, Calling, Knocking.

C. Murray.
Arthur J. Smith.

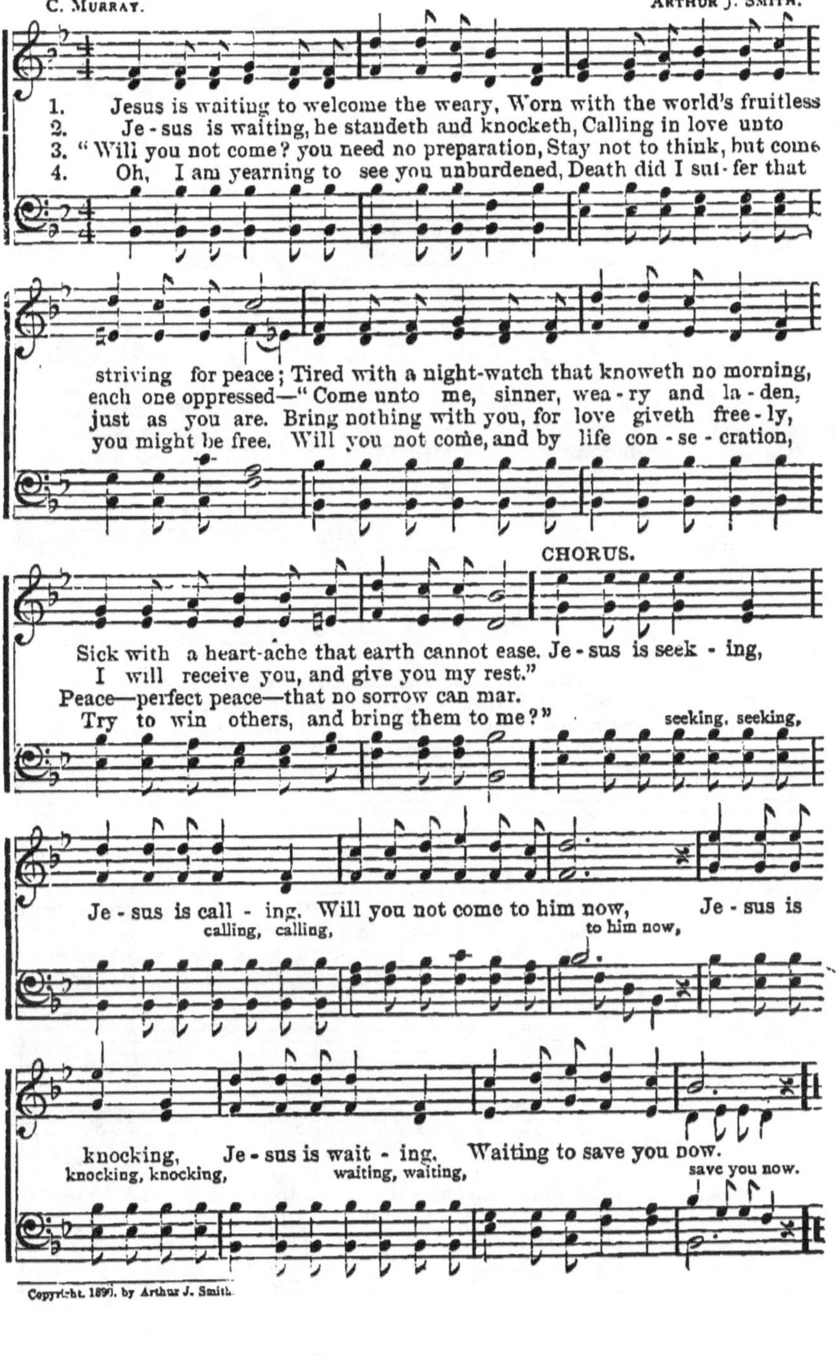

1. Jesus is waiting to welcome the weary, Worn with the world's fruitless striving for peace; Tired with a night-watch that knoweth no morning, Sick with a heart-ache that earth cannot ease.
2. Jesus is waiting, he standeth and knocketh, Calling in love unto each one oppressed—"Come unto me, sinner, weary and laden, I will receive you, and give you my rest."
3. "Will you not come? you need no preparation, Stay not to think, but come just as you are. Bring nothing with you, for love giveth freely, Peace—perfect peace—that no sorrow can mar.
4. Oh, I am yearning to see you unburdened, Death did I suffer that you might be free. Will you not come, and by life consecration, Try to win others, and bring them to me?"

CHORUS.

Jesus is seeking, seeking, Jesus is calling, calling, Will you not come to him now, to him now, Jesus is knocking, knocking, Jesus is waiting, waiting, Waiting to save you now, save you now.

Copyright, 1899, by Arthur J. Smith.

Marching On. 11

JENNIE GARNETT. WM. J. KIRKPATRICK.

1. With our col-ors waving bright in the blaze of gos-pel light We are marshall'd on the world's great field; great field; We are ready for the strife and the bat-tle work of life, Ev-er trusting in the Lord our shield.
2. Oft the tempter we shall meet, but we will not fear de-feat, Though his arrows at our ranks may fly; may fly; Thro' a Saviour's mighty love more than conquerors we shall prove, Shouting, Glo-ry be to God on high.
3. We have gird-ed on the sword and the ar-mor of the Lord, We have ta-ken up the cross he bore; he bore; Oh, the trophies we shall win, oh, the vic-tory o-ver sin, When the bat-tle and the strife are o'er!
4. Soon we'll reach the pearly gate, where the blessed army wait, Soon their welcome, welcome song may ring; may ring; When we lay our armor down and re-ceive a star-ry crown, Shouting, Glo-ry be to God our King.

CHORUS.

Glo-ry to God! we are marching, marching on, Marching to a home above;
Glo-ry to God! we are marching, marching on, Happy in a Saviour's love.

Copyright, 1884, by JOHN J. HOOD.

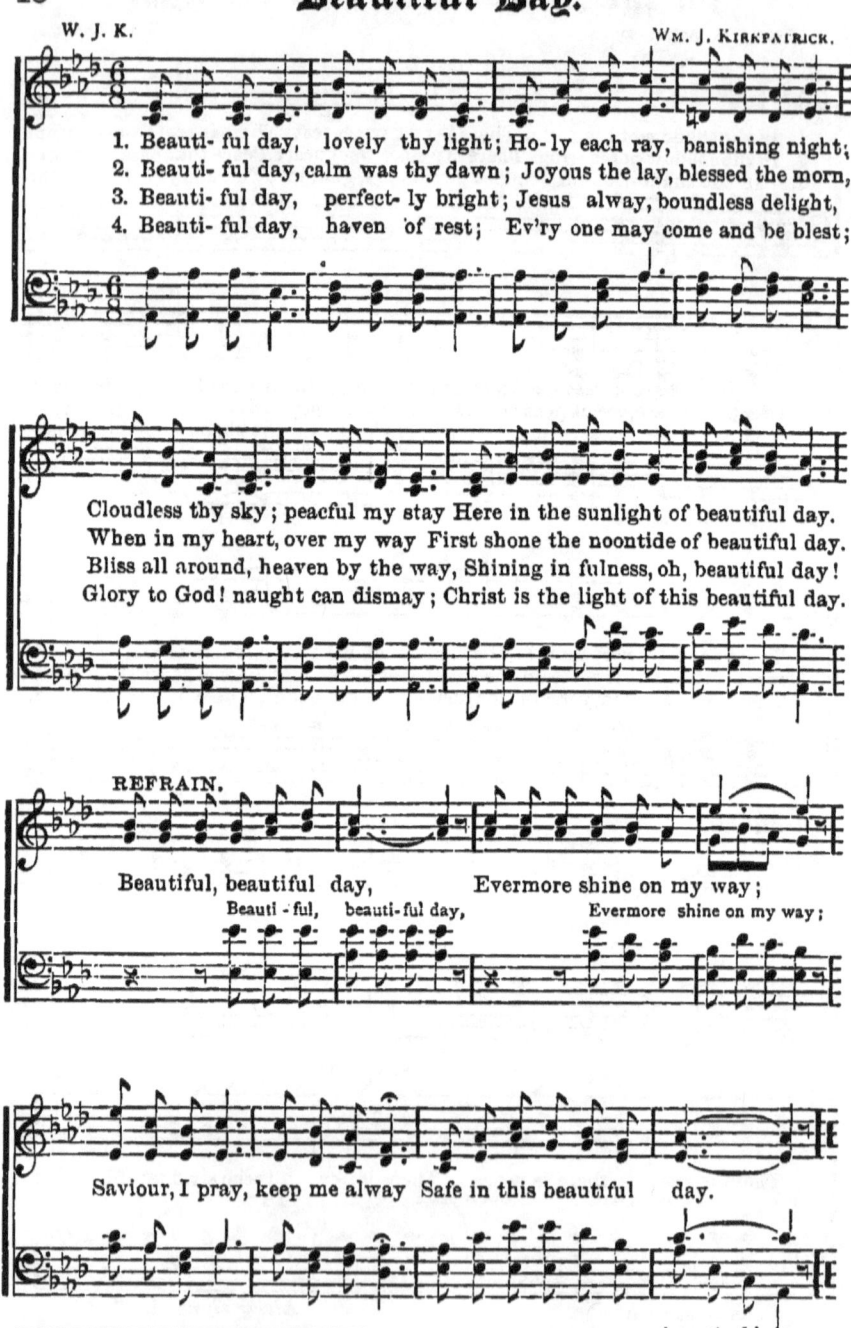

In the Morning.

LIZZIE EDWARDS. JNO. R. SWENEY.

1. We are pilgrims looking home, Sad and weary oft we roam, But we
2. O these tender broken ties, How they dim our aching eyes, But like
3. When our fettered souls are free, Far beyond the narrow sea, And we
4. Thro' our pilgrim journey here, Tho' the night is sometimes drear, Let us

know 'twill all be well in the morning; When, our anchor firmly cast, Ev'ry
jewels they will shine in the morning; When our victor palms we bear, And our
hear the Saviour's voice in the morning; When our golden sheaves we bring To the
watch and persevere till the morning; Then our highest tribute raise For the

storm-y wave is past, And we gather safe at last in the morn-ing.
robes immor-tal wear, We shall know each other there, in the morn-ing.
feet of Christ our King, What a chorus we shall sing in the morn-ing.
love that crowns our days, And to Jesus give the praise in the morn-ing.

D. S.—sun-ny region bright, When we hail the blessed light of the morn-ing.

CHORUS.

When we all meet a-gain in the morn-ing, On the sweet blooming
hills in the morn-ing; Nev-ermore to say good night In that

Copyright, 1884, by JOHN J. HOOD.

In the Book of Life.

Lizzie Edwards. **Wm. J. Kirkpatrick.**

1. In thy book, where glory bright Shines with never-fading light,
2. In the book, whose pages tell Who have tried to serve thee well,
3. In the book, where thou dost keep Record still of years that sleep,
4. O my Saviour, thou canst show What I long so much to know:

Where thy saved thou wilt re-cord, Write my name, my name, O Lord.
O'er my name let mer-cy trace Child of God, redeemed by grace.
Let my name be writ-ten down Heir to life's im-mor-tal crown.
Let my faith be-hold and see That my life is hid with thee.

CHORUS.

Write my name in the book of life, Lamb of God, write it there;
Where thy saved thou wilt re-cord Write my name, my name, O Lord.

Copyright, 1886, by John J. Hood.

At the Cross.

I. WATTS. "Look unto me, and be ye saved,"—Isa. xlv. 22. R. E. HUDSON.

1. A-las! and did my Saviour bleed, And did my Sovereign die?
2. Was it for crimes that I have done, He groaned upon the tree?
3. But drops of grief can ne'er re-pay The debt of love I owe;

Would he devote that sa-cred head For such a worm as I?
A-mazing pit-y, grace unknown, And love beyond de-gree!
Here, Lord, I give my-self a-way, 'Tis all that I can do!

CHORUS.

At the cross, at the cross, where I first saw the light and the burden of my heart rolled a-way, rolled away, It was there by faith I received my sight, And now I am happy all the day.

Copyright, 1885 by R. E. Hudson.

Making Melody.—CONCLUDED. 25

Repeat pp.

I will sing, I will sing, Making melo - dy un - to the Lord.

Jesus, I come to Thee.

FANNY J. CROSBY.   WM. J. KIRKPATRICK.

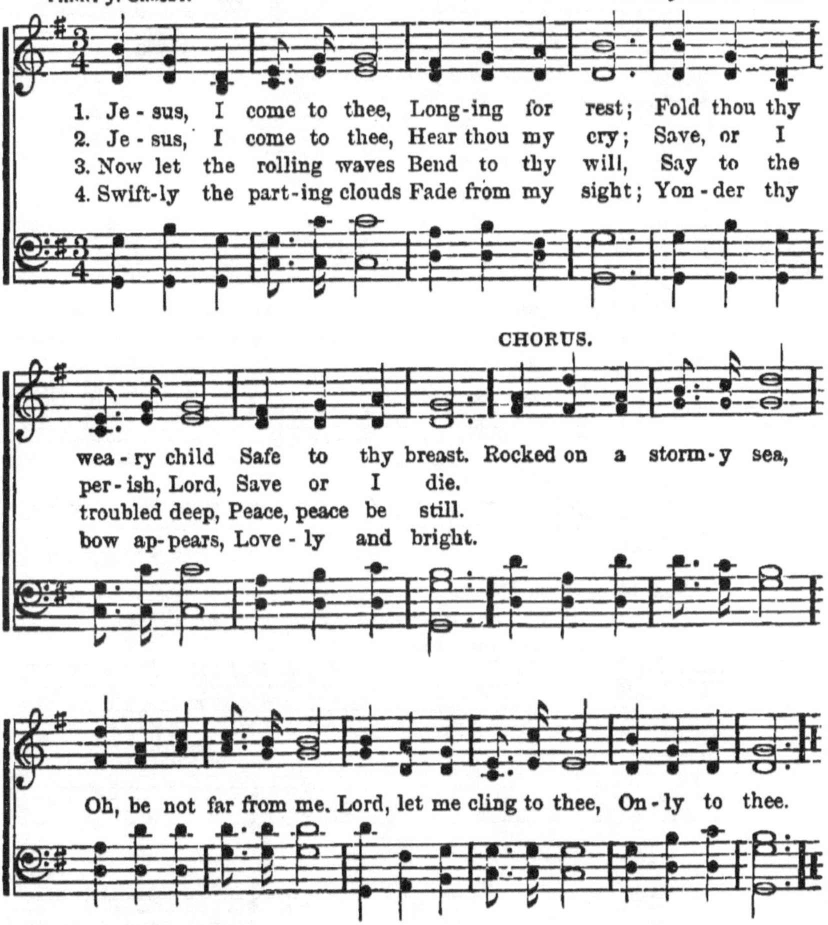

1. Je - sus, I come to thee, Long-ing for rest; Fold thou thy
2. Je - sus, I come to thee, Hear thou my cry; Save, or I
3. Now let the rolling waves Bend to thy will, Say to the
4. Swift-ly the part-ing clouds Fade from my sight; Yon - der thy

CHORUS.

wea - ry child Safe to thy breast. Rocked on a storm-y sea,
per - ish, Lord, Save or I die.
troubled deep, Peace, peace be still.
bow ap-pears, Love - ly and bright.

Oh, be not far from me, Lord, let me cling to thee, On - ly to thee.

Copyright, 1894, by JOHN J. HOOD.

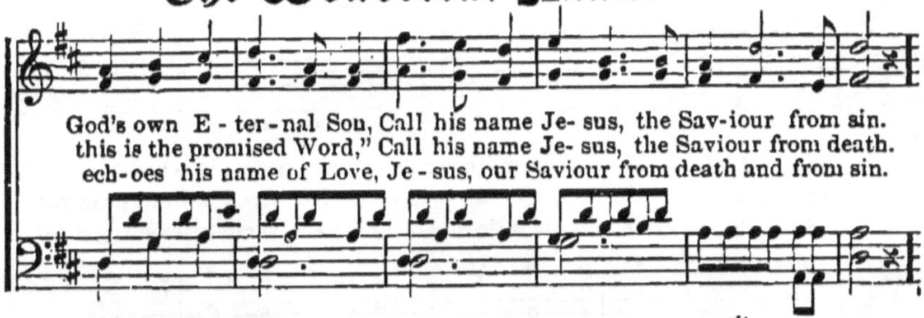

The Wonderful Name.—CONCLUDED.

God's own E-ter-nal Son, Call his name Je-sus, the Sav-iour from sin.
this is the promised Word," Call his name Je-sus, the Saviour from death.
ech-oes his name of Love, Je-sus, our Saviour from death and from sin.

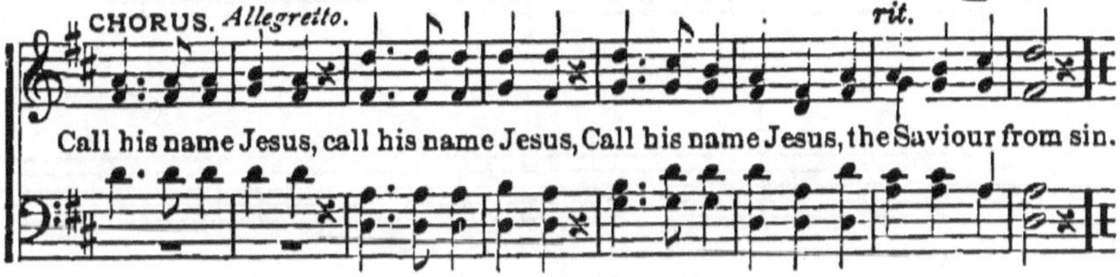

CHORUS. *Allegretto.* *rit.*

Call his name Jesus, call his name Jesus, Call his name Jesus, the Saviour from sin.

Gifts We Bring.

F. G. BURROUGHS.   JOHN J. HOOD.

1. Gifts we bring to our King, Every heart an of-fering,—Loving deeds for
2. Praise we bring to our King, And of God's great love-gift sing, While the story
3. Gifts we bring to our King, While the merry chime-bells ring, Kind words from our

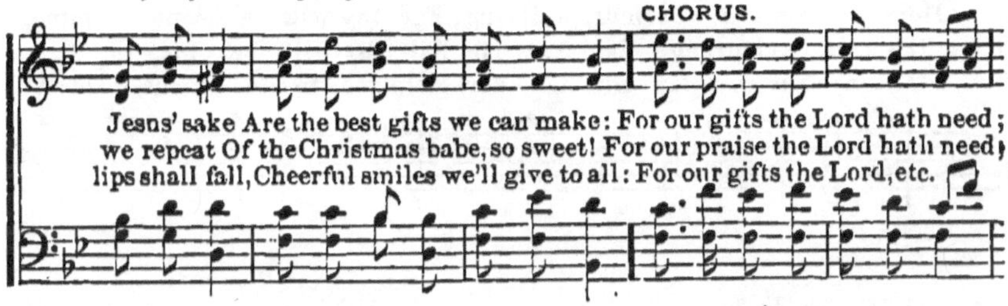

CHORUS.

Jesus' sake Are the best gifts we can make: For our gifts the Lord hath need;
we repeat Of the Christmas babe, so sweet! For our praise the Lord hath need
lips shall fall, Cheerful smiles we'll give to all: For our gifts the Lord, etc.

He will bless each loving deed, He will bless, etc., And the children's off'ring heed.
When we love in truth and deed, When we love, etc., Children's praises he will heed.
He will bless each kindly deed, He will bless, etc., And the words of children heed.

Copyright, 1889, by John J. Hood.

Living Hymns—C

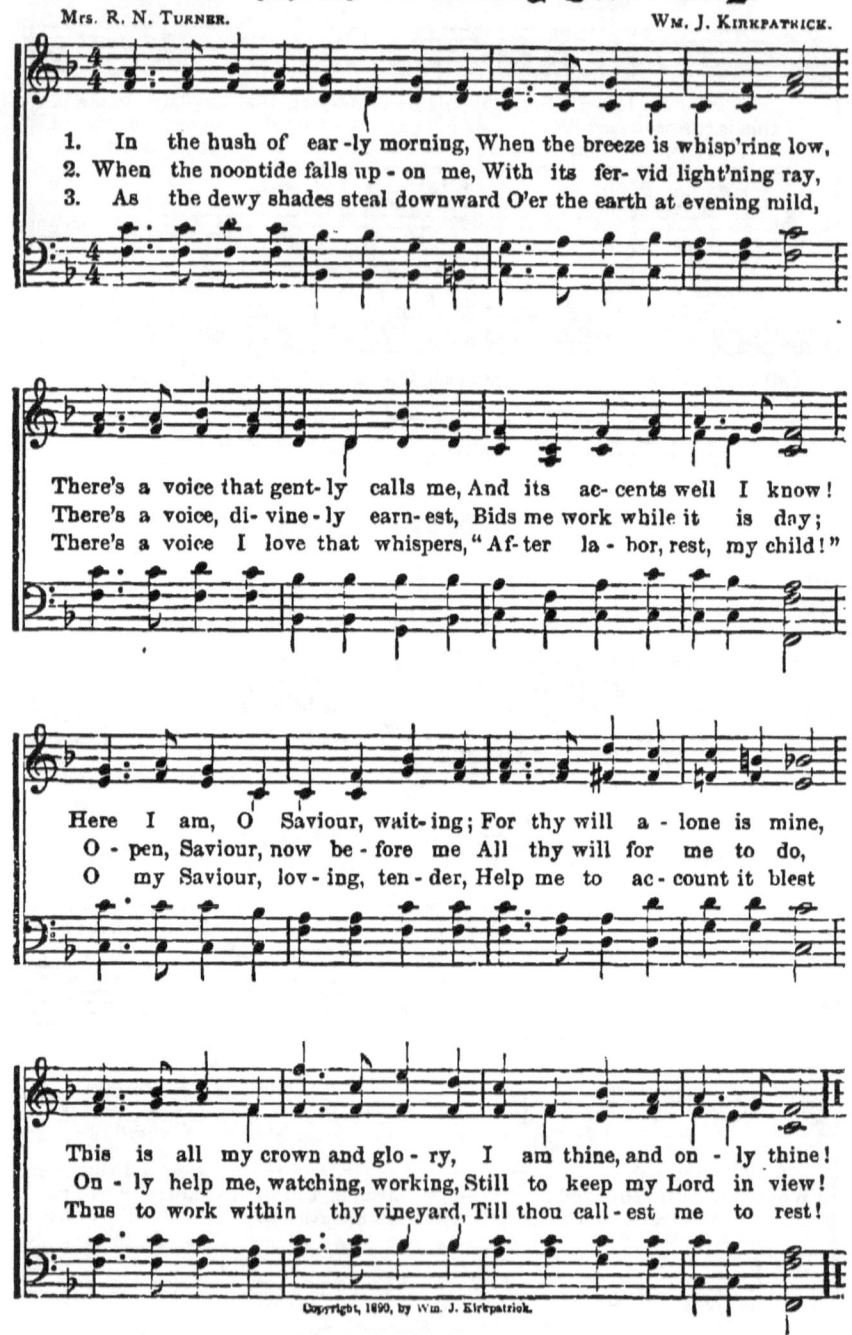

When Jesus Comes.

"Unto them that look for him shall he appear the second time, without sin, unto salvation.—Heb. ix. 28.

P. P. B.   P. P. Bliss.

1. Down life's dark vale we wander, Till Jesus comes; We watch and wait and wonder, Till Jesus comes.
2. Oh, let my lamp be burning When Jesus comes; For him my soul be yearning, When Jesus comes.
3. No more heart-pangs nor sadness, When Jesus comes; All peace and joy and gladness, When Jesus comes.
4. All doubts and fears will vanish, When Jesus comes; All gloom his face will banish, When Jesus comes.

CHORUS.

All joy his loved ones bringing, When Jesus comes; All praise thro' heaven ringing, When Jesus comes; All beauty bright and vernal When Jesus comes; All glory, grand, eternal, When Jesus comes.

5. He'll know the way was dreary, When Jesus comes; He'll know the feet grew weary, When Jesus comes.

6. He'll know what griefs oppressed me, When Jesus comes; Oh, how his arms will rest me! When Jesus comes.

Used by per. The John Church Co., owners of the Copyright.

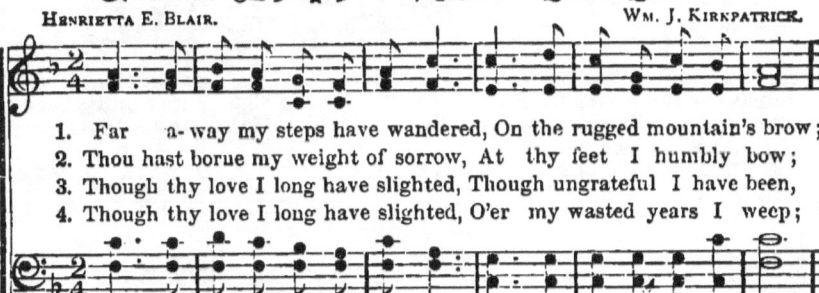

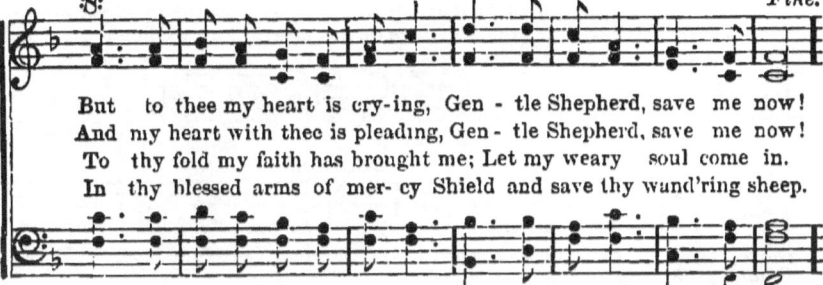

The Everlasting Song.

Lizzie Edwards.   Jno. R. Sweney.

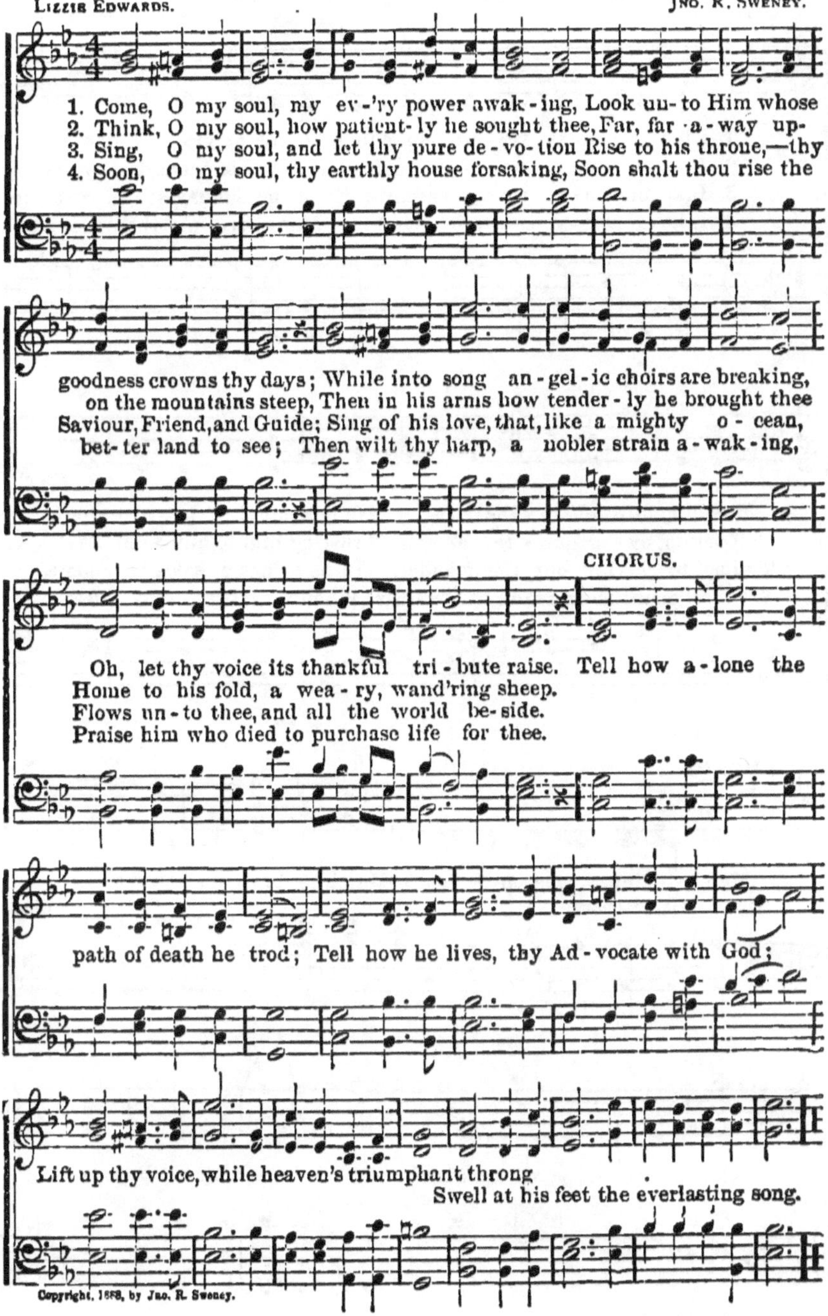

1. Come, O my soul, my ev-'ry power awak-ing, Look un-to Him whose goodness crowns thy days; While into song an-gel-ic choirs are breaking,
2. Think, O my soul, how patient-ly he sought thee, Far, far a-way up-on the mountains steep, Then in his arms how tender-ly he brought thee
3. Sing, O my soul, and let thy pure de-vo-tion Rise to his throne,—thy Saviour, Friend, and Guide; Sing of his love, that, like a mighty o-cean,
4. Soon, O my soul, thy earthly house forsaking, Soon shalt thou rise the bet-ter land to see; Then wilt thy harp, a nobler strain a-wak-ing,

CHORUS.

Oh, let thy voice its thankful tri-bute raise. Tell how a-lone the
Home to his fold, a wea-ry, wand'ring sheep.
Flows un-to thee, and all the world be-side.
Praise him who died to purchase life for thee.

path of death he trod; Tell how he lives, thy Ad-vocate with God;

Lift up thy voice, while heaven's triumphant throng
Swell at his feet the everlasting song.

Copyright, 1888, by Jno. R. Sweney.

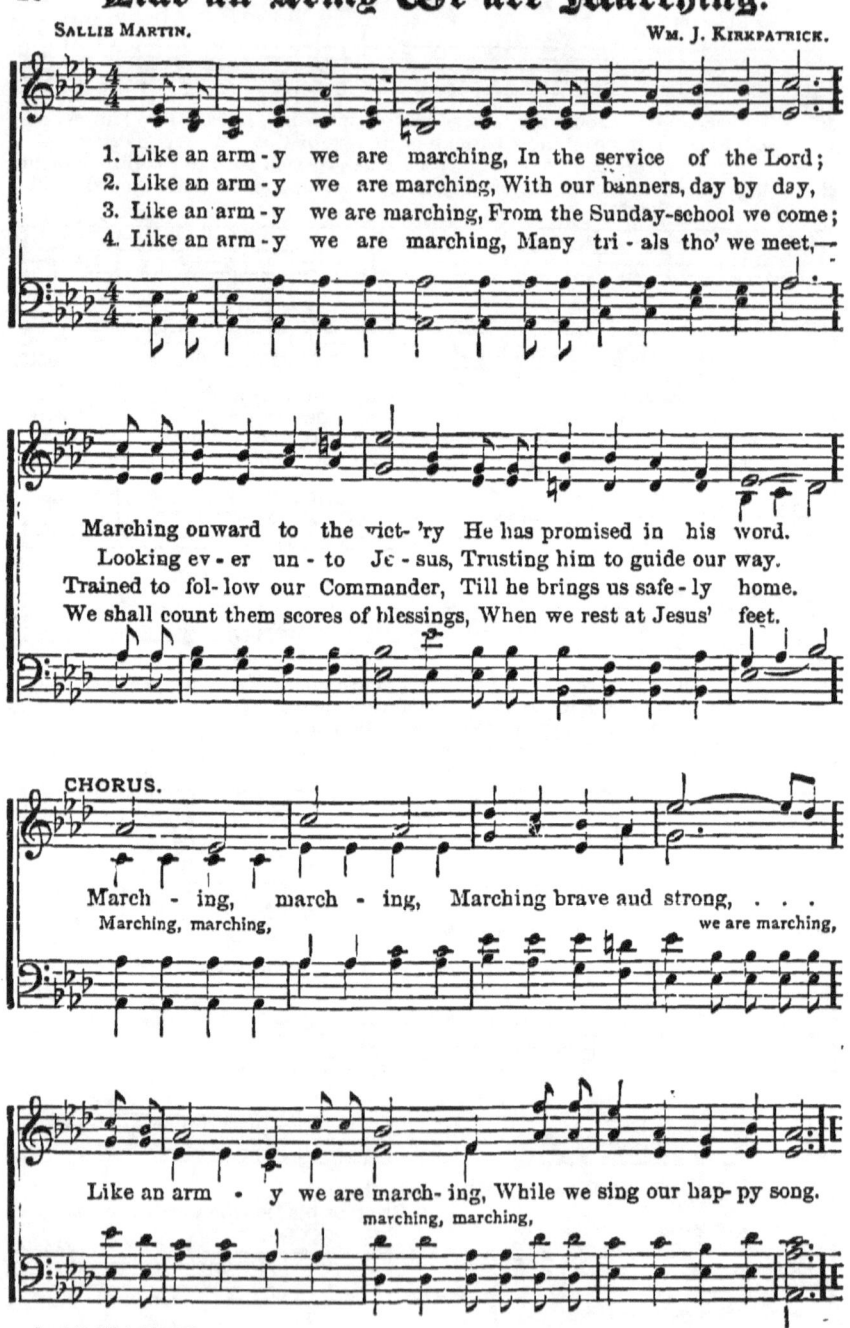

Thou wilt Defend us.

Mable F. Long. Jno. R. Swenby.

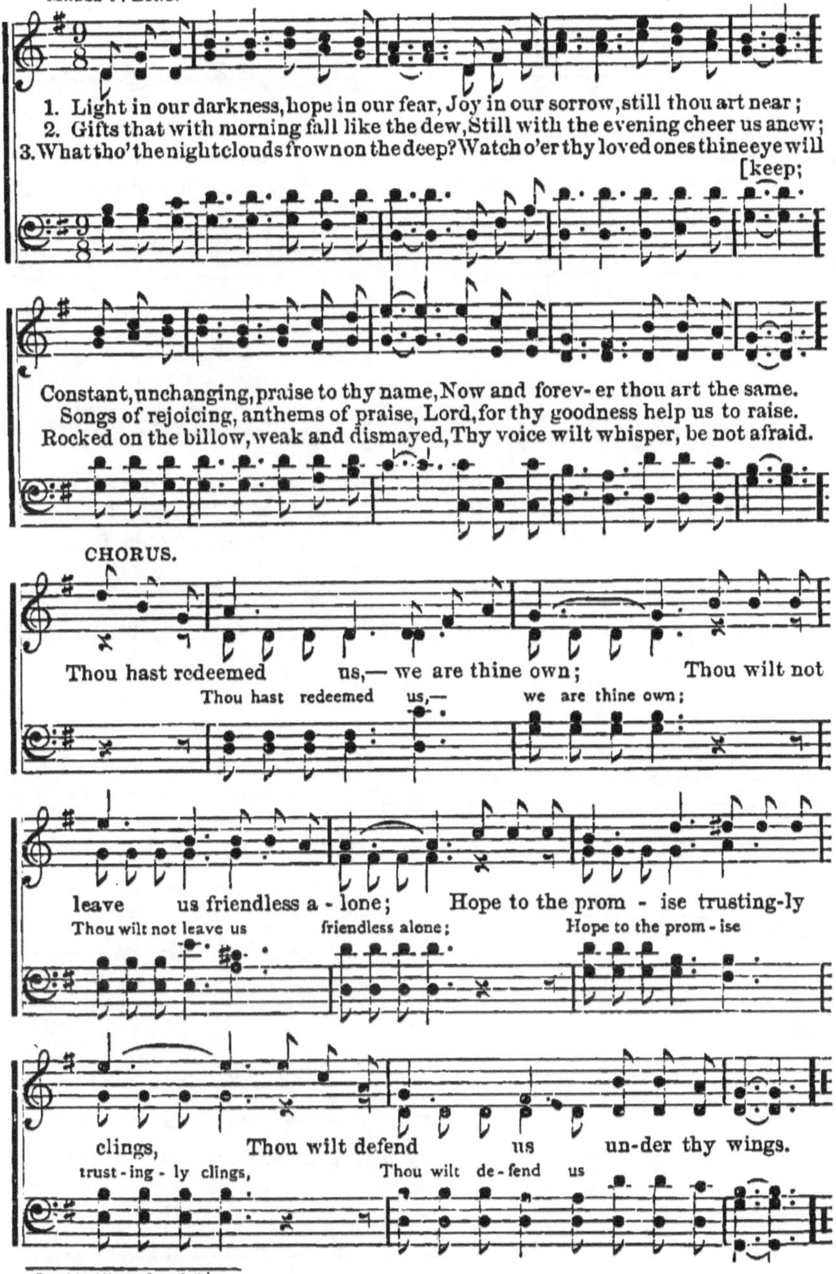
1. Light in our darkness, hope in our fear, Joy in our sorrow, still thou art near;
2. Gifts that with morning fall like the dew, Still with the evening cheer us anew;
3. What tho' the night clouds frown on the deep? Watch o'er thy loved ones thine eye will [keep;
Constant, unchanging, praise to thy name, Now and forev- er thou art the same.
Songs of rejoicing, anthems of praise, Lord, for thy goodness help us to raise.
Rocked on the billow, weak and dismayed, Thy voice wilt whisper, be not afraid.
CHORUS.
Thou hast redeemed us,— we are thine own; Thou wilt not
Thou hast redeemed us,— we are thine own;
leave us friendless a - lone; Hope to the prom - ise trusting-ly
Thou wilt not leave us friendless alone; Hope to the prom - ise
clings, Thou wilt defend us un-der thy wings.
trust - ing - ly clings, Thou wilt de - fend us

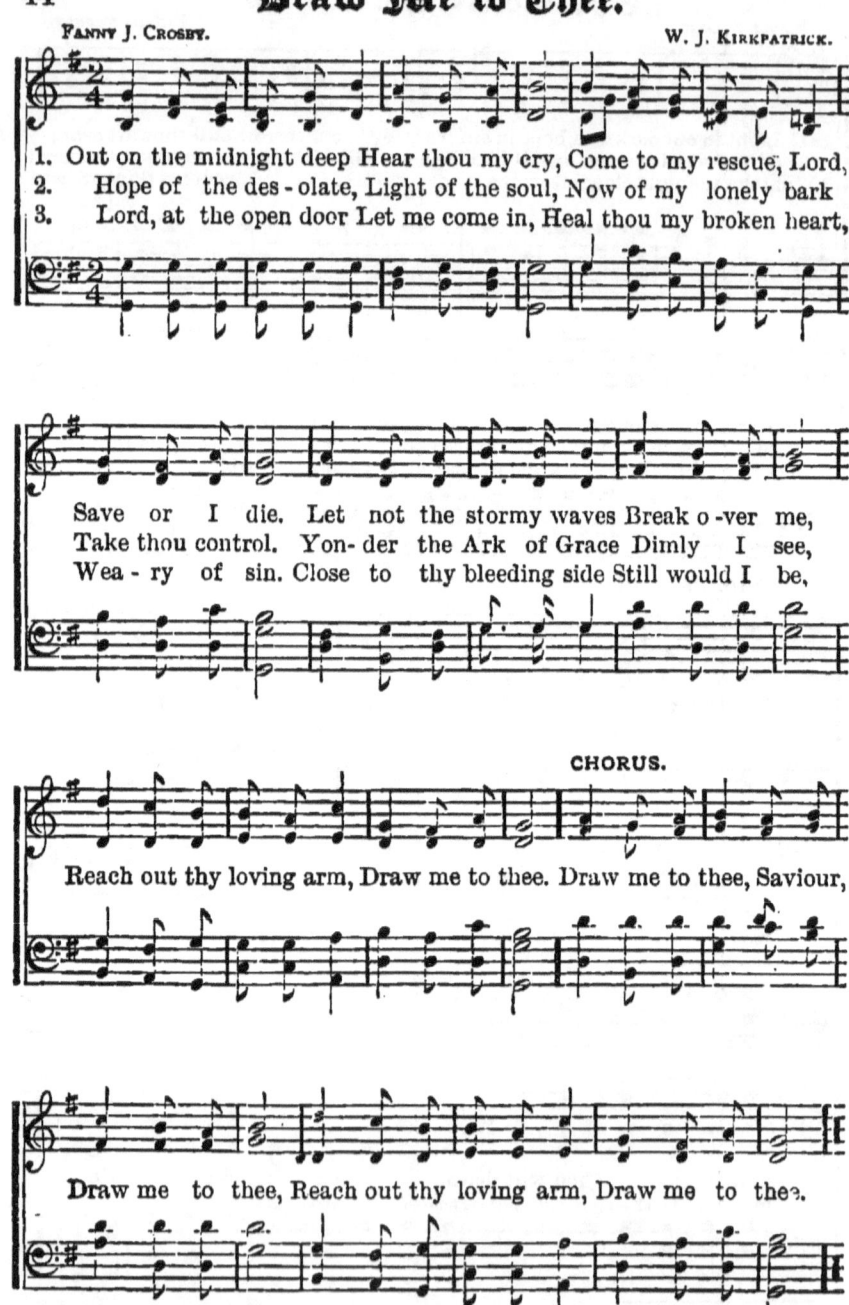

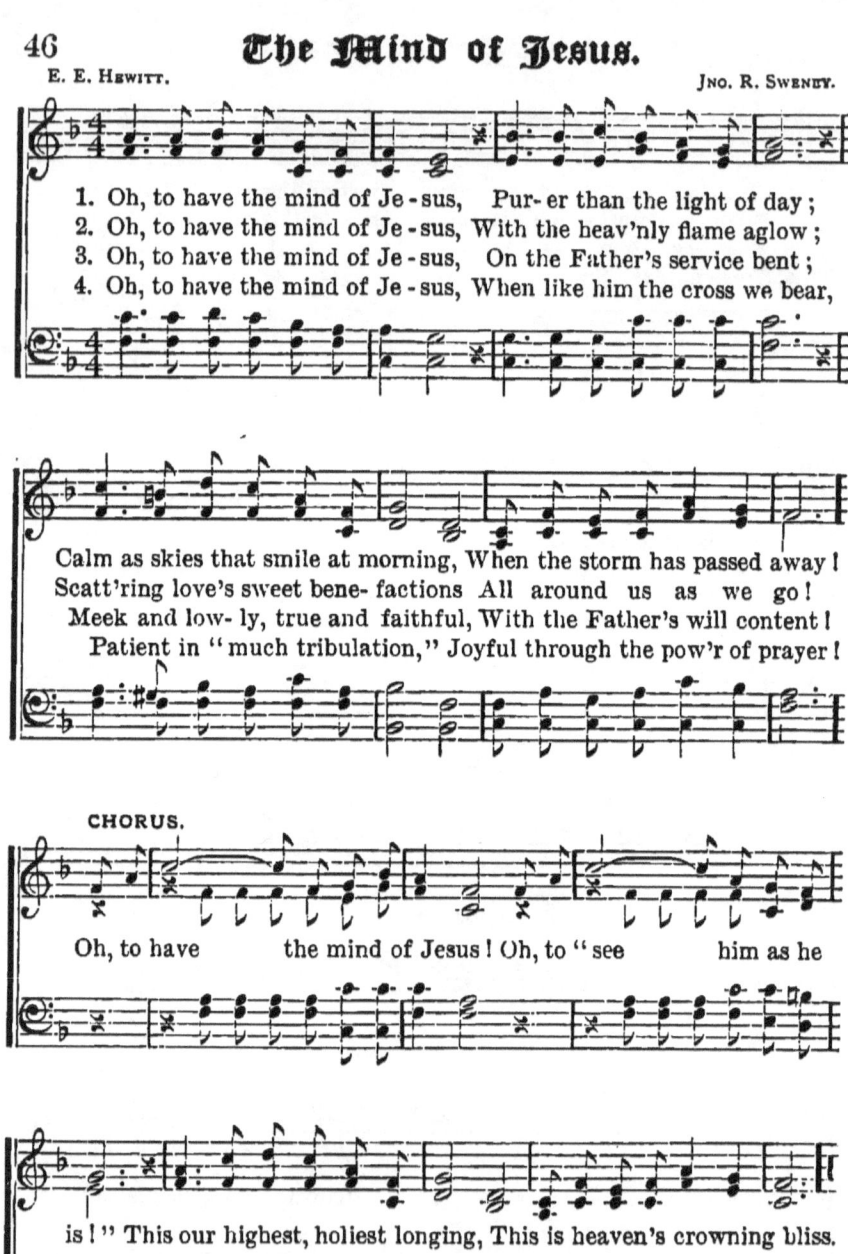

Praise ye the Lord.

FANNY J. CROSBY. **WM. J. KIRKPATRICK.**

1. Praise ye the Lord, the hope of our sal-va-tion; Praise ye the Lord, our soul's a-bid-ing trust; Great are his works and wonderful his counsels; Praise ye the Lord, the only wise and just. Praise ye the Lord, our strength and our Redeemer, Praise ye the Lord, his mighty love recall,—Tell how he came from bondage to de-liv-er, Tell how he came to purchase life for all.

2. Praise ye the Lord, whose throne is everlasting; Praise ye the Lord, whose gifts are ev-er new; Praise ye the Lord, whose tender mercy falleth Pure as the rain and gentle as the dew. Praise ye the Lord, oh, glory! hal-le-lujah! Praise ye the Lord, whose kingdom has no end; Praise ye the Lord, who watcheth o'er the faithful, Praise ye the Lord, our never changing Friend.

CHO.—Praise ye the Lord, for good it is to praise him; O let the earth his ma-jest-y proclaim; Shout, shout for joy and bow the knee before him; Sing to the harp and magnify his name.

Copyright, 1881, by JOHN J. HOOD.

John iii. 36.
5 He that believeth | on the Son, :‖
Hath everlasting | life.

Is. xlv. 22.
6 Look unto me, and | be ye saved, :‖
All the ends of the | earth.

Matt. v. 8.
7 Blessed are the | pure in heart, :‖
For | they shall see | God.

Matt v. 12.
8 Re- | joice and be ex- | ceeding glad, :‖
For | great is your reward in | heaven.

John xiv. 18.
9 I | will not leave you | comfortless, ‖
I will come unto | you.

John vii. 37.
10 If | any man thirst let him | come unto
And drink of the water of | life. [me,:‖

Mark. x. 14.
11 Suffer little children to | come unto
me, :‖ [heaven.
For of | such is the kingdom of |

John xiv. 2.
12 I | go to prepare a | place for you, ‖
In my Fathers' house.

Copyright, 1888, by WM. J. KIRKPATRICK.

The Stranger at the Door.

Rev. iii. 20. T. C. O'Kane.

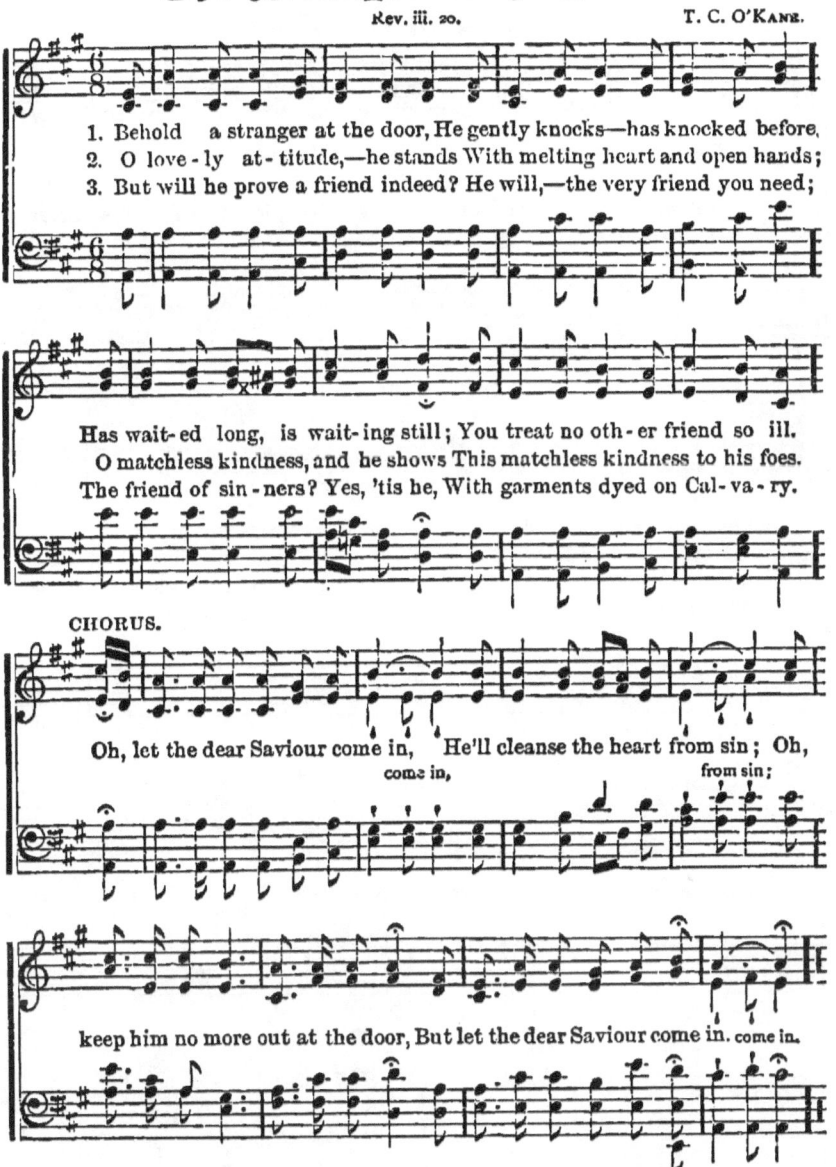

1. Behold a stranger at the door, He gently knocks—has knocked before,
Has wait-ed long, is wait-ing still; You treat no oth-er friend so ill.
2. O love-ly at-titude,—he stands With melting heart and open hands;
O matchless kindness, and he shows This matchless kindness to his foes.
3. But will he prove a friend indeed? He will,—the very friend you need;
The friend of sin-ners? Yes, 'tis he, With garments dyed on Cal-va-ry.

CHORUS.
Oh, let the dear Saviour come in, He'll cleanse the heart from sin; Oh, keep him no more out at the door, But let the dear Saviour come in.

4 Rise, touched with gratitude divine,
Turn out his enemy and thine;
That soul-destroying monster, Sin,
And let the heavenly Stranger in.

5 Admit him, ere his anger burn,—
His feet, departed, ne'er return;
Admit him, or the hour's at hand
You'll at HIS door rejected stand.

By permission.

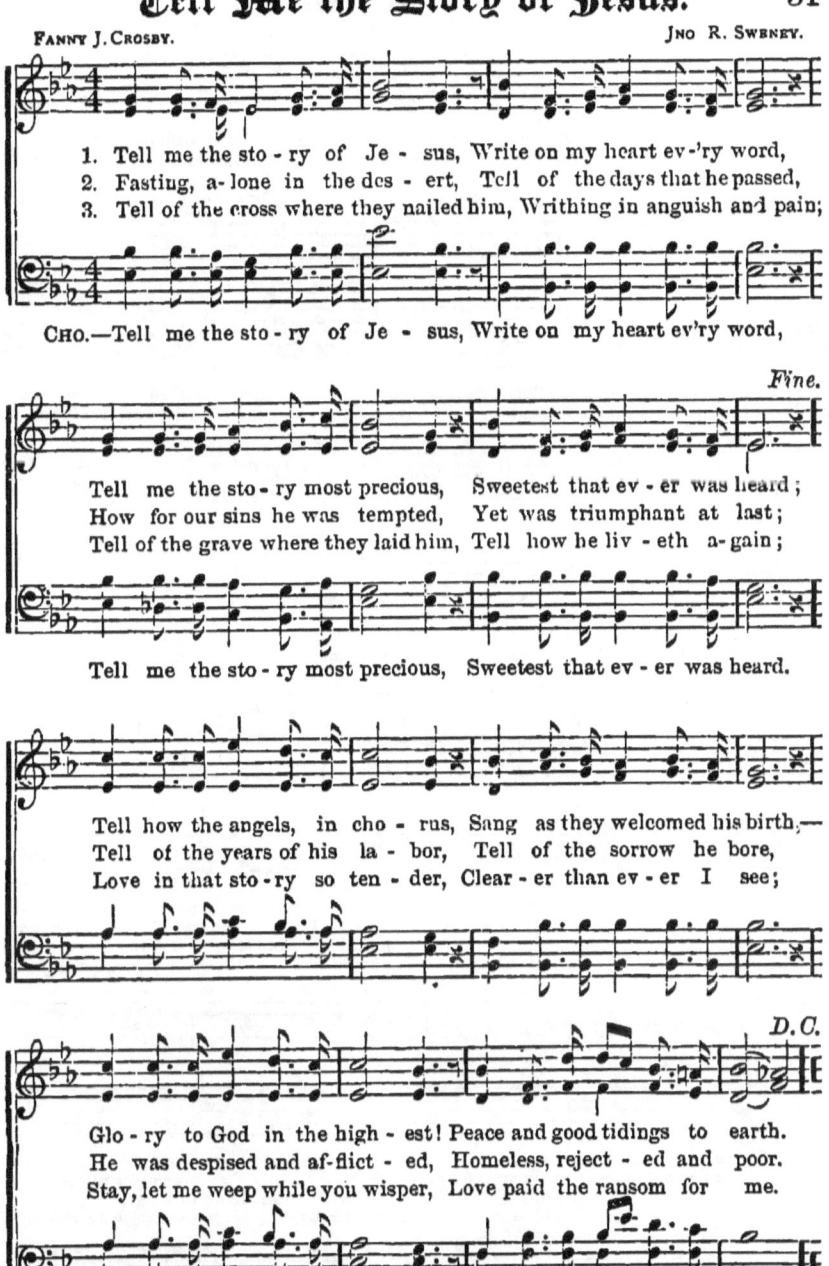

52 O Bless the Lord.

FANNY J. CROSBY.   Psalm ciii.   WM. J. KIRKPATRICK.

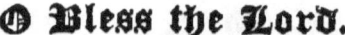

1. O bless the Lord, our souls and all within; O bless the Lord, who pardons ev'ry sin;
2. O bless the Lord, ye worlds beyond the sky; Break forth, ye depths, let rocks and hills reply;

Give thanks to him with ev'ry fleeting breath; Give thanks to him who triumphed over death.
Praise him, ye stars that saw creation's birth, Whose music hailed the pure and shining earth.

O   bless the Lord,   ye an - gels round his throne,
Bless the Lord,   bless the Lord,   bless the Lord,   ye angels round his throne,
O   bless the Lord,   the Prince   of Peace adore,
Bless the Lord,   bless the Lord,   bless the Lord,   the Prince of Peace adore,

Who do his will and make his wonders known;
Bless the Lord,   bless the Lord,   bless the Lord,   and make his wonders known;
And let his love re - sound from shore to shore;
Let his love,   let his love,   let his love   resound from shore to shore;

Strike, strike your harps, ye ran - somed host above,
Strike your harps, strike your harps, strike your harps, ye ransomed host above,
O bless the Lord Je - ho - vah, King of kings,
Bless the Lord, bless the Lord, bless the Lord Je - hovah, King of kings,

Copyright, 1882, by John J. Hood.

O Bless the Lord.—CONCLUDED.

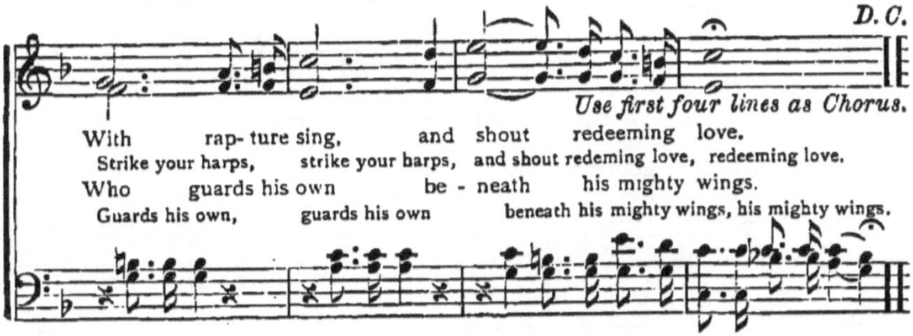

Use first four lines as Chorus.

With rap-ture sing, and shout redeeming love.
Strike your harps, strike your harps, and shout redeming love, redeeming love.
Who guards his own be-neath his mighty wings.
Guards his own, guards his own beneath his mighty wings, his mighty wings.

God Bless our Sabbath=School.

PRISCILLA J. OWENS. RUSSIAN HYMN.

1. God bless our Sabbath-school! Firm-ly u-nit-ed, Un-der thy ban-ner thy glo-ry we sing; Strength of each youth-ful heart, Hope nev-er blight-ed, Be thou our por-tion, Je-sus, our King.
2. God bless our Sabbath-school! Al-migh-ty Fath-er, Shel-ter thy chil-dren in peace 'neath thy wing; Guide in the nar-row way, Heav'nward us gath-er, Be thou our ref-uge, Je-sus, our King.
3. God bless our Sabbath-school! Glorious De-fend-er, Un-der thy ban-ner we march as we sing; Lead us to vic-to-ry; Nev-er sur-ren-der, Thy name must con-quer, Je-sus, our King.

Copyright, 1884, by John J. Hood.

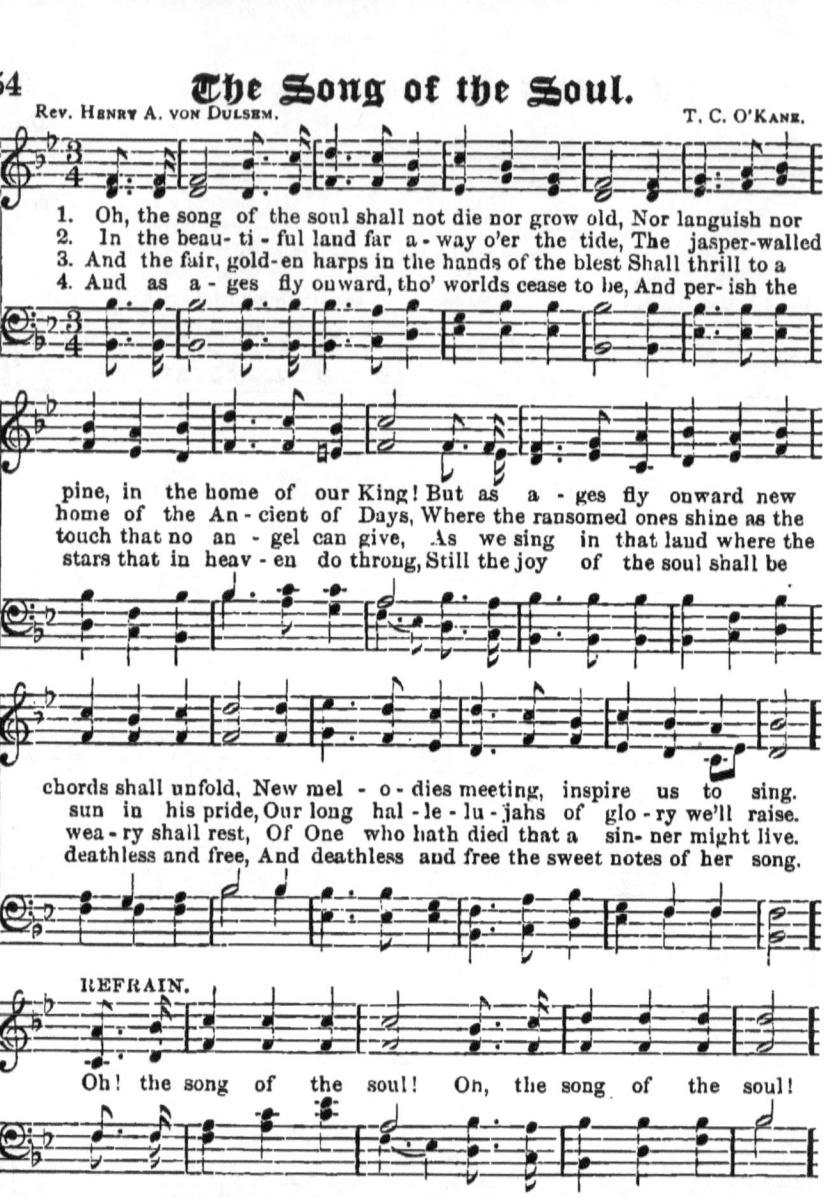

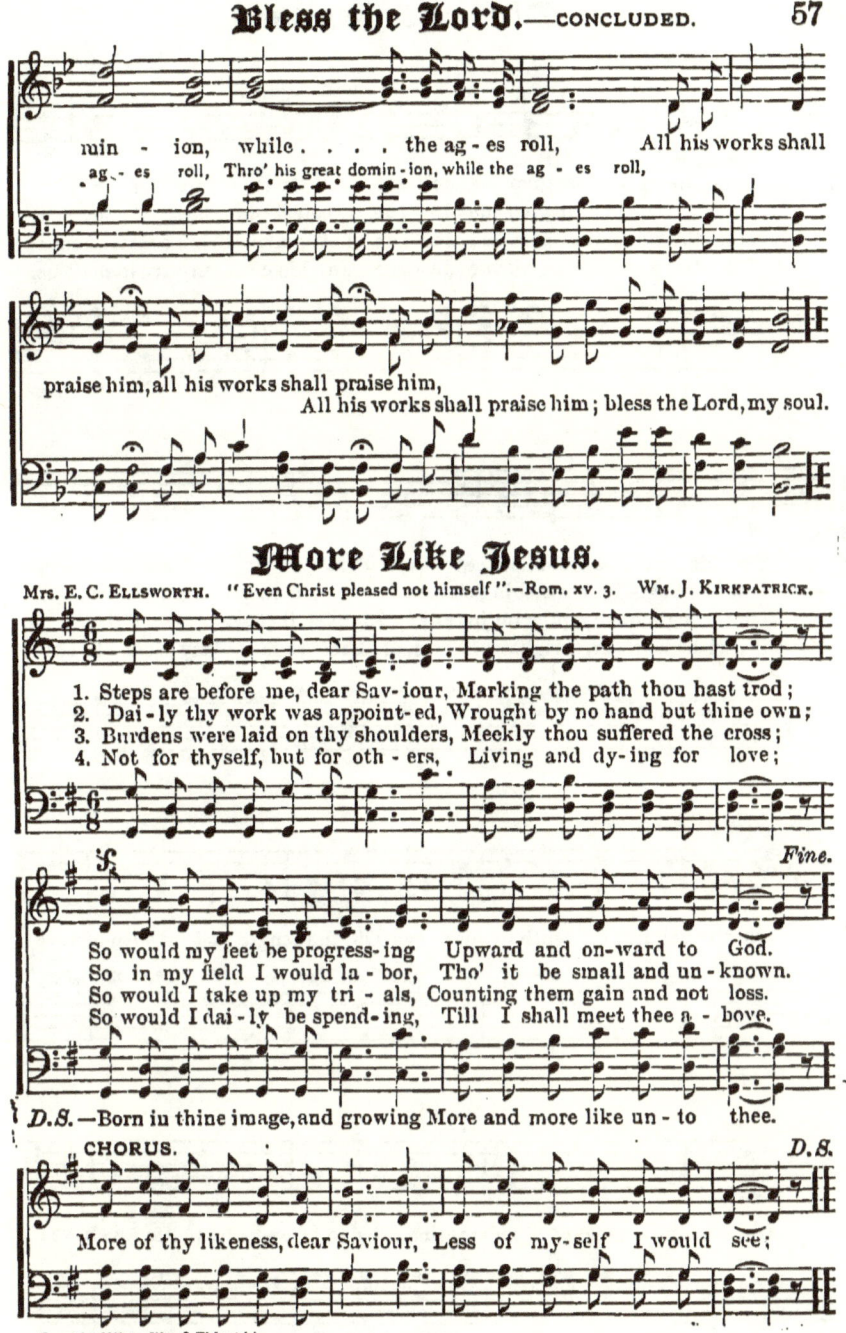

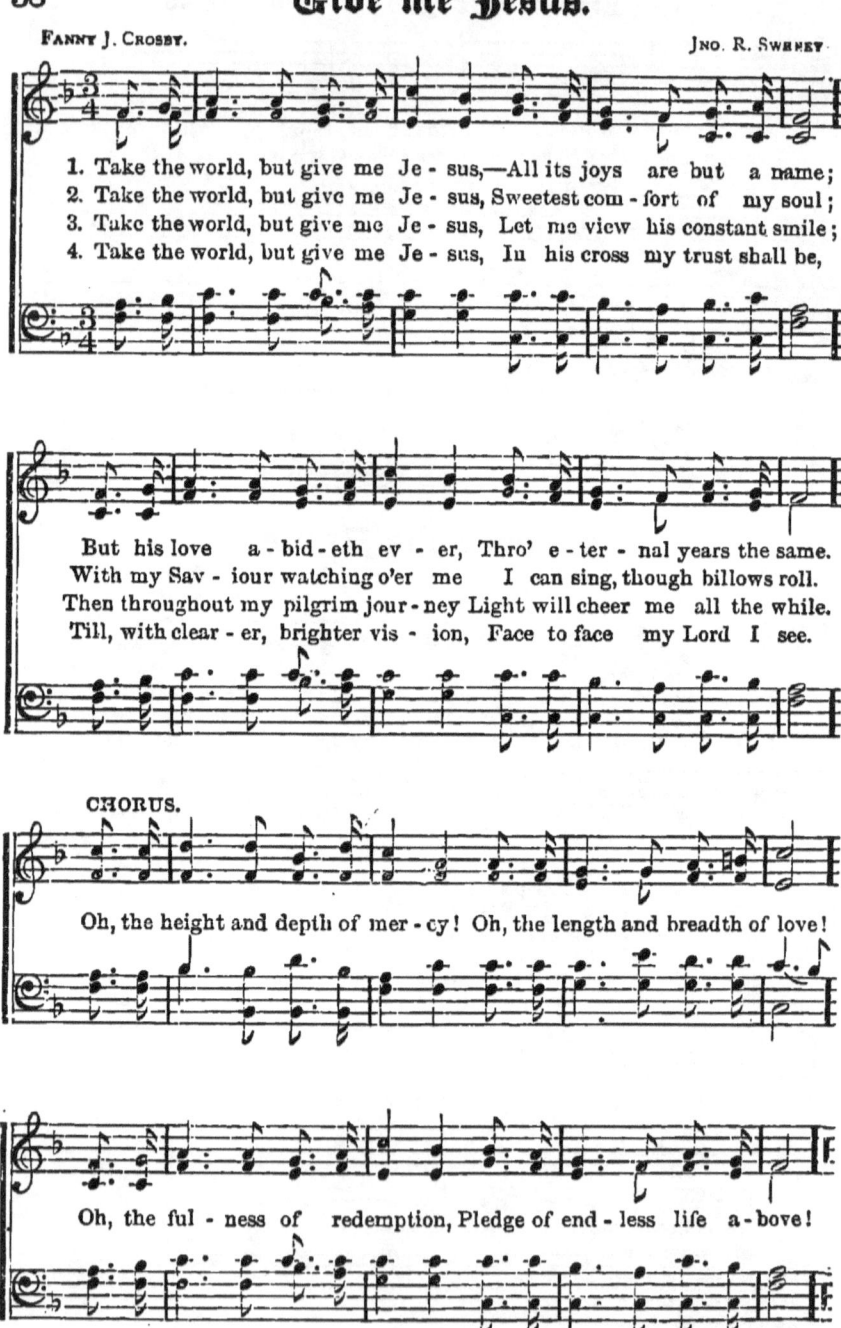

The Lights of Home.—CONCLUDED.

There,... beyond the billows' foam, We see the lights of home.
There, be-yond, beyond

Battling for the Lord.

T. E. PERKINS.

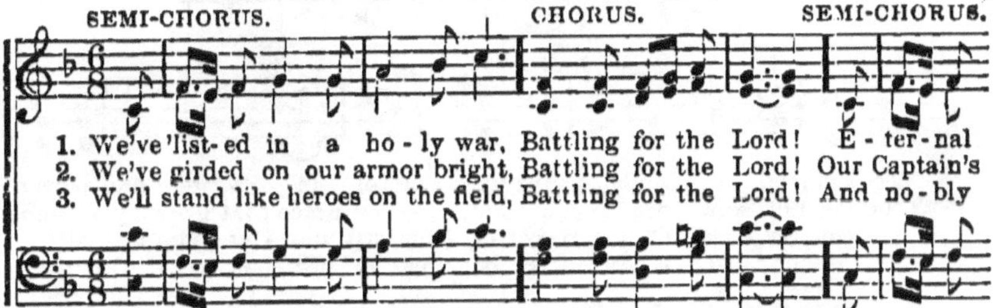

SEMI-CHORUS. / CHORUS. / SEMI-CHORUS.

1. We've 'list-ed in a ho-ly war, Battling for the Lord! E-ter-nal
2. We've girded on our armor bright, Battling for the Lord! Our Captain's
3. We'll stand like heroes on the field, Battling for the Lord! And no-bly

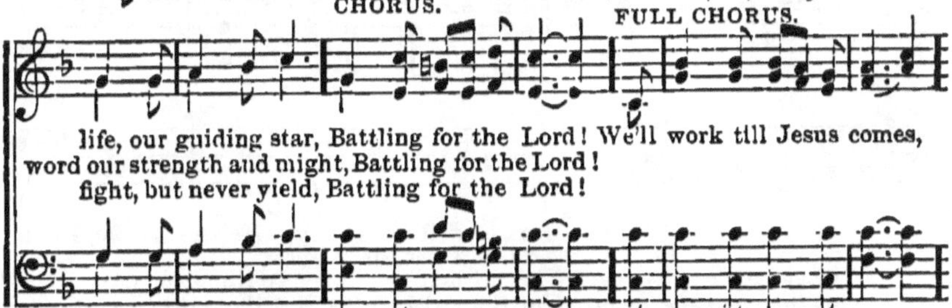

CHORUS. / FULL CHORUS.

life, our guiding star, Battling for the Lord! We'll work till Jesus comes,
word our strength and might, Battling for the Lord!
fight, but never yield, Battling for the Lord!

We'll work till Je-sus comes, We'll work till Je-sus comes, And

then we'll rest at home.

4 Though sin and death our way oppose,
Battling for the Lord!
Through grace we'll conquer all our foes,
Battling for the Lord!

5 And when our glorious war is o'er,
Battling for the Lord!
We'll shout salvation evermore,
Battling for the Lord!

Copyright by T. E. Perkins.

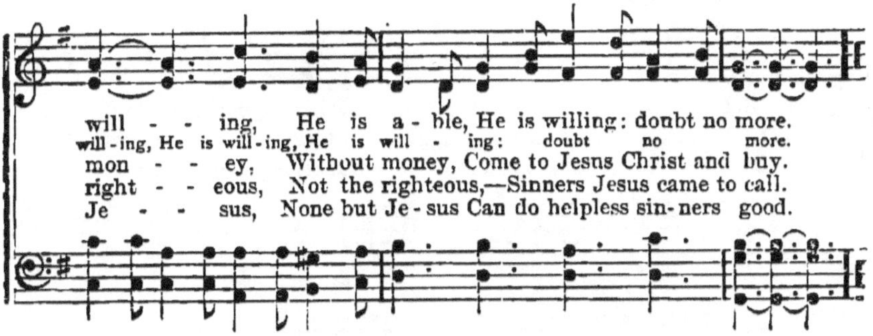

Come, ye Sinners.—CONCLUDED.

will - - ing, He is a - ble, He is willing: doubt no more.
will - ing, He is will - ing, He is will - ing: doubt no more.
mon - - ey, Without money, Come to Jesus Christ and buy.
right - - eous, Not the righteous,—Sinners Jesus came to call.
Je - - sus, None but Je - sus Can do helpless sin-ners good.

Nearer to Thee.

MARTHA J. LANKTON. WM. J. KIRKPATRICK.

1. When doubt and conflict weigh me down, and clouds be-fore me rise,
2. When joys that once I thought so true Have lost each balm - y sweet,
3. While day by day I journey on To reach that world sub- lime,

Whose gath'ring gloom and deep'ning shade With sor - row fills mine eyes,
And withered hopes, like summer flowers, Lie crushed beneath my feet,
That stands in perfect loveliness Be - - yond the shore of time;

'Tis then I lift my fainting soul In prayer that I may be
With quivering lip and yearning heart I pray on bend - ed knee,
My faith looks up and softly breathes The prayer so dear to me,

Lento.

Near - - er, my God, to thee, Near - - er to thee.

Copyright, 1887, by John J. Hood.   *Living Hymns*—E

Anywhere With Jesus.

JESSIE H. BROWN.   "I will trust and not be afraid." Isaiah xli. 2.   D. B. TOWNER. By per.

1. An-ywhere with Je-sus I can safe-ly go, An-ywhere He leads me in this world be-low. Anywhere without him, dearest joys would fade, Anywhere with Je-sus I am not a-fraid.
2. An-ywhere with Je-sus I am not a-lone, Other friends may fail me, He is still my own. Tho' his hand may lead me o-ver drearest ways, Anywhere with Je-sus is a house of praise.
3. An-ywhere with Je-sus I can go to sleep, When the darkling shadows round a-bout me creep; Knowing I shall waken nev-er more to roam, Anywhere with Je-sus will be home, sweet home.

CHORUS.

An-y-where! an-y-where! Fear I can-not know, An-y-where with Je-sus I can safe-ly go.

Copyright, 1887, by D. B. Towner.

70   **"Him that Cometh!"**

The first part may be sung as a Duet or Quartet.

JESSIE C. YOUNG.   JAMES McGRANAHAN.

Moderato.

1. Thy Saviour calls! oh, come and see What things he hath prepared for thee.
2. Thy Saviour calls! oh, can it be That call has no sweet charm for thee!
3. Thy Saviour calls! he knows thy sin: But trust him now, he'll enter in:

Life, love, and joy, from God on high, By Christ himself to thee brought nigh.
Wilt thou not turn and give him heed? Wilt thou not think while he doth plead?
And he thy heart will pu - ri - fy, And ev - 'ry need-ed grace supply.

CHORUS. John vi, 37.
Allegretto.

"Him that cometh, him that cometh, Him that cometh to me, I will in no wise, I will in no wise, I will in no wise cast out; Him that cometh, him that cometh, Him that cometh to me, I will in no wise, I will in no wise, I will in no wise cast out."

Used by per. of James McGranahan, owner of C.pyright

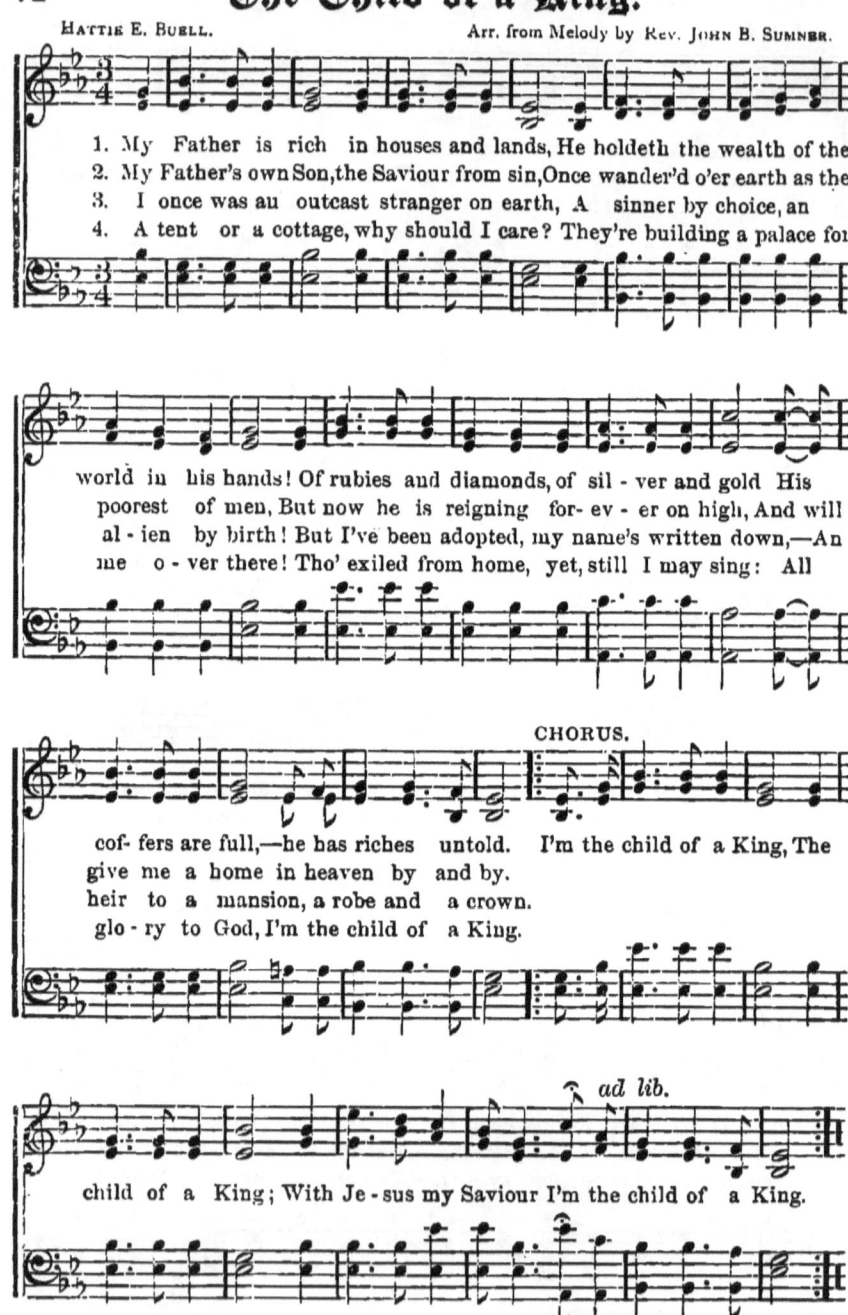

"This I Did for Thee."

H. BONAR.
W. H. DOANE.

1. I gave my life for thee, My precious blood I shed, That thou might'st ransom'd be, And quickened from the dead; I gave my life for thee; What hast thou done for me?
2. I spent long years for thee In weariness and woe, That one e-ter-ni-ty Of joy thou mightest know; I spent long years for thee; Hast thou spent one for me?
3. My Father's house of light, My rainbow-circled throne, I left for earthly night, For wand'rings sad and lone; I left it all all for thee; Hast thou left aught for me?
4. I suffered much for thee,—More than my tongue can tell, Of bitterest agony; To rescue thee from hell; I suffered much for thee; What dost thou bear for me?

CHORUS.

This I did for thee, What hast thou done for me?
This I did for thee, What hast thou done for me? Yes,
This I did for thee, What hast thou done for me?
this I did for thee,

5 And I have brought to thee,
  Down from my house above,
  Salvation full and free.
  My pardon and my love;
  Great gifts I brought to thee;
  What hast thou brought to me?

6 Oh, let thy life be given,
  Thy years for me be spent,
  World fetters all be riven,
  And joy with suffering blent;
  Give thou thyself to me,
  And I will welcome thee!

Used by permission of with W. H. Doane, owner of Copyright.

Onward and Upward.—CONCLUDED.

up - - ward, Onward unto glory, To the perfect day.
upward, marching upward, upward,

The Great Physician.

Rev. Wm. H. Hunter. D. D. Arranged by J H Stockton.

1. The Great Phy-si-cian now is here, The sym-pa-thiz-ing Je-sus:
He speaks the drooping heart to cheer, Oh, hear the voice of Je-sus.

CHORUS.
Sweet-est note in ser-aph song, Sweetest name on mor-tal tongue,
Sweet-est car-ol ev-er sung, Je-sus, bles-sed Je-sus.

2 Your many sins are all forgiven,
  Oh, hear the voice of Jesus;
  Go on your way in peace to heaven,
  And wear a crown with Jesus.

3 All glory to the dying Lamb!
  I now believe in Jesus;
  I love the blessed Saviour's name,
  I love the name of Jesus.

4 The children too, both great and small,
  Who love the name of Jesus,
  May now accept his gracious call
  To work and live for Jesus.

5 Come, brethren, help me sing his praise,
  Oh, praise the name of Jesus;
  Come, sisters, all your voices raise,
  Oh, bless the name of Jesus.

6 His name dispels my guilt and fear,
  No other name but Jesus;
  Oh, how my soul delights to hear
  The precious name of Jesus.

7 And when to that bright world above,
  We rise to see our Jesus,
  We'll sing around the throne of love
  His name, the name of Jesus.

Since I Have Been Redeemed. 79

E. O. E. E. O. EXCELL. By per.

1. I have a song I love to sing, Since I have been redeemed, Of my Re-
2. I have a Christ that satis-fies, Since I have been redeemed, To do his
3. I have a Witness bright and clear, Since I have been redeemed, Dispelling
4. I have a joy I can't express, Since I have been redeemed, All thro' his
5. I have a home prepared for me, Since I have been redeemed, Where I shall

CHORUS.

deemer, Saviour King, Since I have been redeemed. Since I . . . have been re-
will my highest prize, Since I have been redeemed.
every doubt and fear, Since I have been redeemed.
blood and righteousness, Since I have been redeemed.
dwell e-ter-nal-ly, Since I have been redeemed. Since I have been redeemed, since

deemed,   Since I have been redeemed, I will glory in his name, Since
I have been redeemed,

I . . . have been redeemed,   I will glory in the Saviour's name.
I have been redeemed, since I have been redeemed,

Copyright, 1884, by E. O. Excell.

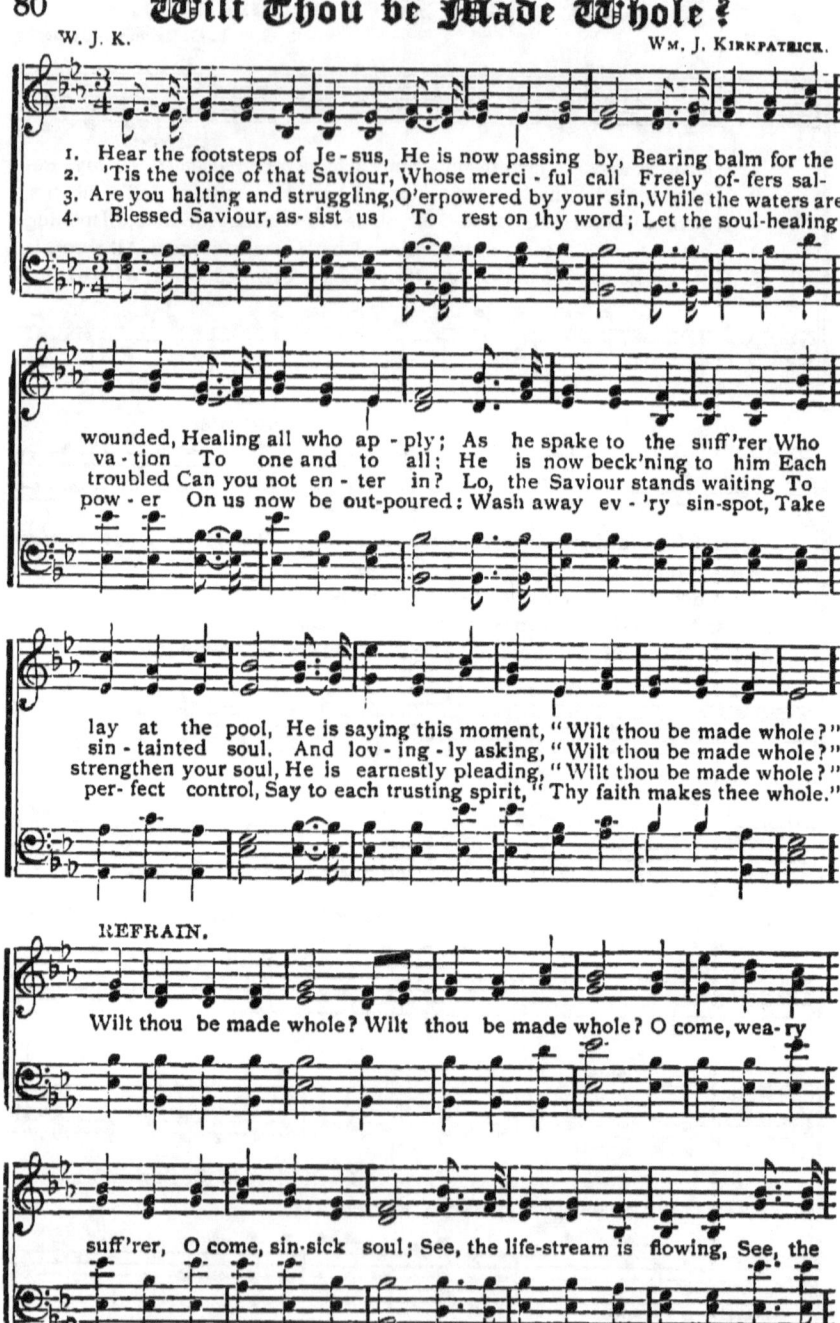

My Shepherd.—CONCLUDED.

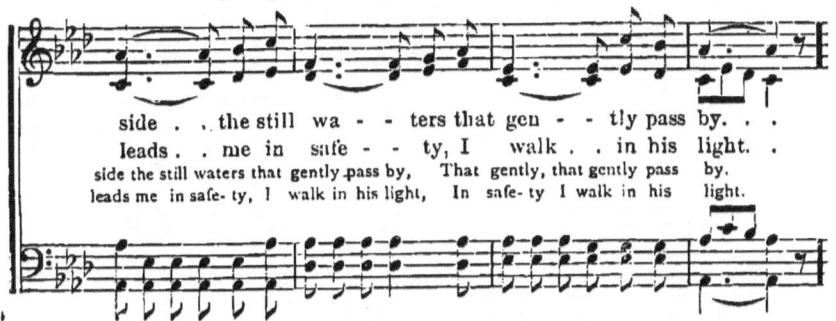

side the still waters that gently pass by, That gently, that gently pass by.
leads me in safety, I walk in his light, In safety I walk in his light.

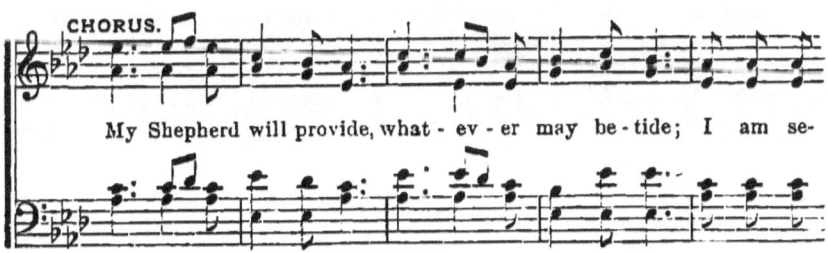

My Shepherd will provide, whatever may betide; I am se-

cure, For his promise is sure, The Lord will provide.

3 When called to surrender my faltering breath,
And pass through the vale of the shadow of death,
The presence of Jesus will brighten the tomb,
With hope and with gladness dispelling its gloom,
         With gladness dispelling its gloom.

4 For me his free bounty a table has spread;
And blessings unmeasured he pours on my head;
My cup with abundance and joy overflows;
He dries all my tears, and he heals all my woes.
         He heals all my woes, all my woes.

5 His goodness and mercy shall crown all my days,
My mouth shall be filled with thanksgiving and praise;
I'll dwell in his temple of glory above,
And sing evermore of his grace and his love.
         And sing of his grace and his love.

84. Only a Beam of Sunshine.

FANNY J. CROSBY.   JNO. R. SWENEY.

1. On-ly a beam of sunshine, But oh, it was warm and bright; The heart of a wea-ry trav-'ler Was cheered by its welcome sight. On-ly a beam of sunshine That fell from the arch a-bove, And ten-der-ly, soft-ly whispered A message of peace and love.

2. On-ly a beam of sunshine, That in-to a dwelling crept, Where o-ver a fad-ing rose-bud, A mother her vig-il kept. On-ly a beam of sunshine That smiled thro' her falling tears, And showed her the bow of promise, Forgot-ten perhaps for years.

3. On-ly a word for Je-sus! Oh, speak it in his dear name; To per-ishing souls a-round you The message of love pro-claim. Go, like the faithful sunbeam, Your mission of joy ful-fil; Re-member the Saviour's promise, That he will be with you still.

CHORUS.

On-ly a word for Je-sus, On-ly a whispered prayer

Copyright, 1884, by John J. Hood.

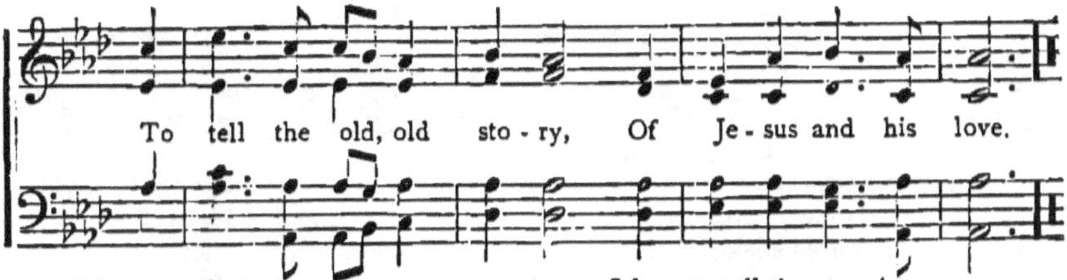

I Love to Tell the Story.—CONCLUDED.

To tell the old, old story, Of Jesus and his love.

3. I love to tell the story!
   'Tis pleasant to repeat
What seems, each time I tell it,
   More wonderfully sweet.
I love to tell the story;
   For some have never heard
The message of salvation
   From God's own Holy Word.

4. I love to tell the story!
   For those who know it best
Seem hungering and thirsting
   'To hear it like the rest.
And when, in scenes of glory,
   I sing the *New, New Song,*
'Twill be the *Old, Old Story,*
   That I have loved so long.

Even Me.

Mrs. E. Codner. Jno. R. Sweney.

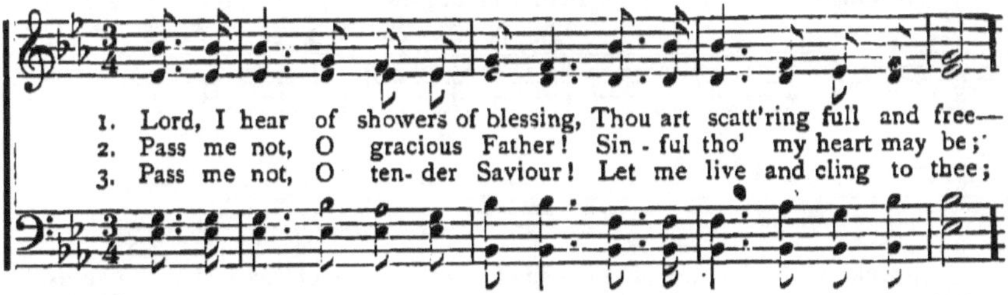

1. Lord, I hear of showers of blessing, Thou art scatt'ring full and free—
2. Pass me not, O gracious Father! Sinful tho' my heart may be;
3. Pass me not, O tender Saviour! Let me live and cling to thee;

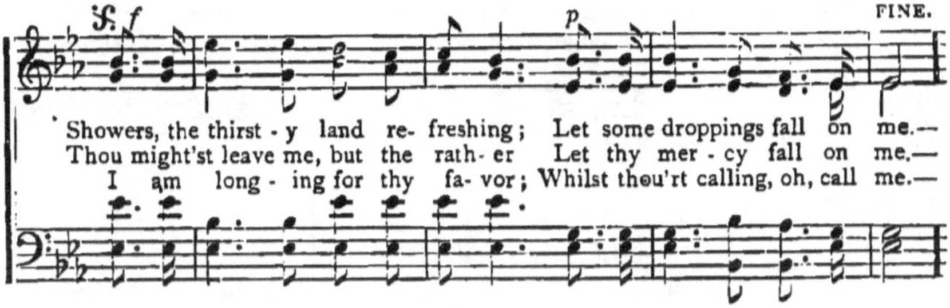

Showers, the thirsty land refreshing; Let some droppings fall on me.—
Thou might'st leave me, but the rather Let thy mercy fall on me.—
I am longing for thy favor; Whilst thou'rt calling, oh, call me.—

E-ven me, E-ven me,
   Yes, e-ven me,   yes, e-ven me.—

4. Pass me not, O mighty Spirit!
      Thou can'st make the blind to see;
   Witnesser of Jesus' merit,
      Speak the word of power to me,—
         Even me, even me, etc.

5. Love of God, so pure and changeless;
      Blood of Christ, so rich and free;
   Grace of God, so strong and boundless,
      Magnify them all in me,—
         Even me, even me, etc.

Bringing in the Sheaves.

"The harvest is the end of the world."—Matt. xiii. 39.

Words from "Songs of Glory." Geo. A. Minor. By per.

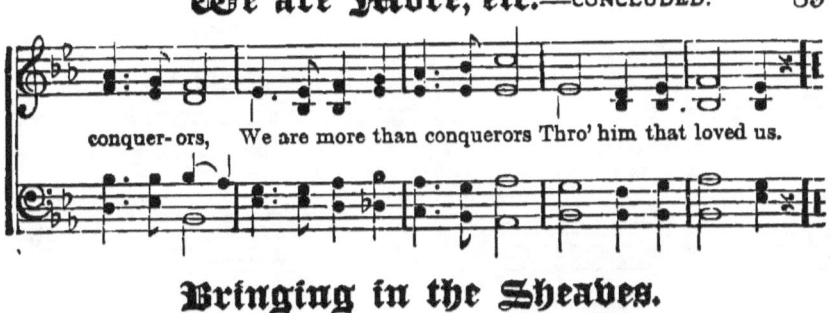

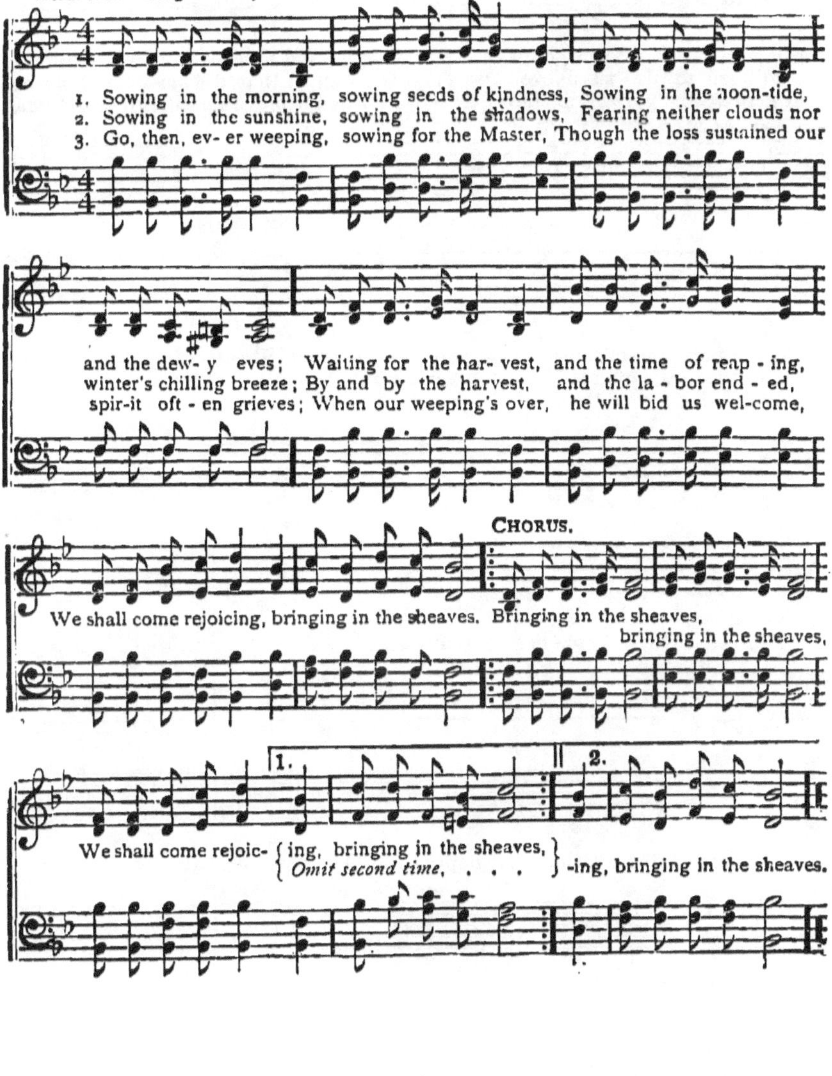

A Blessing in Prayer.

E. E. Hewitt.   Wm. J. Kirkpatrick.

1. There is rest, sweet rest, at the Master's feet, There is favor now at the mer-cy seat, For a-ton-ing blood has been sprinkled there; There is always a blessing, a blessing in prayer.

2. There is grace to help in our time of need, For our friend above is a friend in-deed, We may cast on him ev-'ry grief and care; There is always a blessing, a blessing in prayer.

3. When our songs are glad with the joy of life, When our hearts are sad with its ills and strife, When the powers of sin would the soul ensnare, There is always a blessing, a blessing in prayer.

4. There is perfect peace though the wild waves roll; There are gifts of love for the seek-ing soul; Till we praise the Lord in his home so fair, There is always a blessing, a blessing in prayer.

REFRAIN.

There's a blessing in prayer, in be-lieving prayer; When our Saviour's name to the throne we bear, Then a Father's love will receive us there; There is always a blessing, a blessing in prayer.

Copyright, 1897, by Wm. J. Kirkpatrick.

Oh, to be over Yonder.—CONCLUDED.

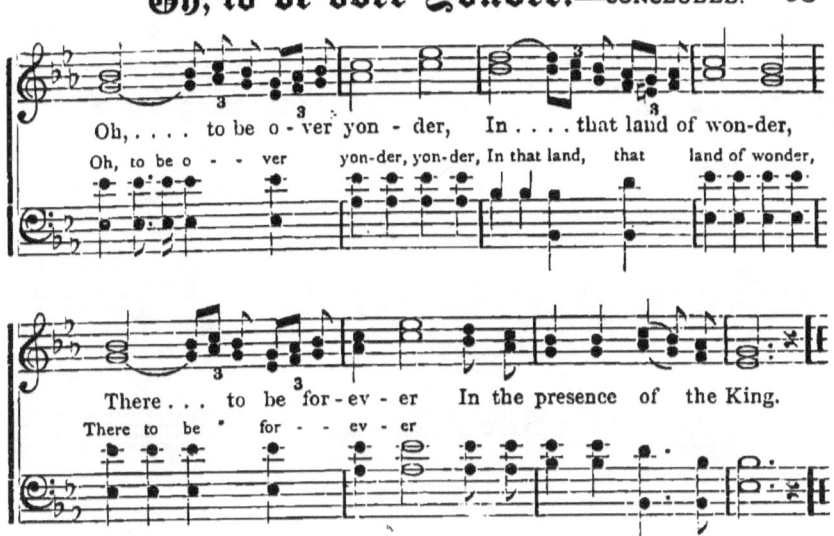

Oh, to be over yonder, In that land of wonder,
There to be forever In the presence of the King.

Saviour, Comfort Me.

JNO. R. SWENEY.

1. In the dark and cloudy day, When earth's riches flee away,
   And the last hope will not stay, Saviour, comfort me.
2. When the secret idol's gone That my poor heart yearned upon,
   Desolate, bereft, alone, Saviour, comfort me.
3. Thou who wast so sorely tried, In the darkness crucified,
   Bid me in thy love confide, Saviour, comfort me.
4. So it shall be good for me Much afflicted now to be,
   If thou wilt but tenderly, Saviour, comfort me.

Copyright, 1875, by John J. Hood

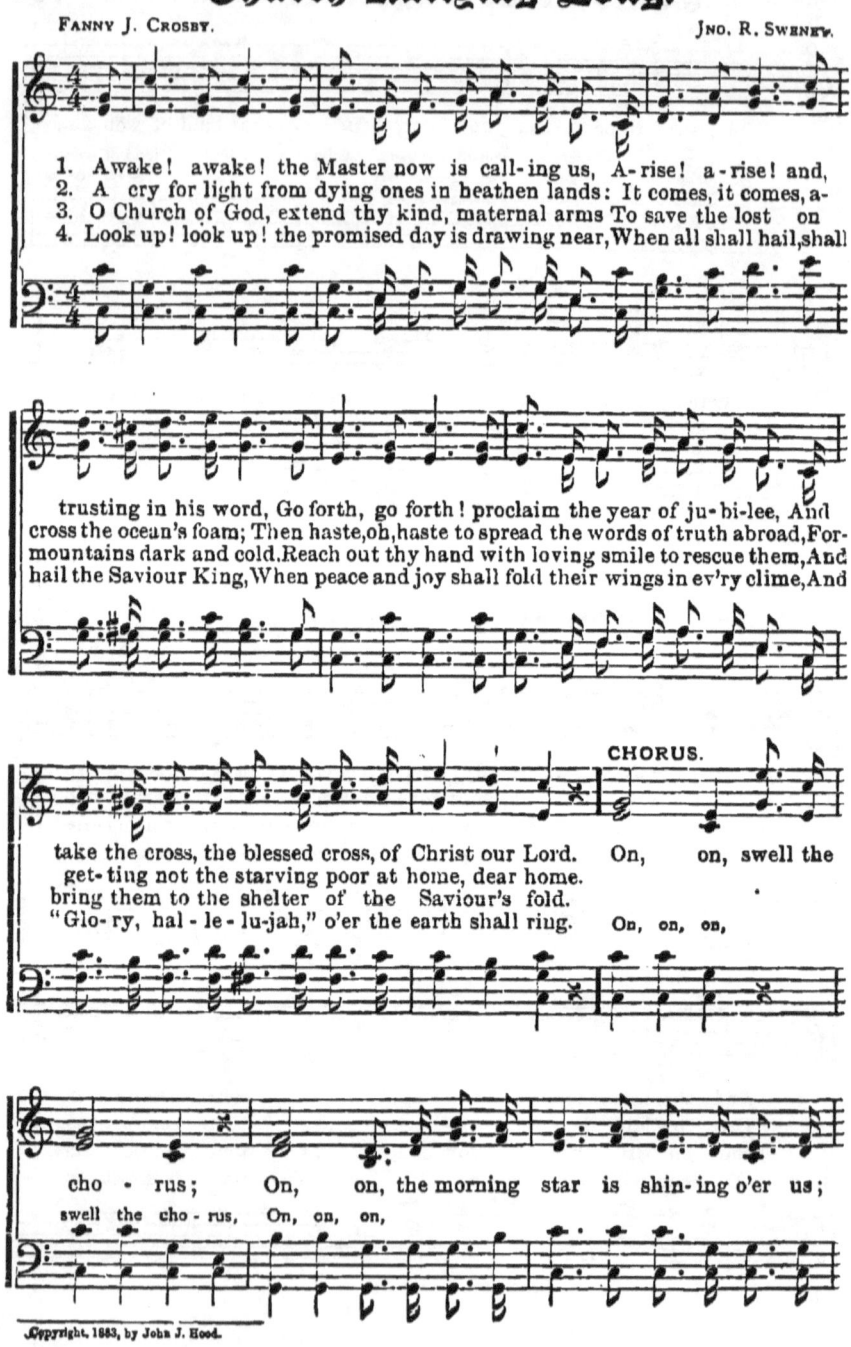

Church Rallying Song.—CONCLUDED. 97

On, on, while before us Our mighty, mighty Saviour leads the way:
Glory, glory, hear the ev-erlasting throng
Shout ho-sanna, while we boldly march along; Faithful soldiers here below,
Only Jesus will we know, Shouting "free salvation" o'er the world we go.

F. J. C. Christmas Carol.—Awake! awake! Tune above.

1 Awake! awake! our festive day is dawning now,
Awake! awake! and hail its golden light;
Rejoice! rejoice! behold the Sun of Righteousness
Arising in its beauty o'er a long, long night.

Cho.—Come, come, join the chorus,
Come, come, the angel hosts are bending o'er us;
Come, come, join the chorus,—
All glory be to God, to God above,
Oh, the rapture of the bright angelic form,
Oh, the rapture while the anthem rolls along.
Hark! the merry, merry bells,
Everywhere their music swells;
Hark! the merry chiming of the grand old bells.

2 Good news, good news resounding o'er the earth again,
Good news, good news: behold a Saviour born;
Make room, make room in every heart to welcome him,
And shout aloud, hosanna! on his birthday morn.

4 He comes, he comes, the captive's cruel chain to break,
He comes, he comes to give his people rest;
Break forth, break forth, his mighty, mighty love proclaim;
In him shall every nation, every clime be blessed.

From "Hood's Carols," by per.

Living Hymns-G

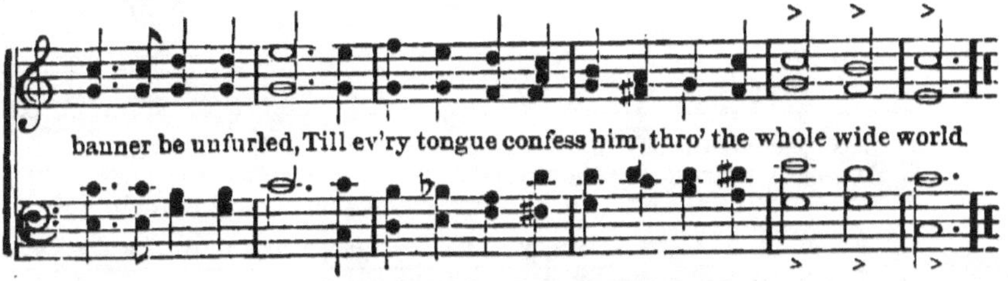

The Whole Wide World.—CONCLUDED 101

banner be unfurled, Till ev'ry tongue confess him, thro' the whole wide world.

Eternity!—Where?

A young man was working alone in a large room in which was a big clock, the loud ticking of which seemed to frame itself into the words, "Eternity!—where?" Unable to endure any longer the reflections thus awakened, he arose and stopped the clock; but the question, "Eternity!—where?" still so haunted him, that he threw down his work, and hurrying home, determined that he would not allow anything to engage his thoughts till he could satisfactorily answer that searching question, "Eternity!—where?"

JNO. R. SWENEY.

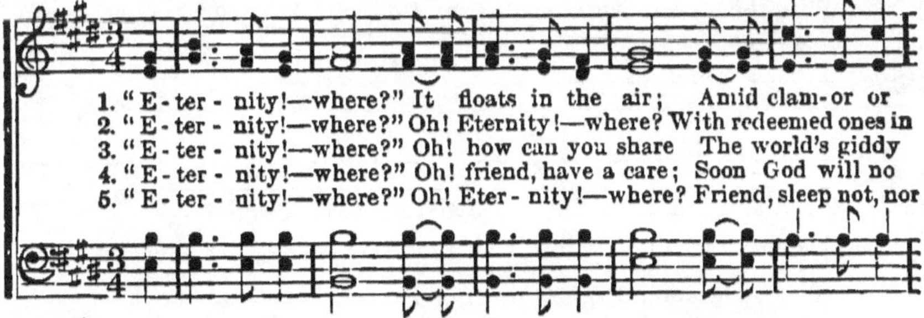

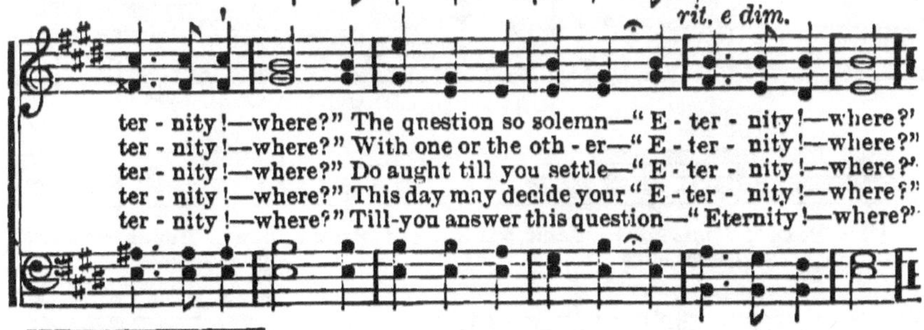

1. "E-ter-nity!—where?" It floats in the air; Amid clam-or or
2. "E-ter-nity!—where?" Oh! Eternity!—where? With redeemed ones in
3. "E-ter-nity!—where?" Oh! how can you share The world's giddy
4. "E-ter-nity!—where?" Oh! friend, have a care; Soon God will no
5. "E-ter-nity!—where?" Oh! Eter-nity!—where? Friend, sleep not, nor

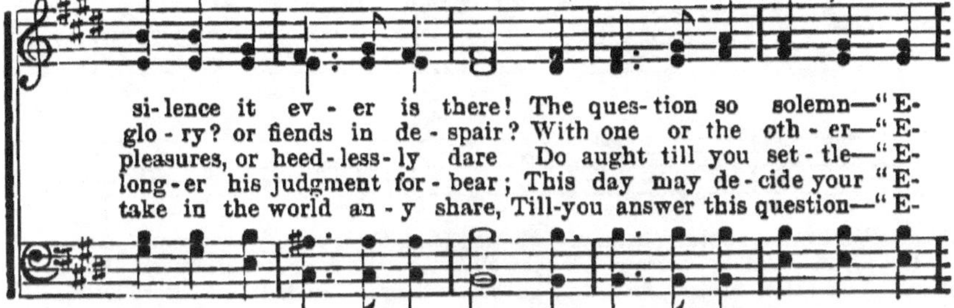

si-lence it ev-er is there! The ques-tion so solemn—"E-
glo-ry? or fiends in de-spair? With one or the oth-er—"E-
pleasures, or heed-less-ly dare Do aught till you set-tle—"E-
long-er his judgment for-bear; This day may de-cide your "E-
take in the world an-y share, Till-you answer this question—"E-

rit. e dim.

ter-nity!—where?" The question so solemn—"E-ter-nity!—where?"
ter-nity!—where?" With one or the oth-er—"E-ter-nity!—where?"
ter-nity!—where?" Do aught till you settle—"E-ter-nity!—where?"
ter-nity!—where?" This day may decide your "E-ter-nity!—where?"
ter-nity!—where?" Till-you answer this question—"Eternity!—where?"

Copyright, 1896, by JOHN J. HOOD.

Passing Homeward.—CONCLUDED.

care, Passing home, to anchor forever; Praise the Lord, we'll soon be there.
care, Passing home, to anchor forev - er; Praise the Lord,

The Prodigal Child.

Mrs. Ellen H. Gates.   "I will arise, and go to my father."   W. H. Doane.

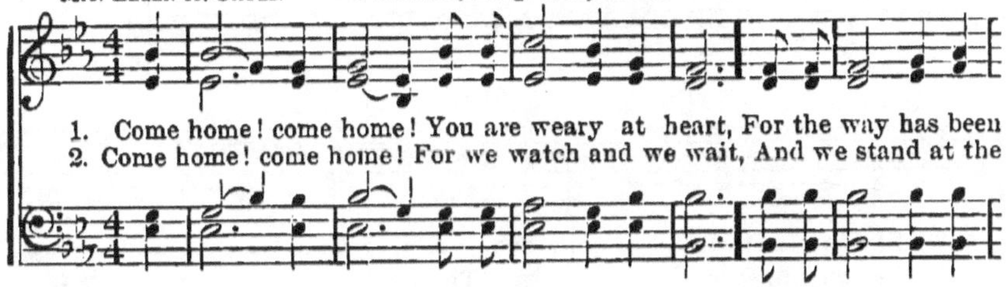

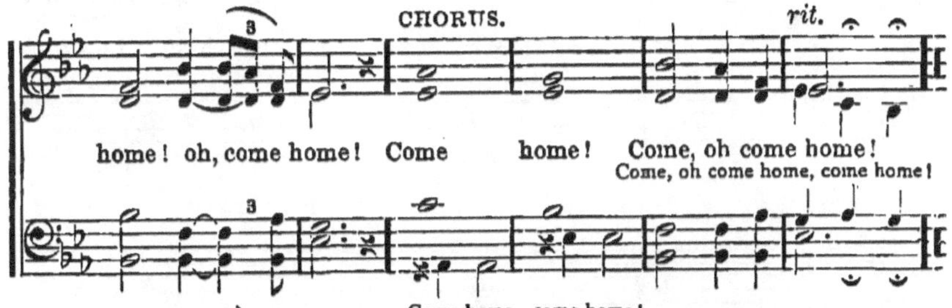

1. Come home! come home! You are weary at heart, For the way has been
2. Come home! come home! For we watch and we wait, And we stand at the

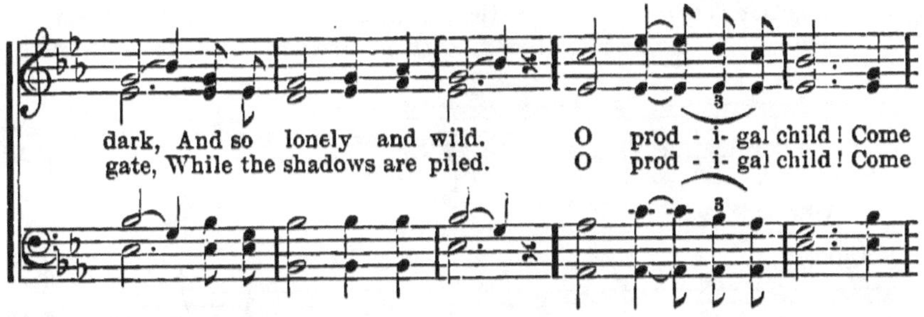

dark, And so lonely and wild.   O prod-i-gal child! Come
gate, While the shadows are piled.   O prod-i-gal child! Come

CHORUS.   *rit.*

home! oh, come home! Come home! Come, oh come home!
Come, oh come home, come home!

Come home, come home!

3 Come home! come home!
From the sorrow and blame,
From the sin and the shame,
And the tempter that smiled,
O prodigal child!
Come home, oh come home!

4 Come home! come home!
There is bread and to spare,
And a warm welcome there,
Then, to friends reconciled,
O prodigal child!
Come home, oh come home.

Used by per. of W. H. Doane, owner of Copyright.

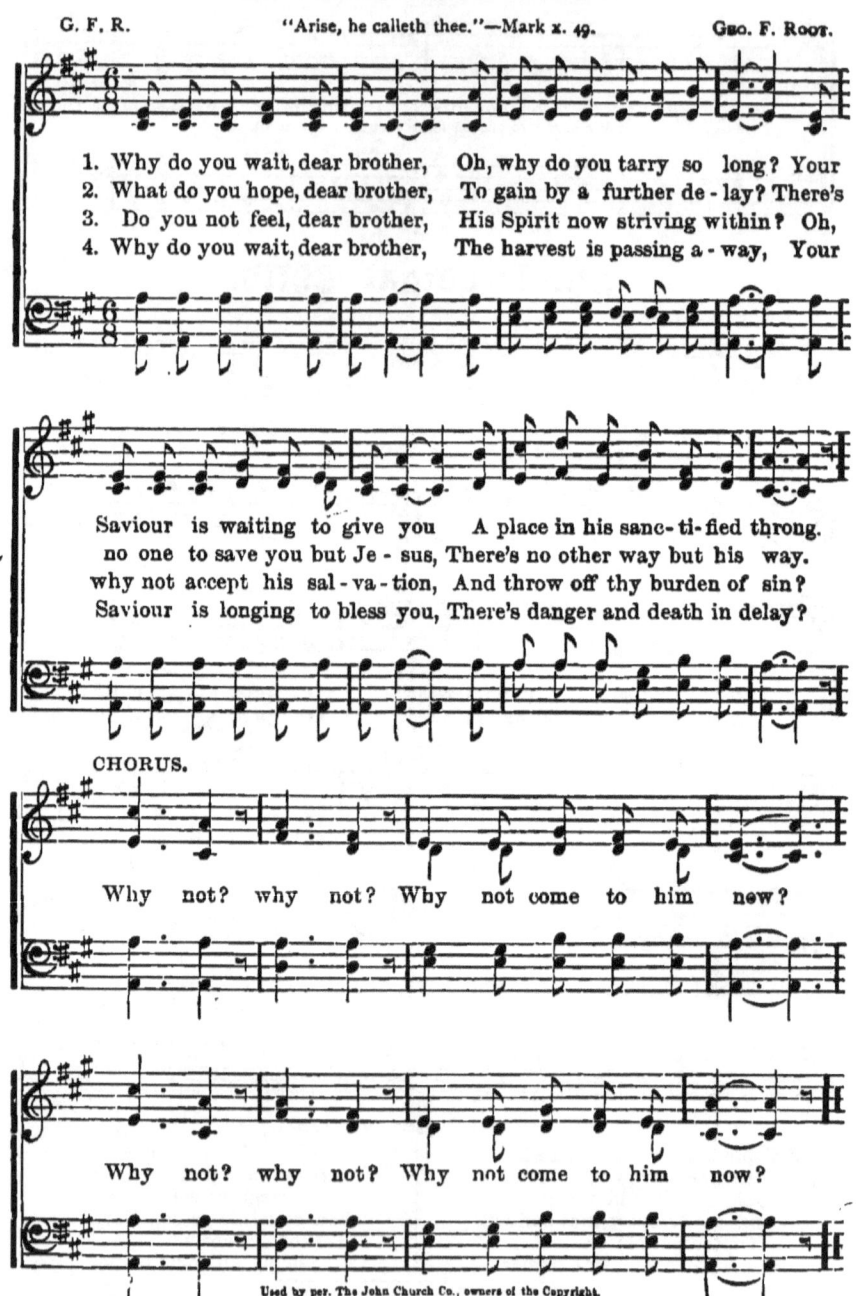

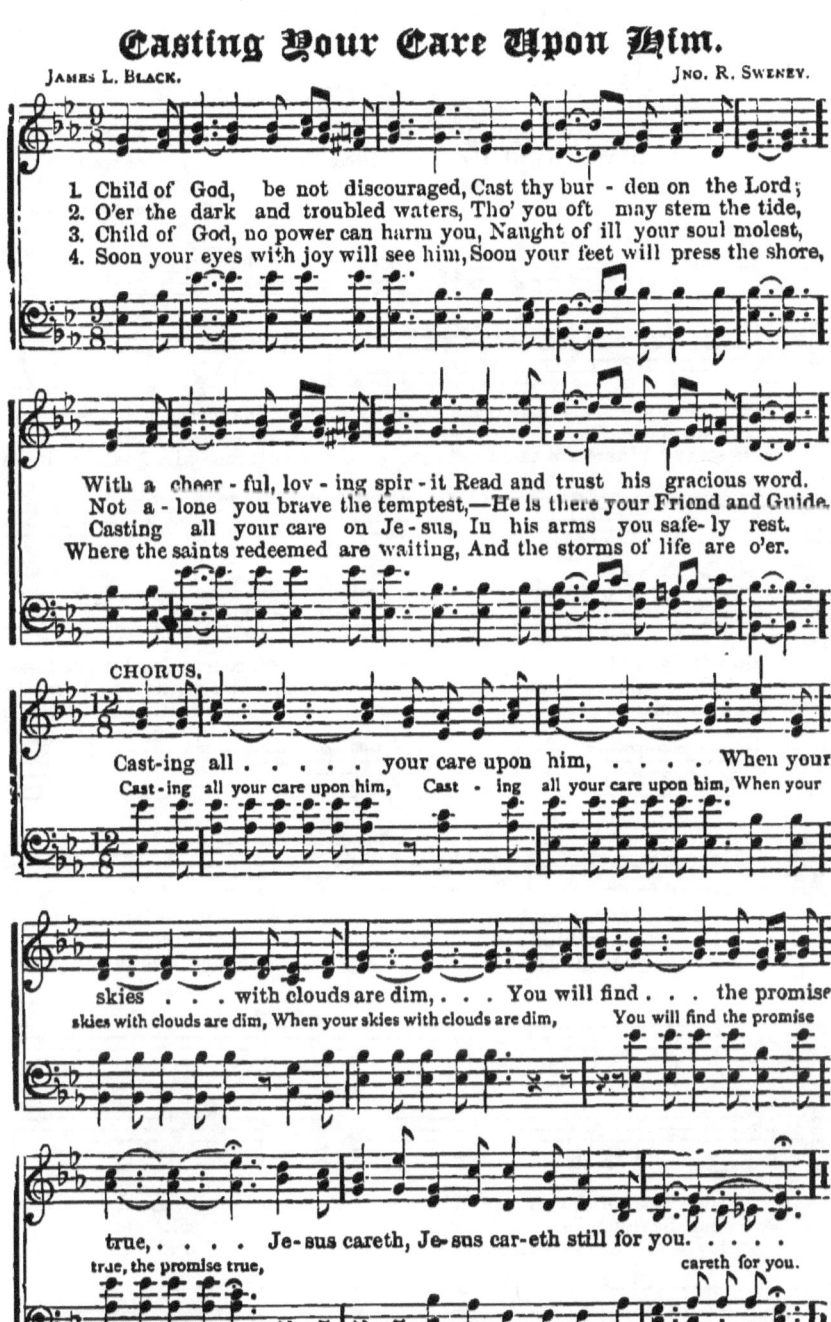

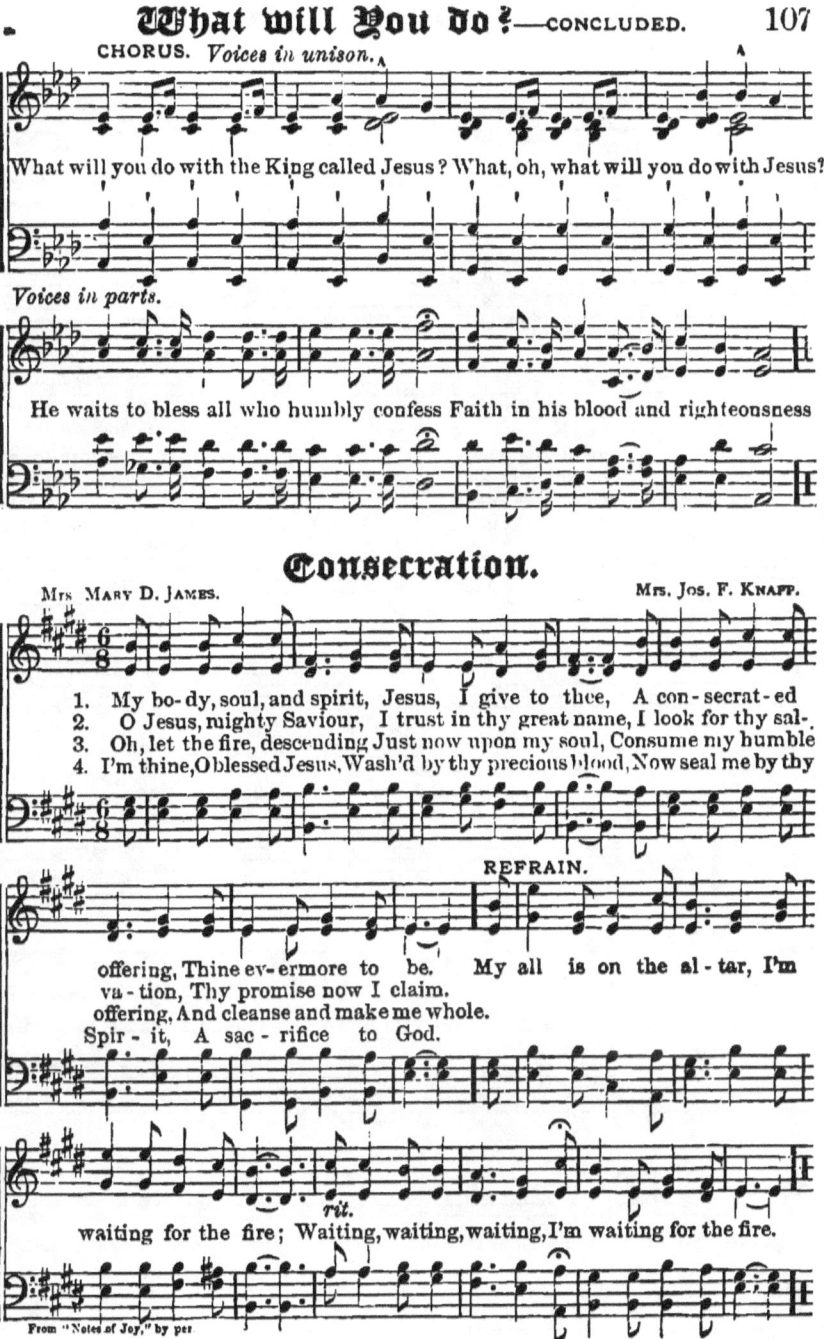

The Endeavor Band.—CONCLUDED.

prayers will ev-er be, That God may bless and keep The Y. P. S. C. E.

Our Sunday School. *Music above.*

1 Our Sunday-school, how sweet, how dear
To meet and learn of Jesus here;
To read his word, whose ev'ry line
Is full of hope and joy divine.

CHO.—Our blessed Sunday-school,
Our bright and happy home,
Within thy peaceful dome
We love, we love to come;
Our thoughts will cling to thee,
And still our prayer will be,
That God may bless and keep our
Sunday-school.

2 Our Sunday school, where all may sing
Glad songs of praise to God our King,
And youthful hearts may find the way
To perfect peace and endless day.

3 Our school is like a garden fair,
Where plants are trained with tender care
To bloom for him, the Lord of all,
Whose loving smiles like sunbeams fall.

4 Our Sunday-school, whose golden hours
From Eden bring refreshing showers,
In thee on earth we learn to live,
For thee our thanks to God we give.

Over the Ocean Wave.

MISSIONARY.   WM. B. BRADBURY. By per.
ANON.

1. O-ver the ocean wave, far, far a-way, There the poor heathen live,
2. Here in this happy land we have the light Shining from God's own word,

CHO.—Pit-y them, pity them, Christians at home, Haste with the bread of life,

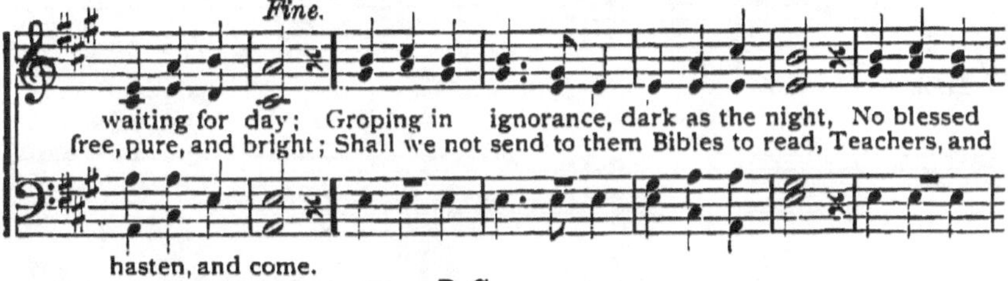

Fine.

waiting for day; Groping in ignorance, dark as the night, No blessed
free, pure, and bright; Shall we not send to them Bibles to read, Teachers, and

hasten, and come.

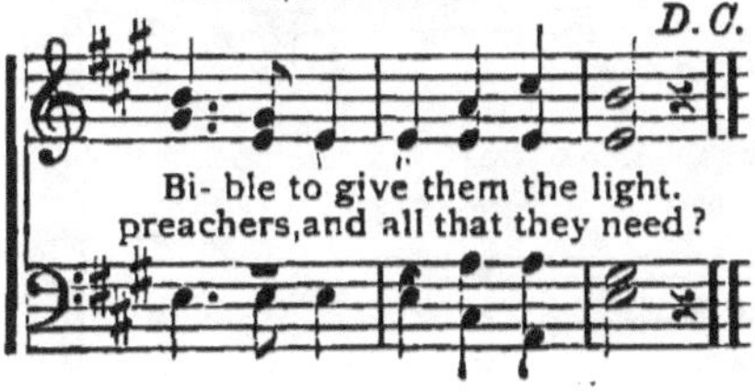

D. C.

Bi-ble to give them the light.
preachers, and all that they need?

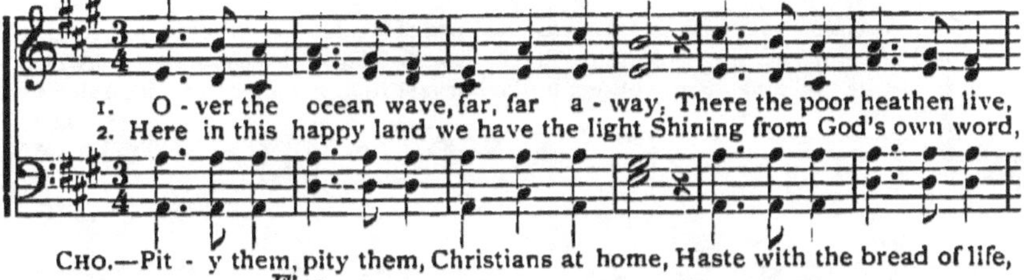

3 Then, while the mission ships glad tidings bring,
List! as that heathen band joyfully sing,
"Over the ocean wave, oh, see them come,
Bringing the bread of life, guiding us home."

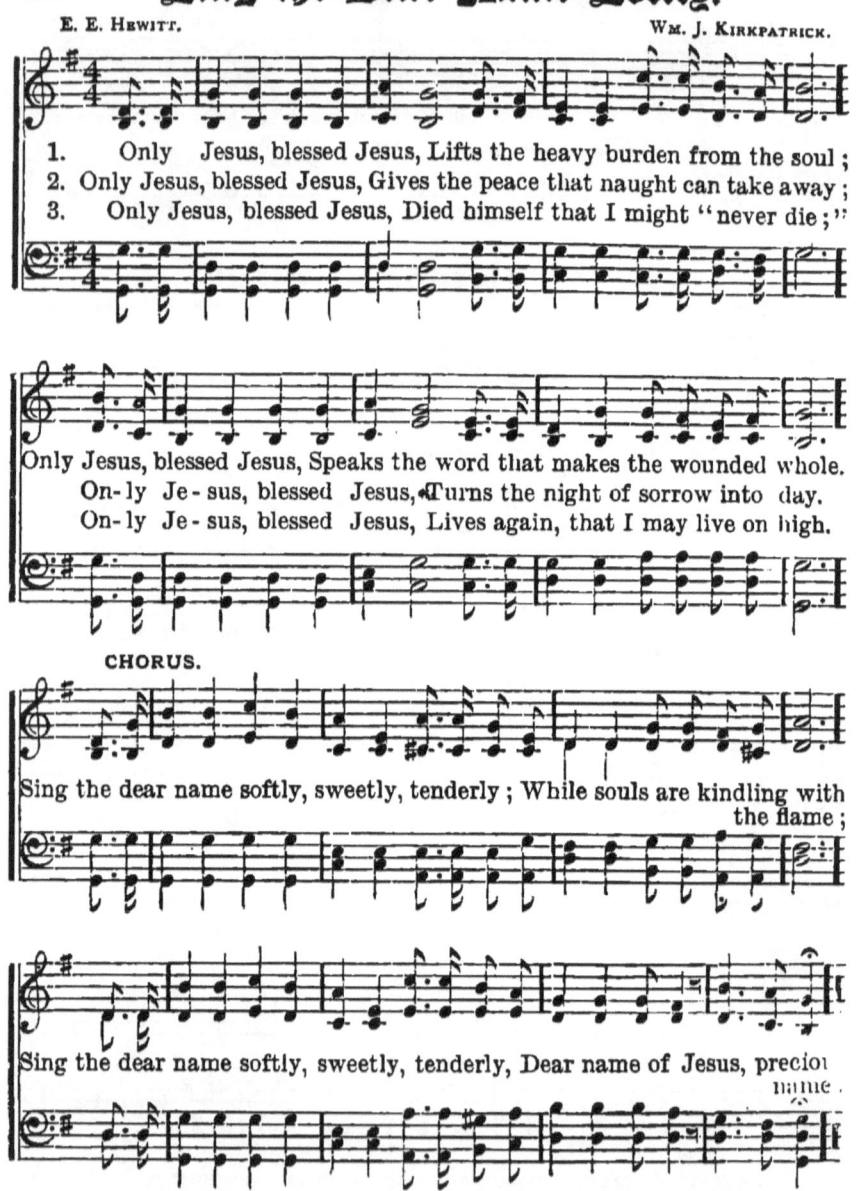

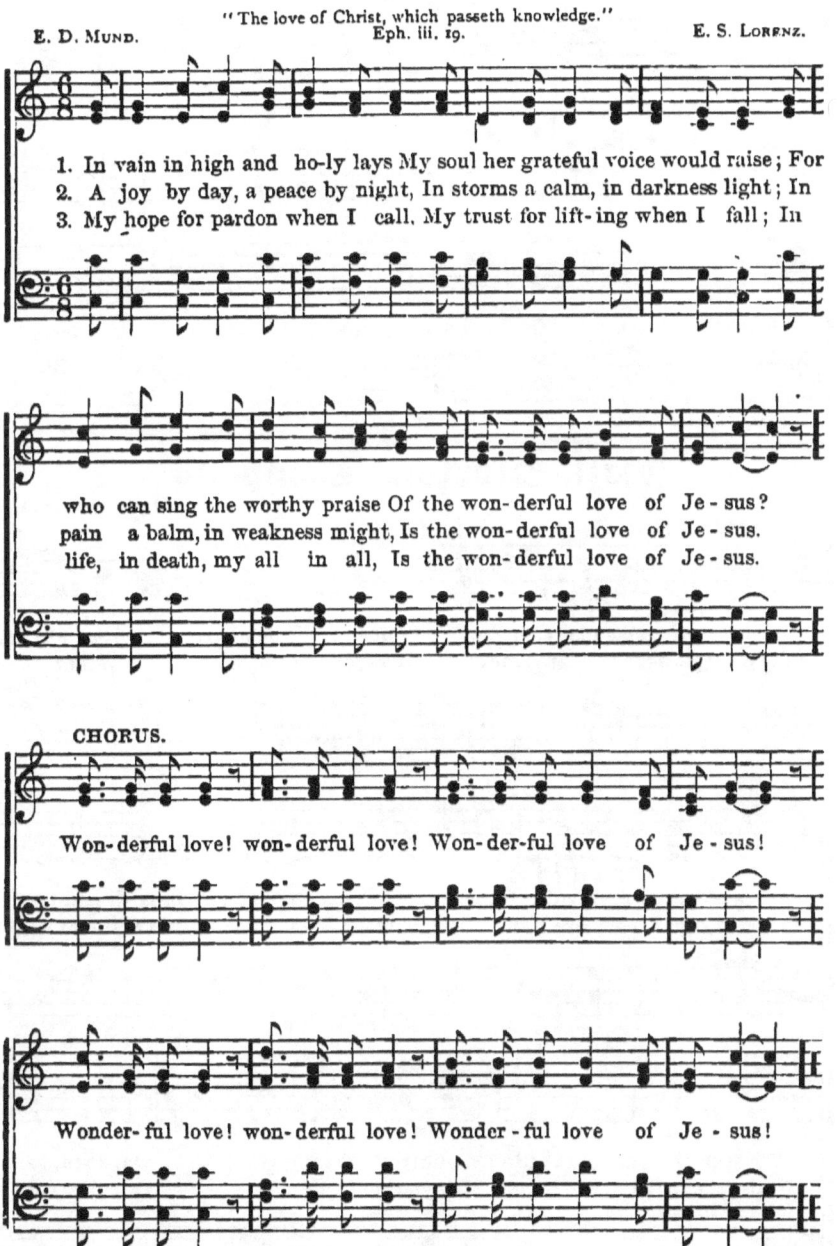

Hail, Glorious Company.—CONCLUDED.

Trust and Obey.

117

Rev. J. H. Sammis. D. B Towner.

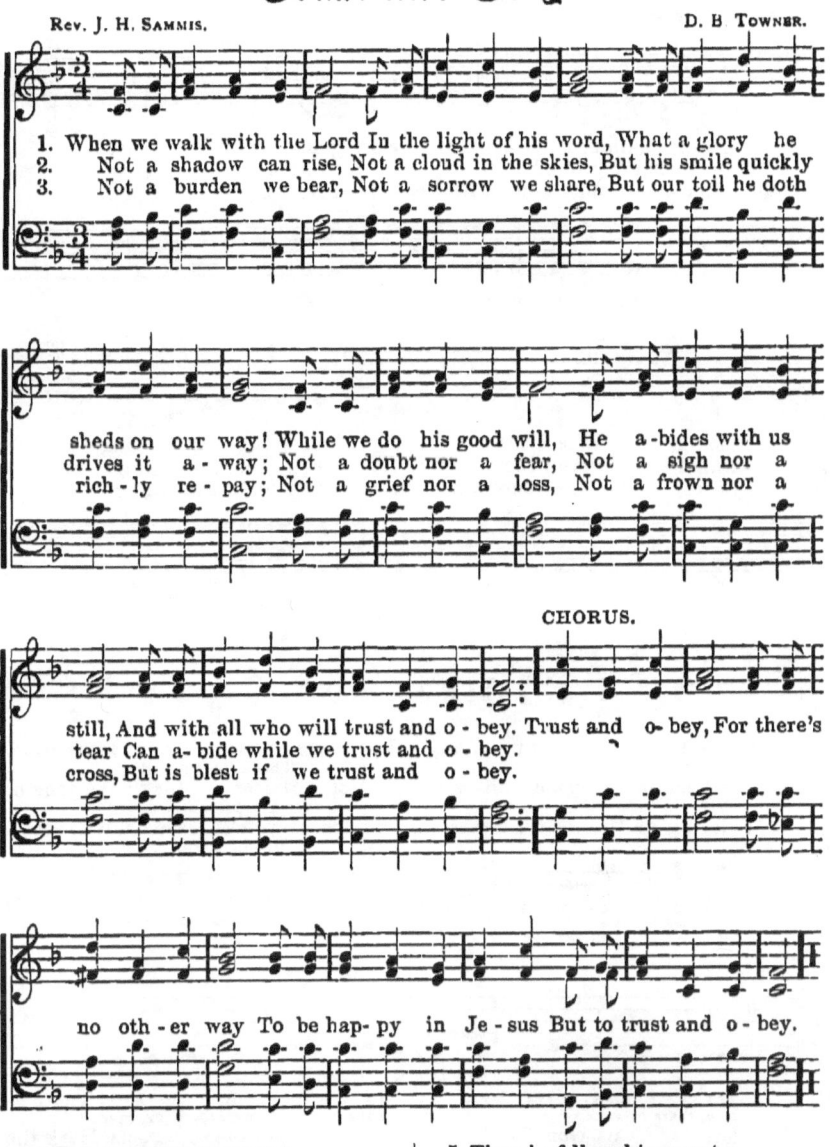

1. When we walk with the Lord In the light of his word, What a glory he sheds on our way! While we do his good will, He abides with us still, And with all who will trust and o-bey.
2. Not a shadow can rise, Not a cloud in the skies, But his smile quickly drives it a-way; Not a doubt nor a fear, Not a sigh nor a tear Can a-bide while we trust and o-bey.
3. Not a burden we bear, Not a sorrow we share, But our toil he doth rich-ly re-pay; Not a grief nor a loss, Not a frown nor a cross, But is blest if we trust and o-bey.

CHORUS.

Trust and o-bey, For there's no oth-er way To be hap-py in Je-sus But to trust and o-bey.

4 But we never can prove
The delights of his love
Until all on the altar we lay,
For the favor he shows,
And the joy he bestows,
Are for all who will trust and obey.

5 Then in fellowship sweet
We will sit at his feet,
Or we'll walk by his side in the way;
What he says we will do,
Where he sends we will go,
Never fear, only trust and obey.

Copyright, 1887, by D. B. Towner. Used by per.

The Summer Land.—CONCLUDED.

119 F. J. C. **The Prince of Peace.** Tune above.

1 'Twas a night of long ago when all were
    sleeping, sleeping, sleeping, [keeping,
When the lonely silent stars a watch were
    Softly o'er the dreaming, dreaming earth ;
Floods of light bursting forth in glory,
    (Pure floods of light, pure floods of light, etc.,)
    Brightest glory, brightest glory,
Harp and voice told the joyful story
    (Sweet harp and voice, sweet harp and voice,)
    Of his birth the Prince of Peace.
Cho.—He has come ; hail the lovely stranger,
    (Yes, he has come, yes, he has come, etc.,)
    Lovely stranger, lovely stranger ;
Lo, the babe cradled in a manger
    (O blessed babe, O blessed babe,)
    Is the King and Prince of Peace.

2 See the rosy blushing morn again is
    breaking, breaking, breaking,
And the melody of song again is waking
    Music in the hearts of all to-day ;
Praise the Lord, come with happy voices,
    (Praise, praise the Lord, praise, praise the Lord,)
    Happy voices, happy voices,
Praise the Lord, how the world rejoices,
    (Praise, praise the Lord, praise, praise the Lord,)
    At his birth the Prince of Peace.

3 Hark the merry silver bells are sweetly
    ringing, ringing, ringing,
And the multitude of angels now are singing
    Glory in the highest evermore ;
Sing aloud, glory ! hallelujah !
    (Sing, sing aloud, sing, sing aloud, etc.,)
    Hallelujah ! hallelujah !
Sing aloud. glory ! hallelujah !
    (Sing, sing aloud, sing, sing aloud,)
    At his birth the Prince of Peace.

From " Hood's Carols for— —Christmas, No. 6," by per.

120. Along the River of Time.

G. F. R.
"Remember how short time is."—Ps. lxxxix. 47.
Geo. F. Root.

1. Along the River of Time we glide, Along the river, along the river, The
2. Along the River of Time we glide, Along the river, along the river; A
3. Along the River of Time we glide, Along the river, along the river; Our

swiftly flowing, resistless tide, The swiftly flowing, the swiftly flowing, And
thousand dangers its currents hide, A thousand dangers, a thousand dangers, And
Saviour only our bark can guide, Our Saviour only, our Saviour only, But

soon, ah, soon the end we'll see: Yes, soon 'twill come, and we will be
near our course the rocks we see: O dreadful thought! a wreck to be,
with him we se-cure may be: No fear, no doubt, but joy to be

p Float-ing, float-ing Out on the sea of e-ter-ni-ty!

pp *rit.* Float-ing, float-ing Out on the sea of e-ter-ni-ty!

by par. of The John Church Co., owners of copyright.

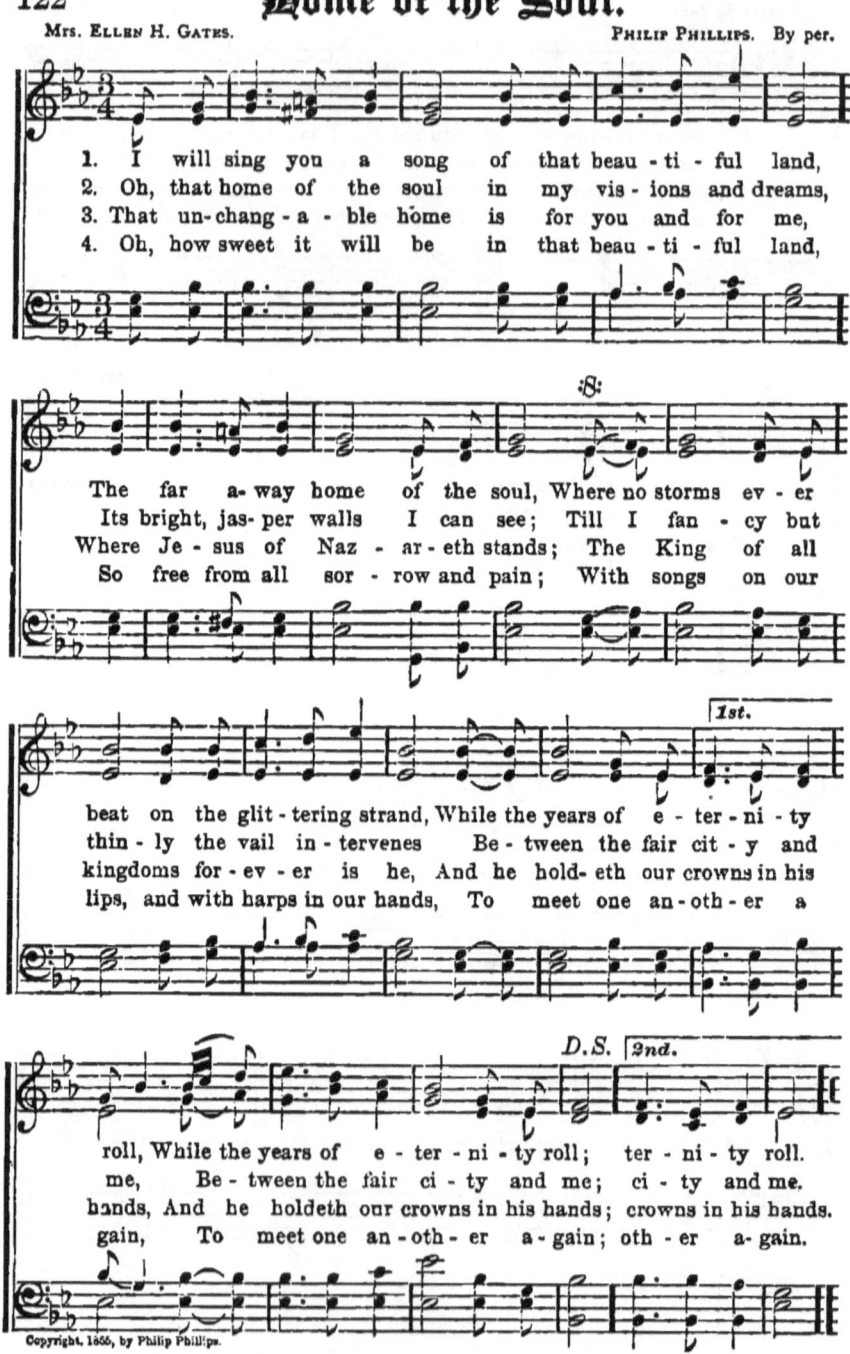

Church of God, Awake.—CONCLUDED.

Send the gos - pel's joyful sound Unto earth's remotest bound.
Oh, send the gos - pel's joy-ful sound

I will Praise Thee.

T. OLIVERS.   C. C. CONVERSE. By per.

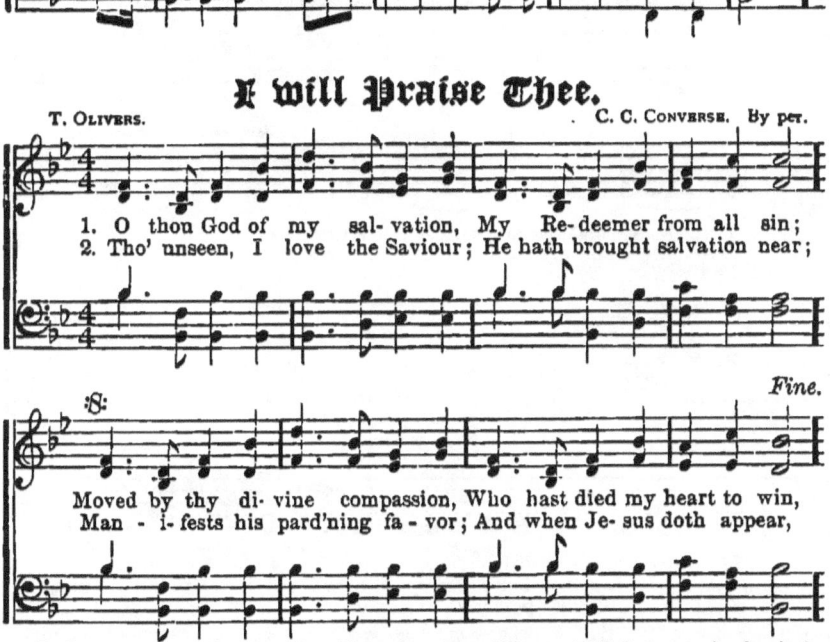

1. O thou God of my sal - vation, My Re-deemer from all sin;
2. Tho' unseen, I love the Saviour; He hath brought salvation near;

Moved by thy di - vine compassion, Who hast died my heart to win,
Man - i - fests his pard'ning fa - vor; And when Je- sus doth appear,

D. S.—I will praise thee, I will praise thee; Where shall I thy praise begin?
Soul and bod - y, soul and bod - y Shall his glorious im - age bear.

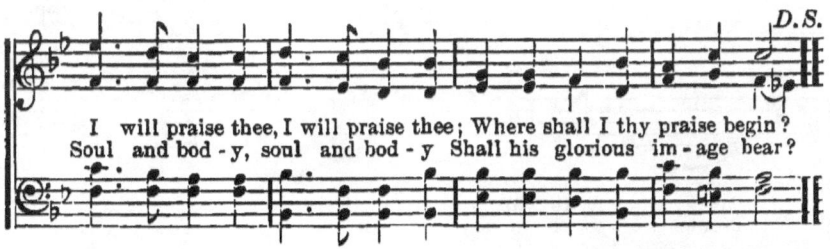

I will praise thee, I will praise thee; Where shall I thy praise begin?
Soul and bod - y, soul and bod - y Shall his glorious im - age bear?

3 While the angel choirs are crying,
  "Glory to the great I AM,"
I with them will still be vying—
  Glory! glory to the Lamb!
    O how precious
Is the sound of Jesus' name!

4 Angels now are hovering round us,
  Unperceived amid the throng;
Wondering at the love that crowned us,
  Glad to join the holy song:
    Hallelujah,
Love and praise to Christ belong!

Living for Jesus.—CONCLUDED.

Je-sus has freed me, Jesus shall lead me, Gladly I fol-low his voice;
Hap-py and grateful, tender and faithful, Ready to work or to wait;
Love's lowly mission, highest am-bition, Crowning each cross with delight;

Use first four lines as Chorus. D.C.

Living for Je-sus, living for Je-sus, Glo-ri-ous portion and choice!
Living for Je-sus, living for Je-sus, Serving him ear-ly and late.
Duty is gladness, shining thro' sadness, Faith will soon grow into sight.

Saviour, Pilot Me.

J. E. GOULD.

1. Jesus, Saviour, pilot me
Over life's tempestuous sea;
Unknown waves before me roll,
Hiding rock and treacherous shoal;
Chart and compass came from thee:
Jesus, Saviour, pilot me.

2. When the Apostles' fragile bark
Struggled with the billows dark,
On the stormy Galilee,
Thou did'st walk across the sea;
And when they beheld thy form,
Safe they glided through the storm.

3. As a mother stills her child
Thou canst hush the ocean wild;
Boisterous waves obey thy will
When thou say'st to them "Be still."
Wondrous Sovereign of the sea,
Jesus, Saviour, pilot me.

4. When at last I near the shore,
And the fearful breakers roar
'Twixt me and the peaceful rest,
Then, while leaning on thy breast,
May I hear thee say to me,
"Fear not, I will pilot thee."

Beautiful Home.—CONCLUDED. 129

Home, home of our Saviour, Bright, beautiful home.
Beautiful,

The New Name.

J. E. H. J. E. HALL.

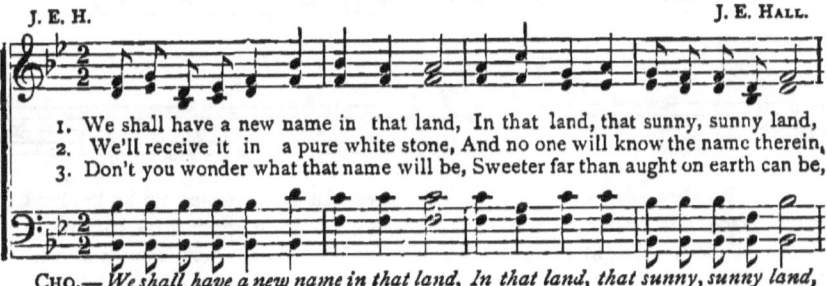

1. We shall have a new name in that land, In that land, that sunny, sunny land,
2. We'll receive it in a pure white stone, And no one will know the name therein,
3. Don't you wonder what that name will be, Sweeter far than aught on earth can be,

CHO.—*We shall have a new name in that land, In that land, that sunny, sunny land,*

Fine.

When we meet that bright angelic band, In that sunny land. A new name, a new name
Only unto him who hath 'tis known, When we're free from sin. A white stone, a white stone
We will be quite satisfied when we Shall that new name know. I wonder, I wonder

When we meet that bright angelic band, In that sunny land.

To Chorus, D.C.

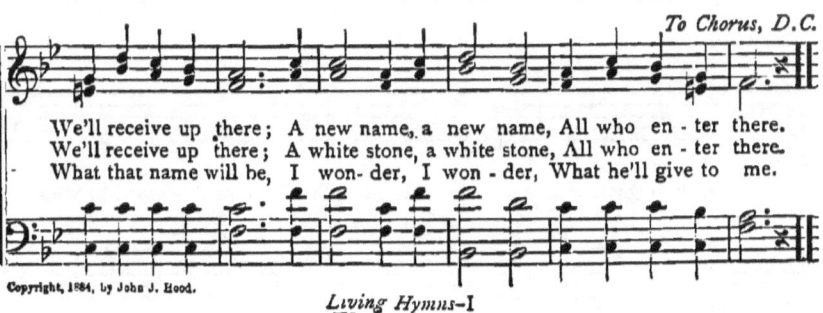

We'll receive up there; A new name, a new name, All who enter there.
We'll receive up there; A white stone, a white stone, All who enter there.
What that name will be, I wonder, I wonder, What he'll give to me.

Copyright, 1884, by John J. Hood.

Living Hymns—I

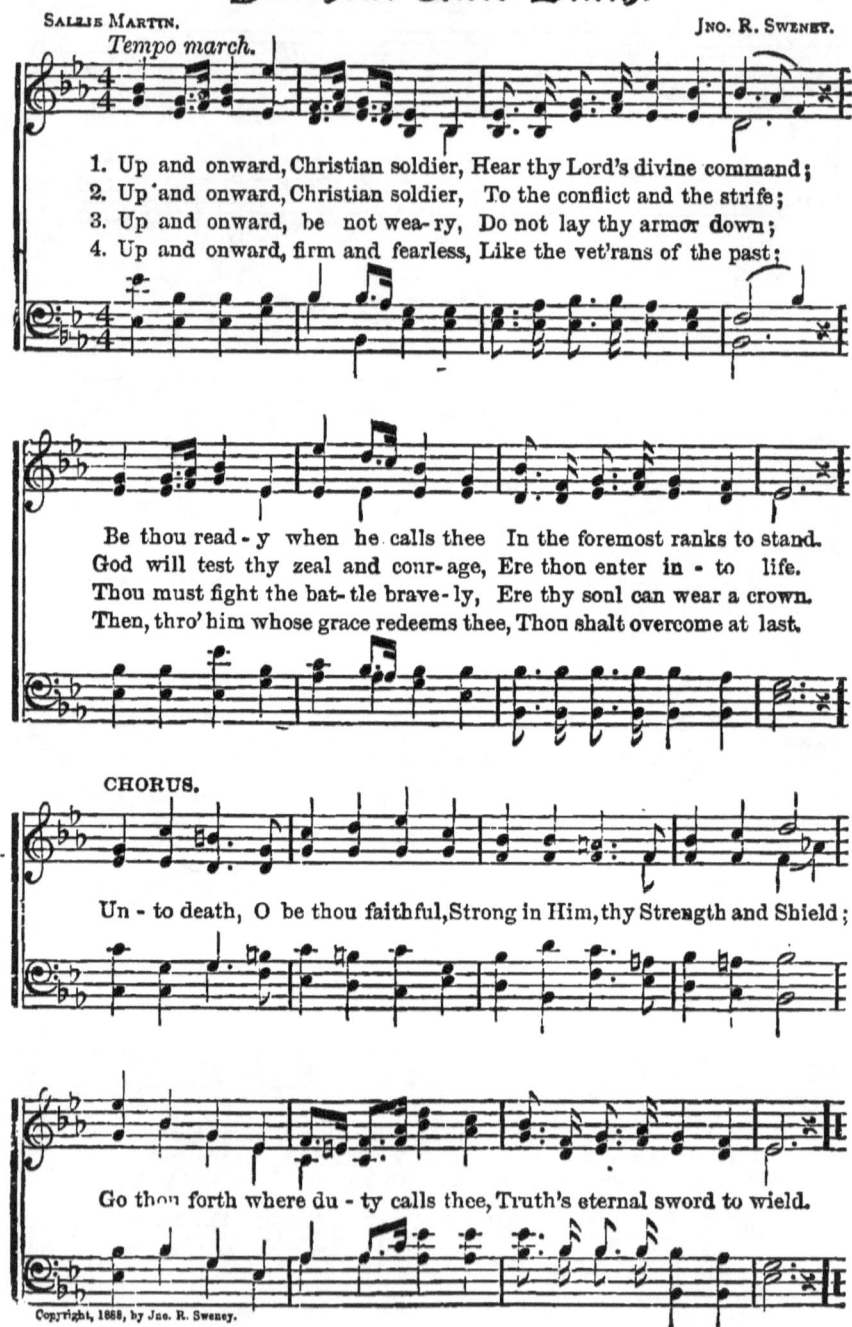

Let Your Light Shine.

131

Words and music by Mrs. G. W. Burroughs.

Earnestly.

1. Brother, you've come to the Lord, You believe in his ho-ly word,
2. Brother, your Lord lived for you As the humblest of humble do,
3. Brother, you may really think, And by this from your duty shrink,
4. Brother, your talents may be Neither five, nor yet two or three,

And its light has shone on your heart; Oh! my brother, ne'er let it depart.
And for you he willingly died, To redeem you, and all men beside.
That for you there's nothing to do, But, my brother, that can't be, no! no!
But you certainly must have one, Then, arouse you! before that is gone.

CHORUS.

Let your light shine, Oh, let it now shine, Out from your heart o'er the world;

Do something, tho' it's lit-tle, Out of love for your Lord.

Copyright, 1890, by John. J. Hood.

He will Hide Me.—CONCLUDED. 133

hide me In the shad - - ow of His hand.

safe - ly hide me In the shad - ow of His hand.

In the Hour of Trial.

"I have prayed for thee that thy faith fail not."

JAMES MONTGOMERY.   SPENCER LANE.

1. In the hour of tri - al, Je-sus, plead for me; Lest by base de-ni - al
2. With forbidden pleasures Would this vain world charm; Or its sordid treasures
3. Should Thy mercy send me Sorrow, toil, and woe; Or should pain attend me
4. When my last hour cometh, Fraught with strife and pain, When my dust returneth

I depart from Thee, When Thou see'st me waver, With a look re -
Spread to work me harm; Bring to my remembrance Sad Geth-sem-a -
On my path be - low: Grant that I may nev - er Fail Thy hand to
To the dust a - gain; On Thy truth re-ly - ing, Through that mortal

call, Nor for fear or fa - vor Suf-fer me to fall.
ne, Or, in dark- er semblance, Cross-crowned Calvary. A-men.
see; Grant that I may ev - er Cast my care on Thee.
strife, Je - sus, take me, dy - ing, To e - ter - nal life.

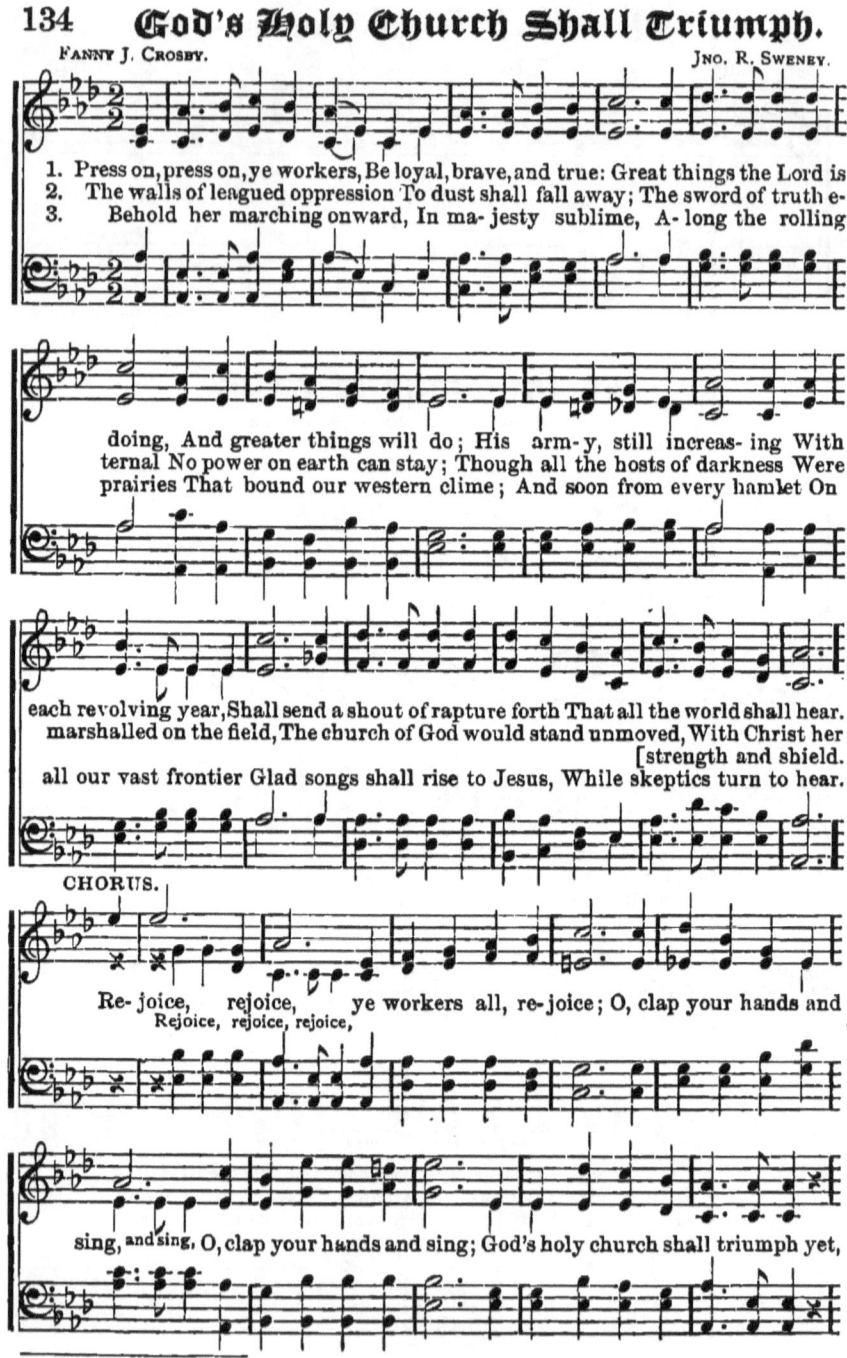

God's Holy Church.—CONCLUDED.

triumph yet, triumph yet, And he shall reign our King, shall reign our King.

Light after Darkness.

JNO. R. SWENEY.

DUET.

1. Light af-ter dark-ness, Gain af-ter loss, Strength af-ter
2. Sheaves af-ter sow-ing, Sun af-ter rain, Sight af-ter
3. Near af-ter dis-tant, Gleam af-ter gloom, Love af-ter

weak-ness, Crown af-ter cross, Sweet af-ter bit-ter,
mys-tery, Peace af-ter pain, Joy af-ter sor-row,
loneliness, Life af-ter tomb; Af-ter long a-go-ny,

Song af-ter fears, Home af-ter wan-der-ing, Praise af-ter tears.
Calm af-ter blast, Rest af-ter wea-riness,—Sweet rest at last.
Rap-ture of bliss; Right was the path-way Leading to this!

From "Goodly Pearls," by par

Joy in Heaven.

Priscilla J. Owens.
Wm. J. Kirkpatrick.

There is joy, there is joy, There is joy in heaven:

1. A ransomed soul re-turns, The path of sin for-sak-ing,
2. A weep-ing sin-ner kneels, The chains of death are brok-en,
3. No news of pain or care, The jas-per sea o'er-reaching,
4. O then to God re-turn,—Come back and be for-giv-en,

And while his sad heart mourns, The harps of God are wak-ing.
And soon his glad heart feels The Saviour's welcome spok-en.
But sweet is echoed there The contrite heart's beseech-ing.
And soon thy heart shall learn To know the joy of heav-en.

CHORUS.

{ All the golden bells are ringing,
  All the angel choirs are singing, } All the lov-ing an-gels say,

"There is joy in heav'n to-day, There is joy, there is joy, joy, joy to-day."

Copyright, 1882, by John J. Hood.

Glory to Jesus, He Saves.

P. B.
P. BILHORN.

1. Glo-ry to Je-sus who died on the tree, Paid the great price that my soul might be free; Now I can sing hal-le-lu-jah to God,
2. Once in my heart there was sin and despair, Now the dear Saviour him-self dwelleth there, And from his pres-ence comes peace to my soul,
3. Come, then, ye wea-ry, who long to be free, Come to the Saviour, he wait-eth for thee; Then with the ransomed this song you can sing,

CHORUS.

Glo-ry! he saves, he saves. Glo-ry! he saves, glo-ry! he saves, Saves a poor sin-ner like me; Glo-ry! he saves, glo-ry! he saves, Saves a poor sin-ner like me. like me.

Copyright, 1886, by P. Bilhorn.

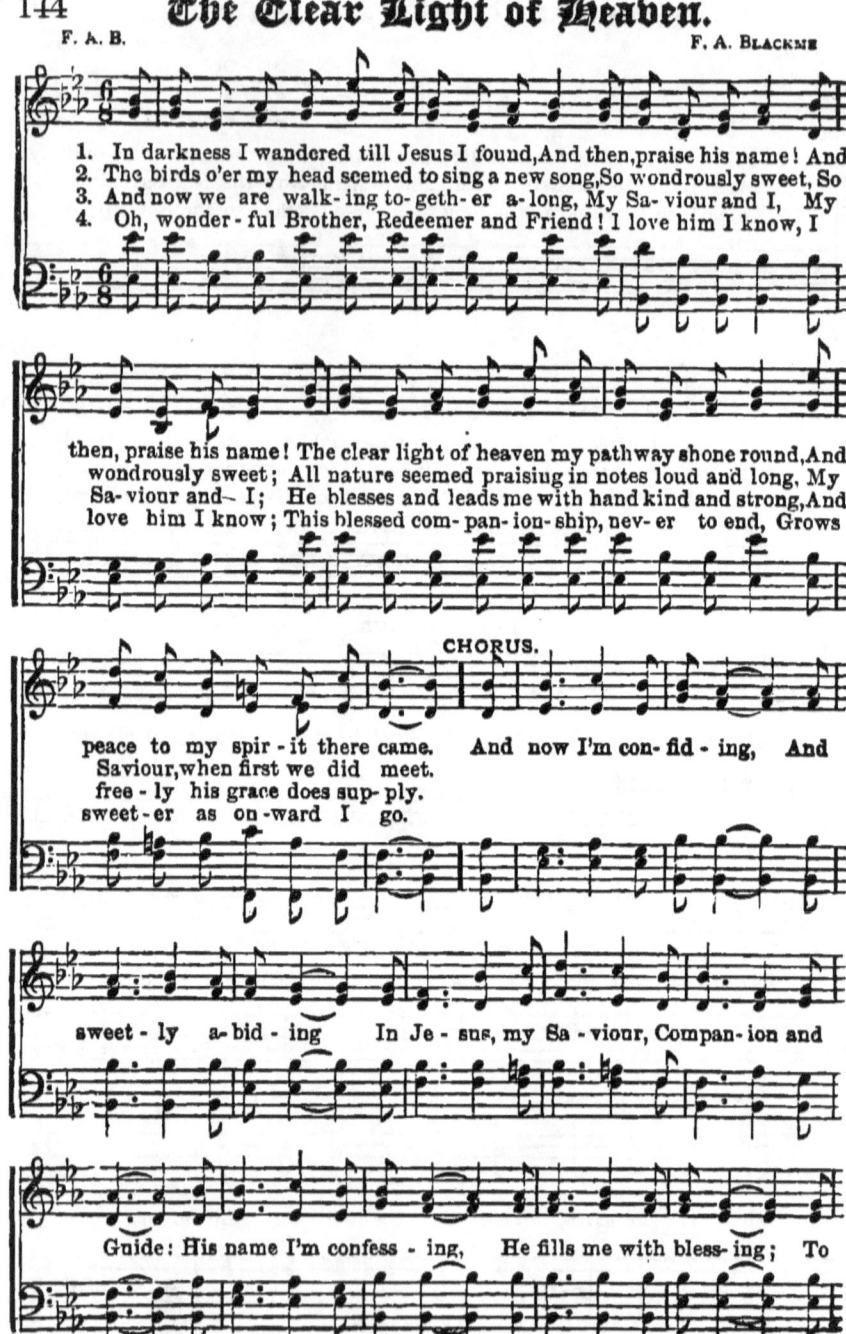

The Clear Light, etc.—CONCLUDED.

me he's far dear-er Than all else be-side.

It Fills My Heart with Joy.

E. E. Hewitt. JNO. R. Sweney.

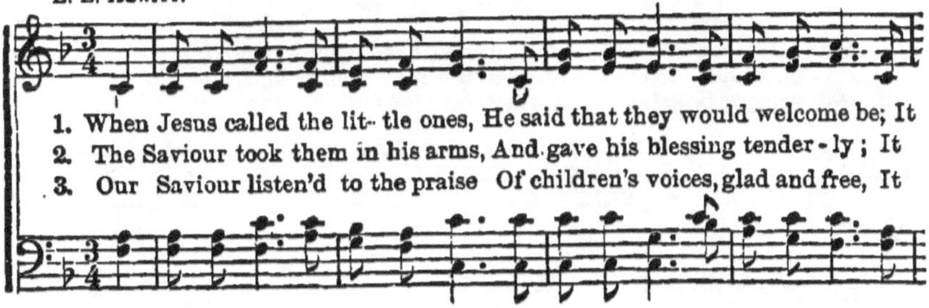

1. When Jesus called the lit- tle ones, He said that they would welcome be; It
2. The Saviour took them in his arms, And gave his blessing tender-ly; It
3. Our Saviour listen'd to the praise Of children's voices, glad and free, It

fills my heart with joy to know He spoke those words for me, For me, for me, He
fills my heart with joy to know His blessing is for me, For me, for me, His
fills my heart with joy to know He listens now to me, To me, to me, He

[me.
spoke those words for me, It fills my heart with joy to know, He spoke those words for
bless-ing is for me, It fills my heart with joy to know, His blessing is for me.
listens now to me, It fills my heart with joy to know, He listens now to me.

Copyright, 1890, by Jno. R. Sweney. *Living Hymns*—K

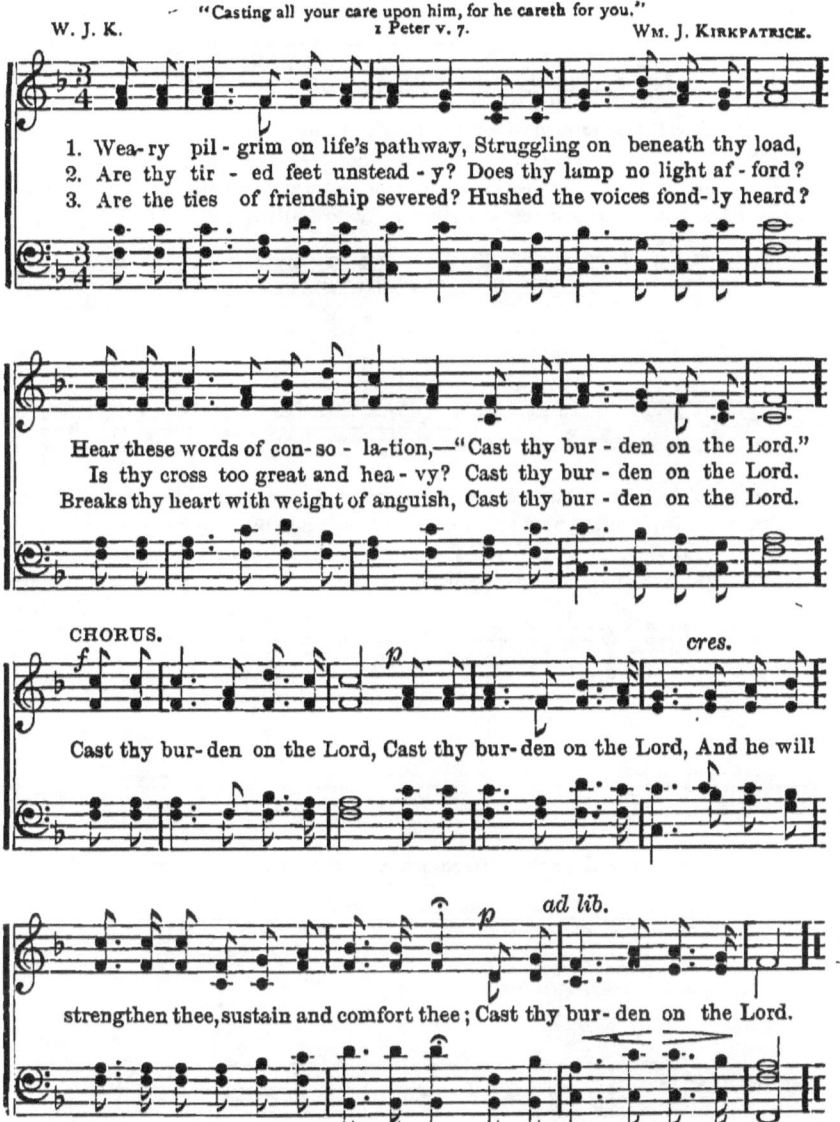

4 Does thy heart with faintness falter?
　Does thy mind forget his word?
　Does thy strength succumb to weak-
　Cast thy burden on the Lord. [ness?

5 He will hold thee up from falling,
　He will guide thy steps aright;
　He will strengthen each endeavor;
　He will keep thee by his might.

5 I dreamed that hoary time had fled,
   And earth and sea gave up their dead,
   A fire dissolved this ball,
   I saw the church's ransomed throng,
   I heard the burden of their song,
   'Twas "Christ is all in all."

6 Then come to Christ, oh, come to-day,
   The Father, Son, and Spirit say;
   The Bride repeats the call,
   For he will cleanse your guilty stains,
   His love will soothe your weary pains,
   For "Christ is all in all."

By permission

Keep Thy Faith Steady.

MARTHA J. LANKTON.   WM. J. KIRKPATRICK.

1. Keep thy faith steady, my brother, Shedding its beautiful ray,
2. Keep thy faith steady, my brother, Firm as a rock let it be;
3. Keep thy faith steady, my brother, Looking to Jesus alone;
4. Keep thy faith steady, my brother, Souls by its light may be won;

Clear as the brow of the morning, Bright as the eye of the day.
Pray, and believe when thou prayest, Love hath an answer for thee.
Then will the blessing thou seekest Drop like the dew from his throne.
Trust till thy journey is over, Trust till thy life-work is done.

CHORUS.

Tranquilly shining, never declining,
Tranquilly, tranquilly shining, never, no, never declining,

Keep ... thy faith steady, and wait, oh, wait on the Lord.
Keep thy faith steady, keep thy faith steady,

Copyright, 1896, by John J. Hood.

He Comes.

FANNY J. CROSBY. JNO. R. SWENEY.

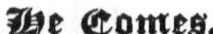

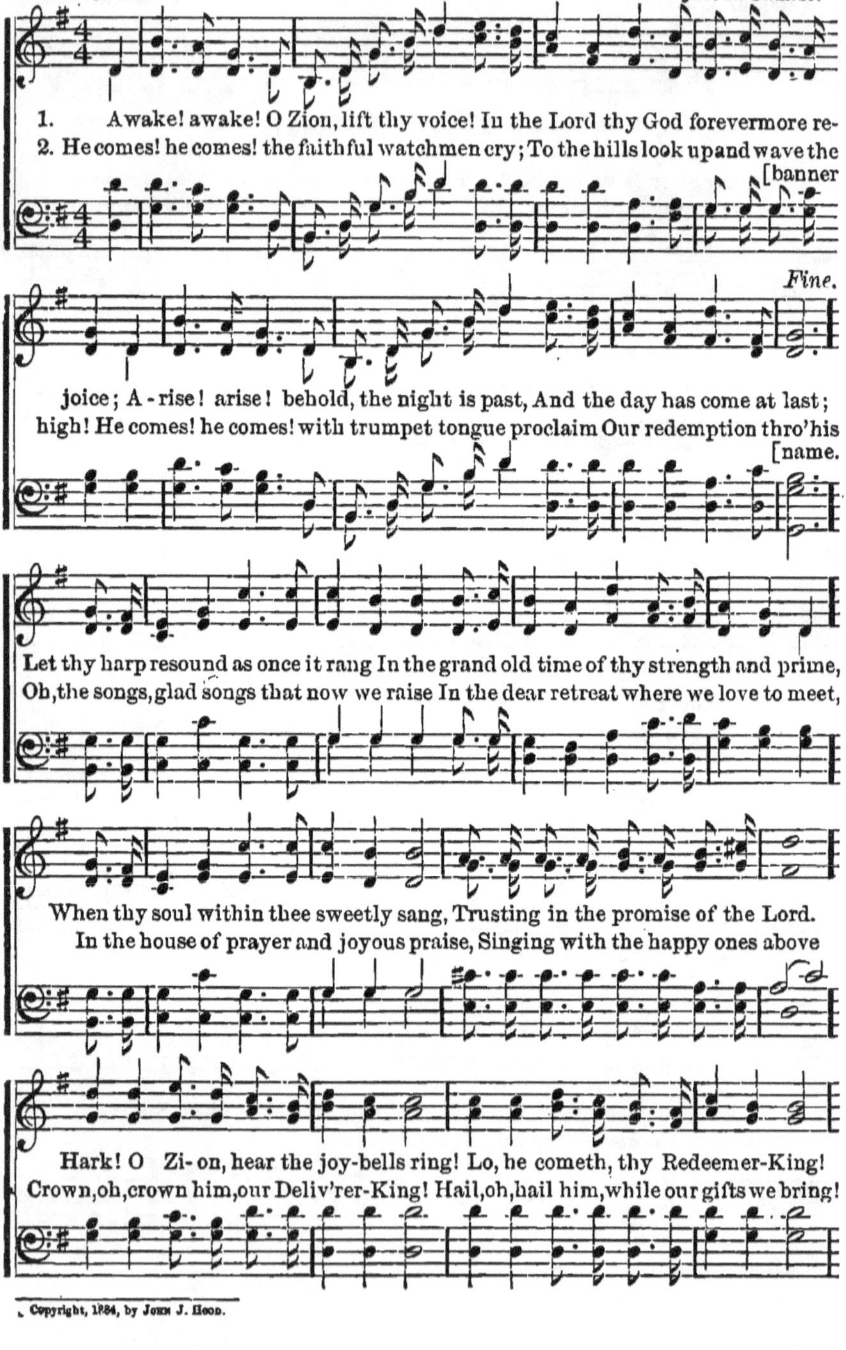

He Comes.—CONCLUDED. 155

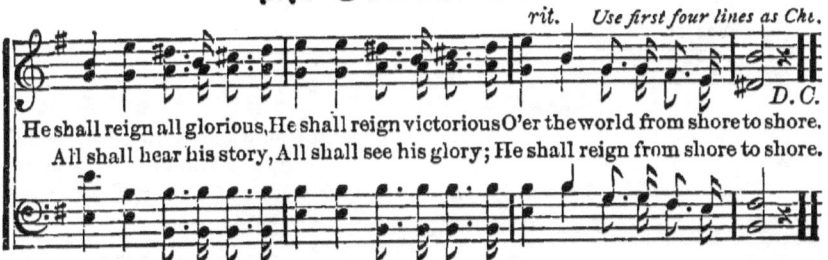

He shall reign all glorious, He shall reign victorious O'er the world from shore to shore.
All shall hear his story, All shall see his glory; He shall reign from shore to shore.

By Grace I Will.

E. E. HEWITT.   WM. J. KIRKPATRICK.

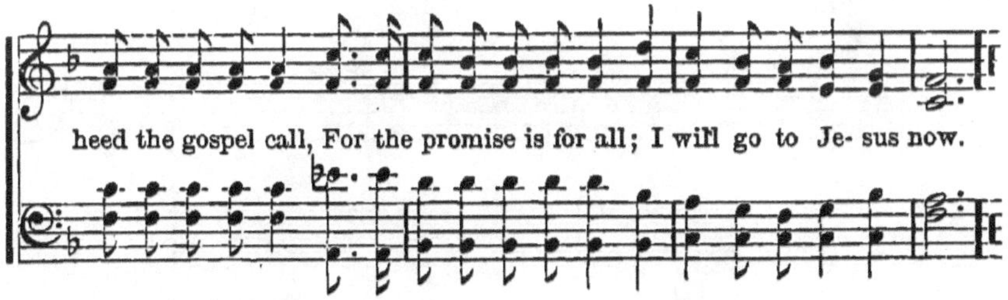

1. Will you go to Jesus now, dear friend? He is calling you to-day;
   Will you seek the bright and better land, By "the true and living way?
2. Would you know the Saviour's boundless love, And his mercy rich and free?
   Will you seek the saving, cleansing blood, That was shed for you and me.

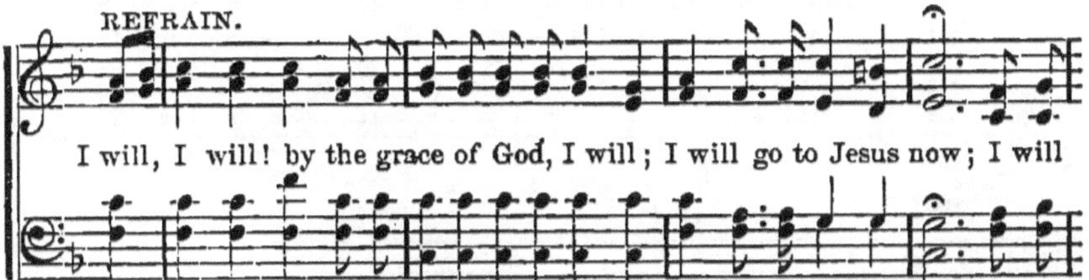

REFRAIN.

I will, I will! by the grace of God, I will; I will go to Jesus now; I will heed the gospel call, For the promise is for all; I will go to Jesus now.

3 Will you consecrate your life to him,
    To be ever his alone?
  And your loving service freely yield,
    To the King upon his throne.

4 Will you follow where the Master leads,
    Choosing only his renown,
  Will you daily bear the cross for him,
    Till he bids you wear the crown?

Copyright, 1888, by WM. J. KIRKPATRICK.

156. Beautiful Robes.

E. E. Hewitt.
Wm. J. Kirkpatrick.

Not too fast.

1. We shall walk with him in white, In that country pure and bright, Where shall enter naught that may defile; Where the day-beam ne'er declines, For the blessed light that shines Is the glory of the Saviour's smile.
2. We shall walk with him in white, Where faith yields to blissful sight, When the beauty of the King we see; Holding converse full and sweet, In a fellowship complete; Waking songs of holy melody.
3. We shall walk with him in white, By the fountains of delight, Where the Lamb his ransomed ones shall lead, For his blood shall wash each stain, Till no spot of sin remain, And the soul forevermore is freed.

CHORUS.

Beau - - tiful robes, . . Beau - - tiful robes, . .
Beautiful robes, beautiful robes, Beautiful robes, beautiful robes,
Beau - - - ti- ful robes we then shall wear, . .
Beau-ti-ful robes we then shall wear, Beau-ti-ful robes we then shall wear,

Copyright, 1890, by Wm. J. Kirkpatrick.

Beautiful Robes.—CONCLUDED.

The Golden Key.

"Prayer is the key to unlock the door, and the bolt to shut in the night."

JNO. R. SWENEY.

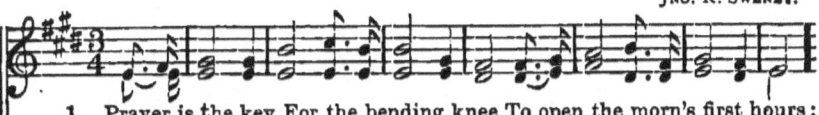

1. Prayer is the key For the bending knee To open the morn's first hours;
2. Not a soul so sad, Nor a heart so glad, When cometh the shades of night,
3. Take the golden key In your hand and see, As the night tide drifts away,

See the incense rise To the starry skies, Like per-fume from the flow'rs.
But the daybreak song Will the joy prolong, And some darkness turn to light.
How its blessed hold Is a crown of gold, Thro' the weary hours of day.

4 When the shadows fall,
  And the vesper call
Is sobbing its low refrain,
  'Tis a garland sweet
  To the toil dent feet,
And an antidote for pain

5 Soon the year's dark door
  Shall be shut no more:
Life's tears shall be wiped away,
  As the pearl gates swing,
  And the gold harps ring,
And the sun unsheathe for aye.

Copyright, 1875, by John J. Hood.

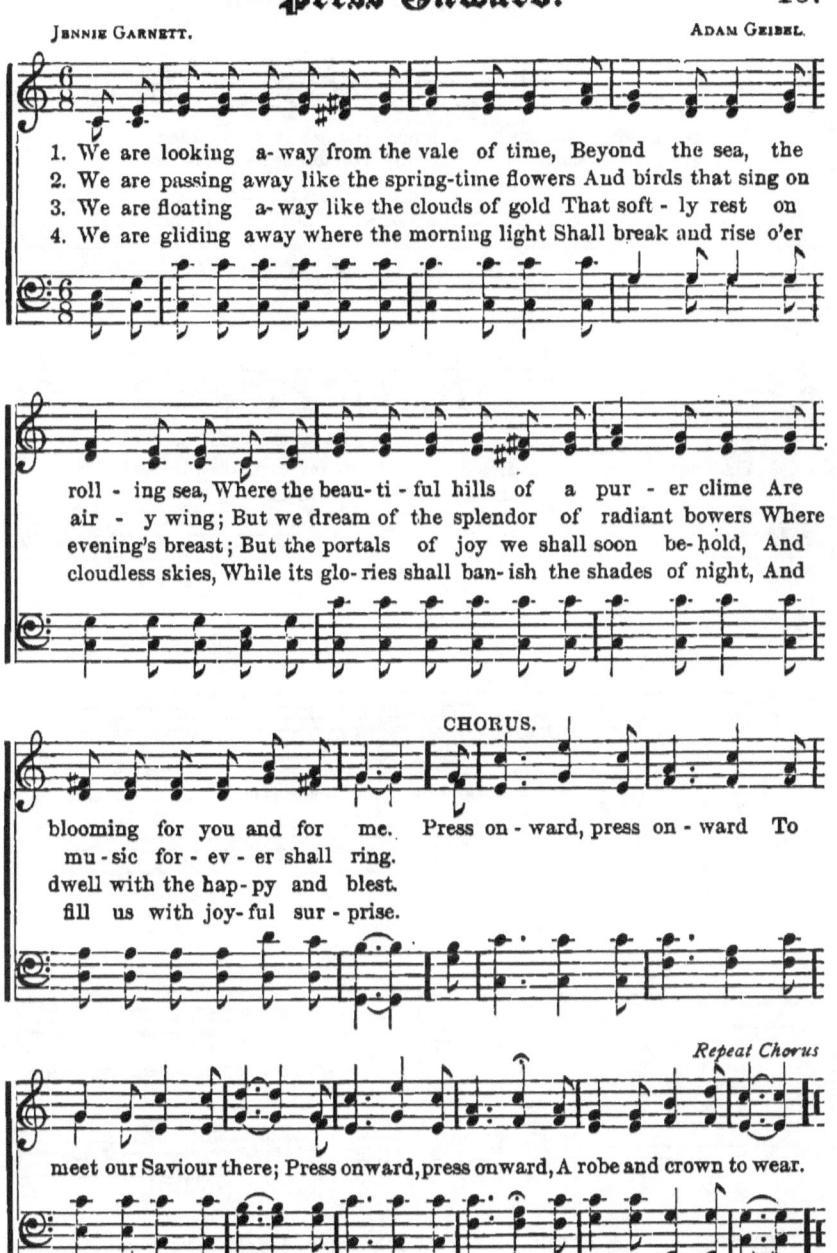

Leaning on Jesus.

Rev. W. F. Crafts. Wm. J. Kirkpatrick.

1. Wea-ry with walking a-lone, Long heav-y-laden with sin;
2. Fearing to stand for my Lord, Trembling for weakness in prayer;

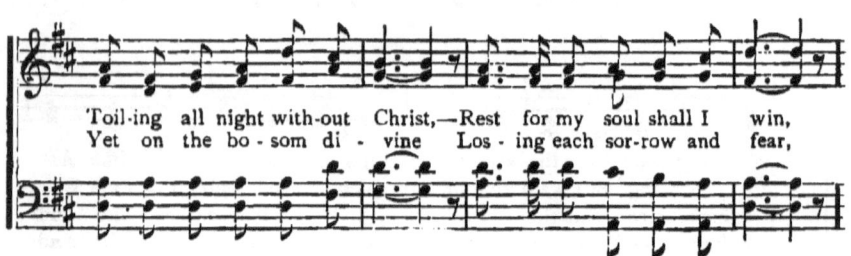

Toil-ing all night with-out Christ,—Rest for my soul shall I win,
Yet on the bo-som di-vine Los-ing each sor-row and fear,

CHORUS.

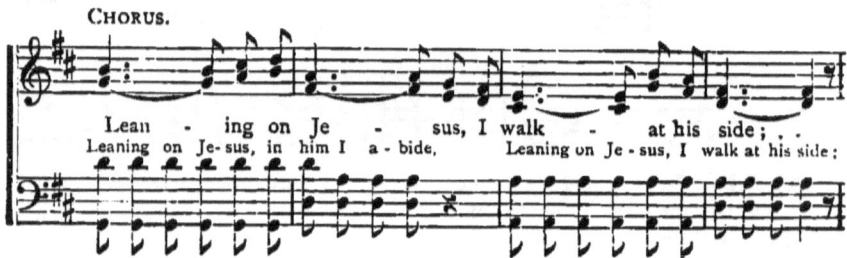

Lean - ing on Je - sus, I walk at his side;
Leaning on Je-sus, in him I a-bide.   Leaning on Je-sus, I walk at his side;

Lean - ing on Je - sus, I trust him, my Shepherd and Guide.
Leaning on Je-sus, what-ev-er be-tide,

3 Anxious no longer for self,
  Shrinking no longer from pain,
  Leaning on Jesus alone,
  He all my care will sustain.

4 Leaning, I walk in "the way,"
  Leaning, "the truth" I shall know;
  Leaning on heart-throbs of Christ,
  Safe into "life" I may go.

From "Leaflet Gems." by permission of John J. Hood.

The New Song.—CONCLUDED.

3 Can my lips be mute, or my heart be sad,
When the gracious Master hath made me
glad? [be,
When he points where the many mansions
And sweetly says, 'There is one for thee'?

4 I shall catch the gleam of its jasper wall
When I come to the gloom of the evenfall,
For I know that the shadows, dreary and
dim,
Have a path of light that will lead to him.

From "Gems of Praise," by per.

My All to Thee.

HAVERGAL.   T. C. O'KANE. By per.

2 My *heart* to thee I bring,
  The heart I cannot read;
A faithless, wand'ring thing—
  An evil heart indeed;
I bring it, Saviour, now to thee,
That fixed and faithful it may be.

3 I bring my *grief* to thee,
  The grief I cannot tell,
No words shall needed be,
  Thou knowest all so well;
I bring the sorrow laid on me,
O suffering Saviour, all to thee.

4 My *joys* to thee I bring,
  The joys thy love has given,
That each may be a wing
  To lift me nearer heaven;
I bring them, Saviour, all to thee,
Who hast procured them all for me.

5 My *life* I bring to thee,
  I would not be my own;
O Saviour, let me be
  Thine, ever thine alone:
My heart, my life, my all, I bring
To thee, my Saviour and my King.

We shall Know.—CONCLUDED.

Must Jesus Bear the Cross.

THOMAS SHEPHERD. Alt.
Tune, MAITLAND. C. M.

1. Must Je-sus bear the cross a-lone, And all the world go free?
No, there's a cross for ev-'ry one, And there's a cross for me.

2 How happy are the saints above,
  Who once went sorrowing here!
  But now they taste unmingled love,
  And joy without a tear.

3 The consecrated cross I'll bear,
  Till death shall set me free;
  And then go home my crown to wear,
  For there's a crown for me.

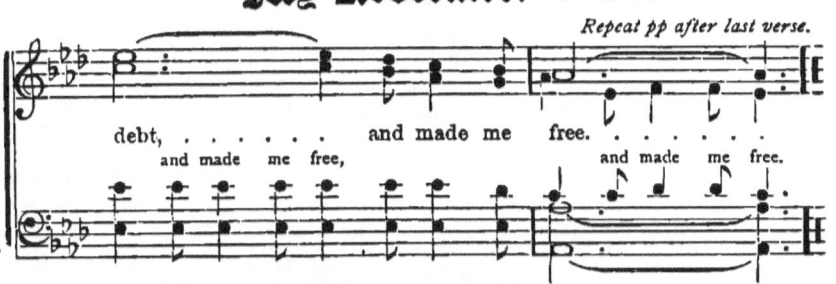

O Receive Him.

FOR PRIMARY CLASS.

Lizzie Edwards.   Jno. R. Sweney.

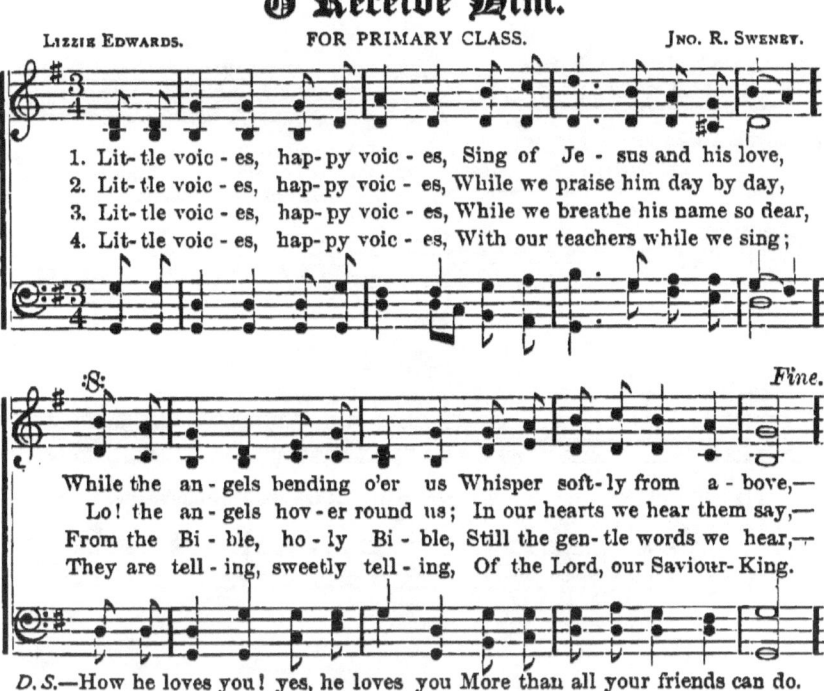

1. Lit-tle voic-es, hap-py voic-es, Sing of Je-sus and his love,
2. Lit-tle voic-es, hap-py voic-es, While we praise him day by day,
3. Lit-tle voic-es, hap-py voic-es, While we breathe his name so dear,
4. Lit-tle voic-es, hap-py voic-es, With our teachers while we sing;

While the an-gels bending o'er us Whisper soft-ly from a-bove,—
Lo! the an-gels hov-er round us; In our hearts we hear them say,—
From the Bi-ble, ho-ly Bi-ble, Still the gen-tle words we hear,—
They are tell-ing, sweetly tell-ing, Of the Lord, our Saviour-King.

D.S.—How he loves you! yes, he loves you More than all your friends can do.

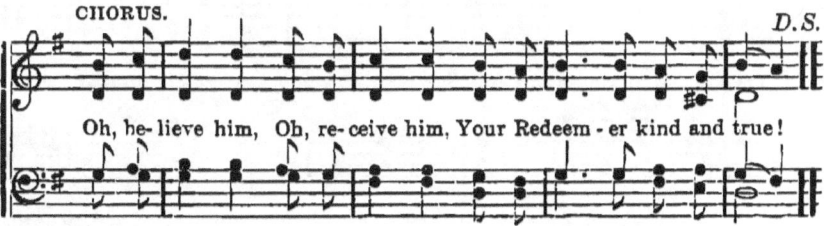

Oh, be-lieve him, Oh, re-ceive him, Your Redeem-er kind and true!

Copyright, 1886, by John J. Hood.

176. He will Gather the Wheat.

HARRIET B. M'KEEVER. JNO. R. SWENEY.

1. When Jesus shall gather the nations Before him at last to appear,
Then how shall we stand in the judgment, When summoned our sentence to hear?

2. Shall we hear, from the lips of the Saviour, The words, 'Faithful servant, well done;'
Or, trembling with fear and with anguish, Be banished away from his throne.

3. He will smile when he looks on his children, And sees on the ransomed his seal;
He will clothe them in heavenly beauty, As low at his footstool they kneel.

CHORUS.
He will gather the wheat in his garner, But the chaff will he scatter away;
Then how shall we stand in the judgment, Oh, how shall it be in that day?

4 Then let us be watching and waiting,—
Our lamps burning steady and bright,—
When the Bridegroom shall call to the wedding
Our spirits made ready for flight.

5 Thus living with hearts fixed on Jesus,
In patience we wait for the time,
When, the days of our pilgrimage ended,
We'll bask in his presence divine.

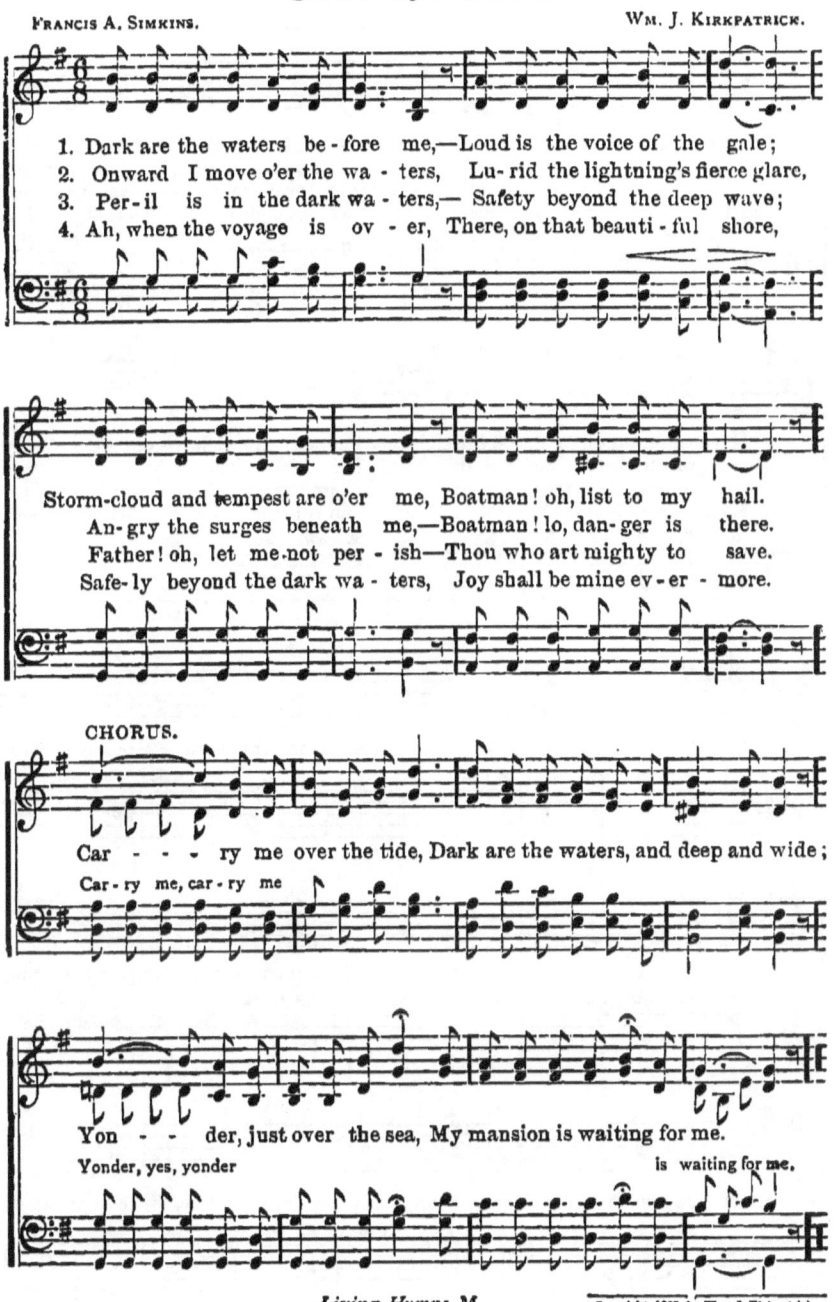

Will You Meet Me.

179

E. O. E.
E. O. Excell.

1. Will you meet me in the morn-ing, On that bright and golden shore?
2. Oh, to meet on that bright morning, When the clouds have passed away!
3. When we meet our loving Sav-iour, What a hap-py hour 'twill be,
4. Oh, this thought should make us happy, And we all should love him more,

Will your lamp be trimmed and burning When He comes to take you o'er?
Oh, to walk and talk with Je-sus, There to dwell with him for aye!
When we're gathered with our loved ones, And their hap-py fa-ces see.
For he'll come, and will not tar-ry, Come to bear us safe-ly o'er.

CHORUS.

Yes, I'll meet .... you in the morn - - - ing, When I
 I'll meet you there,   that morning fair,

hear ... the Saviour's call, ... "Come, ye bless - - - ed of my
 the Saviou'r call,   the Saviour's call,   ye blessed, come,

Fa - - - ther, To a home .. prepared for all. ....
 ye blessed, come,   To a home prepared for all, prepared for all.

Copyright, 1881, by John J. Hood.

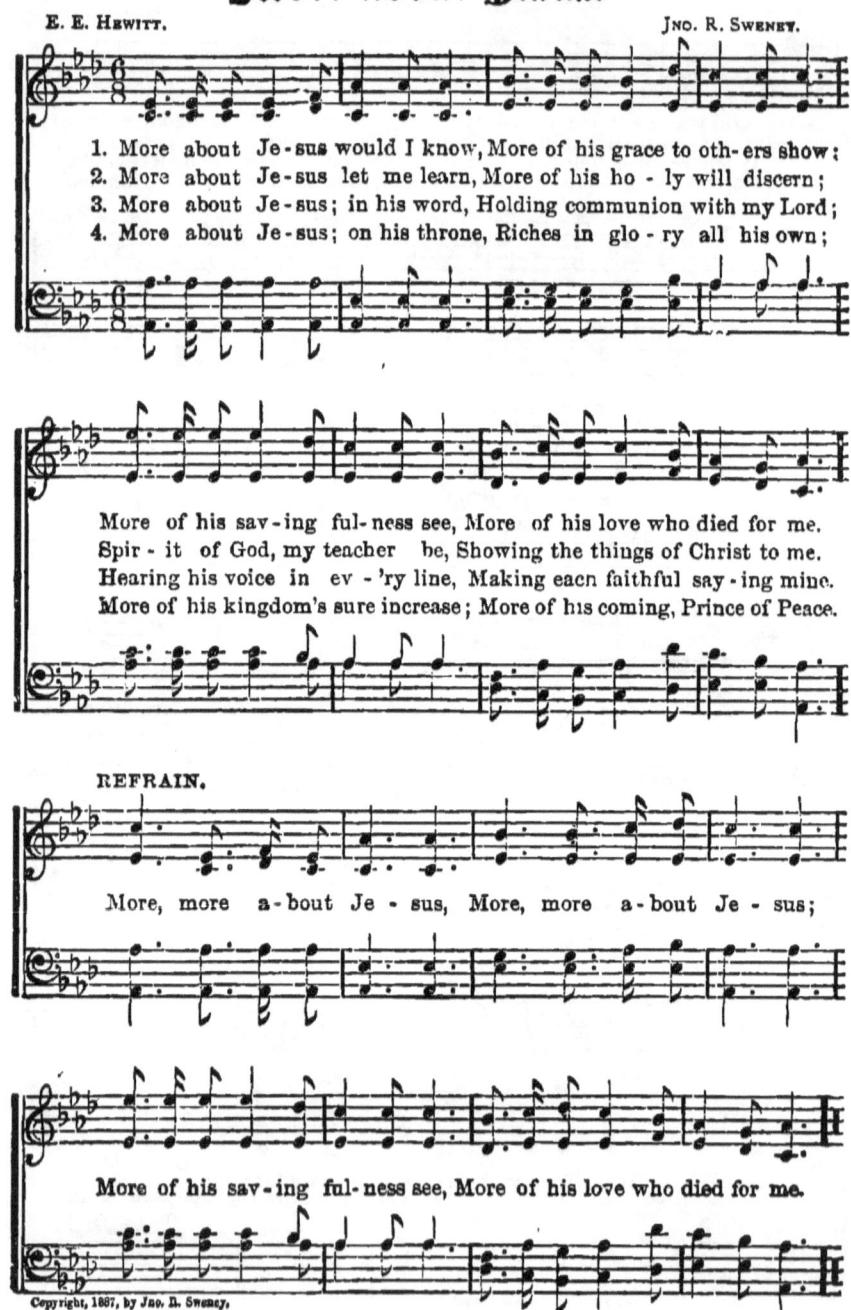

That Gentle Whisper.

E. E. Hewitt. — Adam Geibel.

1. Do you hear that gentle whisper? Sweeter accents cannot be;
2. Wait not till the evening shadows Close around your dark'ning way,
3. Come, and bring your fresh affections, Youth's bright flowers of joy and love,
4. Leave these shallow streams untasted, Nev-er can they sat-is-fy,

'Tis the Saviour's in-vi-ta-tion, "Come, my child, oh, come to me."
Come, while morning dew-drops sparkle, Come, while ear-ly sunbeams play.
Come, to find e-ternal treasures, Find your tru-est Friend above.
Come, to drink of living wa-ters, Freely flowing from on high.

CHORUS.

Come to me, ... come to me;
Come to me, come to me; Sweetly breathes that gentle whisper, "Come to me, oh, come to me," Breathes the Saviour's in-vi-ta-tion, Come to me, oh, come to me.

Copyright, 1890, by John J. Hood.

184. Oh, Where are the Reapers?

EBEN E. REXFORD.   GEO. F. ROOT.

Moderato.

1. Oh, where are the reap-ers that gar-ner in The sheaves of the good from the fields of sin; With sickles of truth must the work be done, And no one may rest till the "harvest home."
2. Go out in the by-ways and search them all; The wheat may be there, tho' the weeds are tall; Then search in the highway, and pass none by, But gath-er from all for the home on high.
3. The fields all are ripe-ning, and far and wide The world now is wait-ing the harvest-tide: But reapers are few, and the work is great, And much will be lost should the harvest wait.
4. So come with your sick-les, ye sons of men, And gath-er to-geth-er the gold-en grain; Toil on till the Lord of the harvest come, Then share ye his joy in the "harvest home."

CHORUS.

Where are the reapers! oh, who will come And share in the glo-ry of the "harvest home?" Oh, who will help us to gar-ner in The sheaves of good from the fields of sin?

Used by per. The John Church Co., owners of the Copyright.

Rest by and by.

185

MAY L. CLAYTON. JNO. R. SWENEY.

1. I've been to the field with the reapers, And there I have gleaned all day;
2. O sweet was the song of the reapers, And bright was their golden grain,
3. And still by the side of the reapers I ask that my place may be,

But my task was light, and my heart was glad, For I heard the Master say:
As it waved in the light of the mid-day sun, And it smiled o'er the harvest plain.
Till the sun shall set, and my work is done, And the Master calls me home.

CHORUS.

Rest by and by, rest by and by, Rest in the field a-bove; There is
rest by and by, happy rest by and by, And a crown of e-ter-nal love.

Copyright, 1886, by JOHN J. HOOD.

A Handful of Leaves.—CONCLUDED.

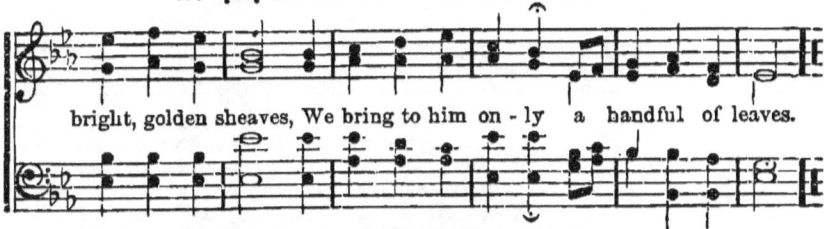

bright, golden sheaves, We bring to him on-ly a handful of leaves.

Why not To-night?

ANON.   J. S. H.

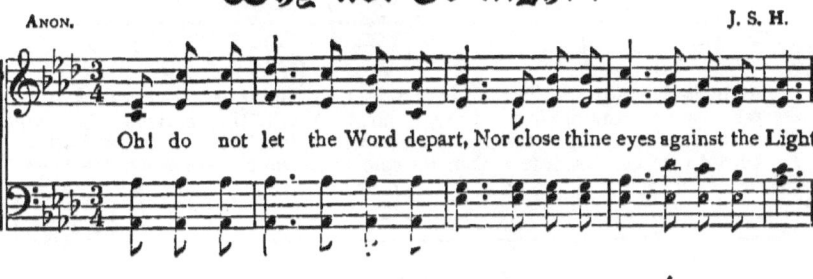

Oh! do not let the Word depart, Nor close thine eyes against the Light, Poor sinner, harden not your heart, Thou would'st be saved, why not to-night?

REFRAIN.   Rit.

Why not to-night? why not to-night? Thou would'st be saved, why not to-night?

2 To-morrow's sun may never rise
    To bless thy long-deluded sight,
  This is the time, oh, then, be wise!
    Thou would'st be saved, why not to-night?

3 Our God in pity lingers still,
    And wilt thou thus his love requite?
  Renounce at length thy stubborn will,
    Thou would'st be saved, why not to-night?

4 The world has nothing left to give,
    It has no new, no pure delight;
  Oh, try the life which Christians live,
    Thou would'st be saved, why not to-night?

5 Our blessed Lord refuses none
    Who would to him their souls unite,
  Then be the work of grace begun,
    Thou would'st be saved, why not to-night?

192. Come, oh, Come with Me.

Mrs Edward Anderson.
Jno. R. Sweney.

1. Come, oh, come with me where love is beaming, Come, oh, come with me where light is streaming, Light and love divine, in Christ reveal-ing God him-self to you and me.
2. Come with all your sins, al-though a mountain, Come unto the cross, from whence a foun-tain Flows, divinely clear, to heal the nations; Come and wash, and make you clean.
3. None can be too vile for love so beam-ing, None can be too dark for light so streaming, Christ will make you whole, thro' faith revealing Full sal-va-tion un-to you.
4. Come and let us kneel where Je-sus meets us, Let us ev-er stay where Christ receives us, Safe within the fold no harm can reach us; Hast-en hast-en to the fold.

CHORUS. *Faster.*

Hal-le-lu-jah, hal-le-lu-jah; I love thee my Saviour: Hal-le-lu-jah, hal-le-lu-jah; I trust but in thee:

1st. ... *D.S.*

2d. Saviour: Hal-le-lu-jah, hal-le-lu-jah; I trust but in thee.

Copyright, 1881, by John J. Hood.

194. Not Half has ever been Told.

"And the building of the wall it was of jasper; and the city was pure gold, like unto clear glass."—Rev. 21. 18.

Rev. J. B. Atchinson.   O. F. Presbrey. By per.

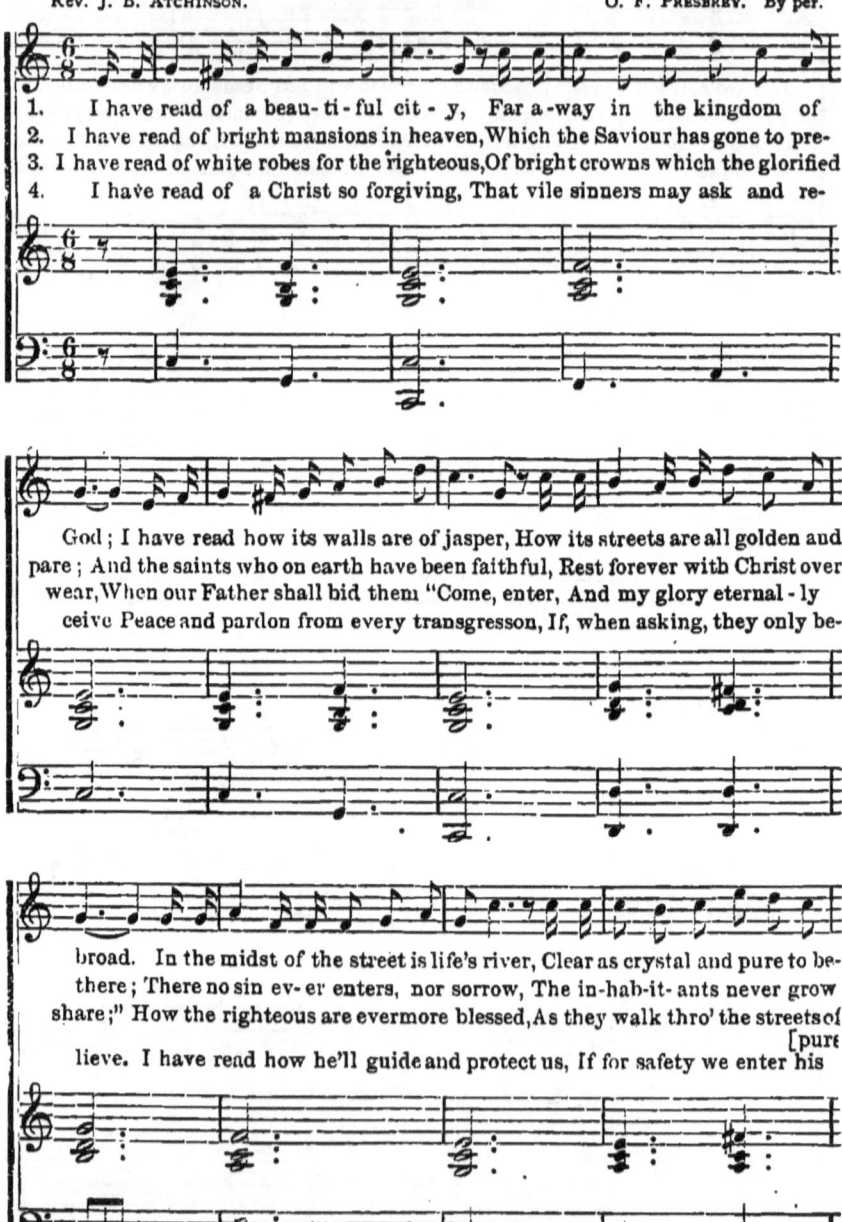

1. I have read of a beau-ti-ful cit-y, Far a-way in the kingdom of God; I have read how its walls are of jasper, How its streets are all golden and broad. In the midst of the street is life's river, Clear as crystal and pure to be-
2. I have read of bright mansions in heaven, Which the Saviour has gone to pre-pare; And the saints who on earth have been faithful, Rest forever with Christ over there; There no sin ev-er enters, nor sorrow, The in-hab-it-ants never grow
3. I have read of white robes for the righteous, Of bright crowns which the glorified wear, When our Father shall bid them "Come, enter, And my glory eternal-ly share;" How the righteous are evermore blessed, As they walk thro' the streets of
4. I have read of a Christ so forgiving, That vile sinners may ask and re-ceive Peace and pardon from every transgresson, If, when asking, they only be-lieve. I have read how he'll guide and protect us, If for safety we enter his

[pure

Not Half has, etc.—CONCLUDED.

hold; But not half of that city's bright glory To mortals has ever been told.
old; But not half of the joys that await them To mortals has ever been told.
gold; But not half of the wonderful sto-ry To mortals has ever been told.
fold; But not half of his goodness and mercy To mortals has ever been told.

CHORUS.

Not half has ev-er been told; Not half has ev-er been told; Not half of that city's bright glo-ry To mortals has ev-er been told.

Repeat the Chorus p.

To-day the Saviour Calls.

SALLIE F. SMITH.   LOWELL MASON.

1. To-day the Saviour calls; Ye wand'rers, come; O ye be-night-ed souls, Why long-er roam?
2. To-day the Saviour calls; Oh, hear him now; Within these sac-red walls To Je-sus bow.

3 To-day the Saviour calls,
   For refuge fly;
The storm of justice falls,
   And death is nigh.

4 The Spirit calls to-day;
   Yield to his power;
Oh, grieve him not away,
   'Tis mercy's hour.

By the Grace of God, etc.—CONCLUDED.

Faithful Guide.

M. M. WELLS. By per.

1. Ho-ly Spir-it, faith-ful guide, Ev-er near the Christian's side;
Gen-tly lead us by the hand, Pil-grims in a des-ert land;
D.C. Whisp'ring soft-ly, wand'rer, come! Follow me, I'll guide thee home.

Wea-ry souls for e'er re-joice, While they hear that sweet-est voice,

2 Ever present, truest Friend,
Ever near thine aid to lend,
Leave us not to doubt and fear,
Groping on in darkness drear,
When the storms are raging sore,
Hearts grow faint, and hopes give o'er,
Whispering softly, wanderer, come!
Follow me, I'll guide thee home.

3 When our days of toil shall cease,
Waiting still for sweet release,
Nothing left but heaven and prayer,
Wond'ring if our names were there;
Wading deep the dismal flood,
Pleading nought but Jesus' blood;
Whispering softly, wanderer, come!
Follow me, I'll guide thee home!

Praise Him. 199

Miss M. A. Baker.   H. R. Palmer. By per.

1. Praise the Saviour, O ye people! Praise and bless his ho-ly name!
2. Praise him for his mighty actions; Praise him for his ten-derness,

Praise and worship him; children, worship him, For a child from heav'n he came;
When he loving-ly held the lit-tle ones In his arms to save and bless;

Praise him from the hills and mountains, From the vales and cities
Praise him, all ye wise and no-ble, Men and maid - ens, old and

Cho.—Praise him in the sanctu - a - ry; Let the chil - dren swell the

all; Hail him king of earth and heav-en, Who was once a child so
young; Let redeem - ing love and mer - cy Be the theme of ev-'ry

strain, And at morn, and noon and e - ven, Echo still the sweet re-

D.S. *Fine.*

small; Hail him king of earth and heaven, Who was once a child so small.
tongue; Let redeem - ing love and mercy Be the theme of ev'ry tongue.

frain; And at morn, and noon and e - ven, Echo still the sweet refrain.

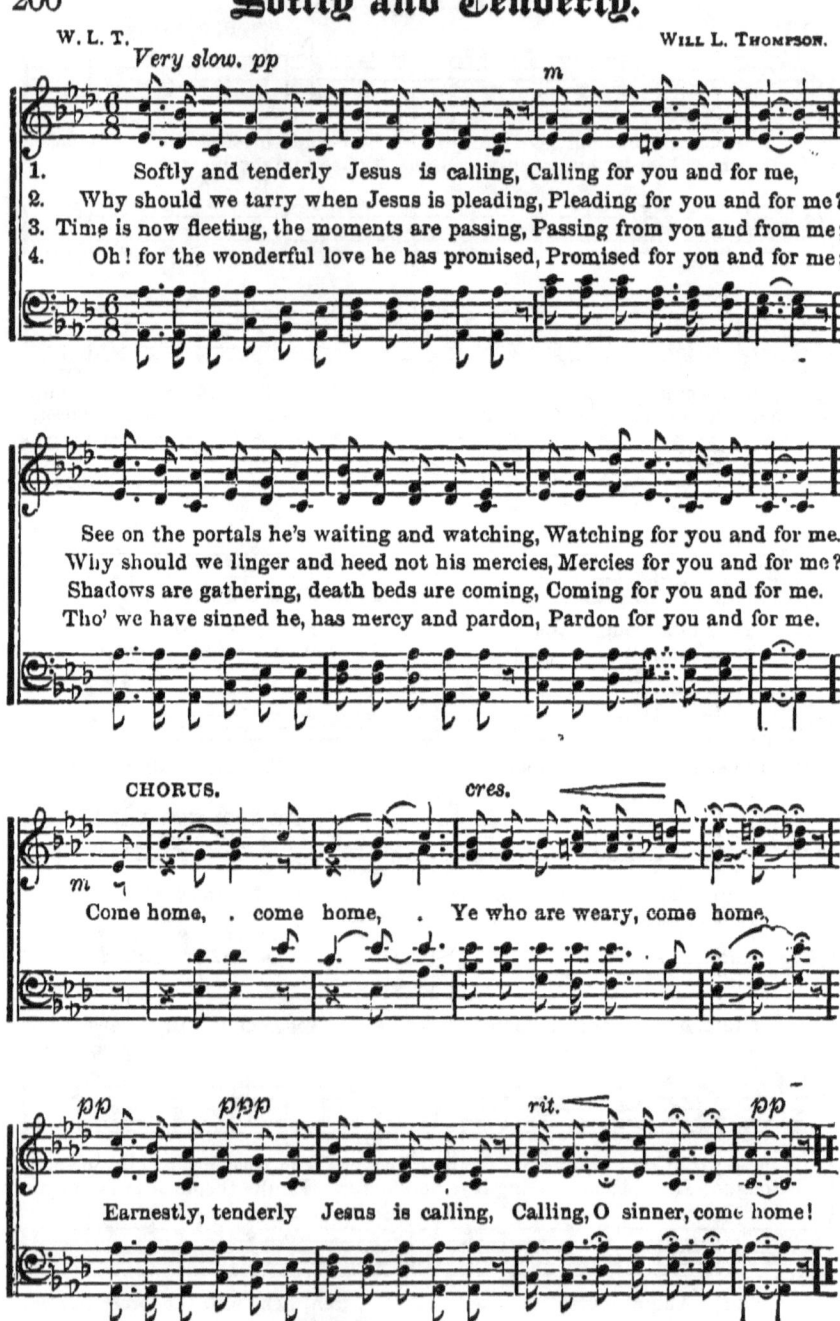

Treasures in Heaven.

1. There's a crown in heaven for the striving soul, Which the blessed Jesus himself will place On the head of each who shall faithful prove, Ev-en unto death, in the heavenly race.
2. There's a joy in heaven for the mourning soul, Tho' the tears may fall all the earth-ly night; Yet the clouds of sad-ness will break a-way, And rejoicing come with the morning light.
3. There's a home in heaven for the faithful soul, In the many mansions prepared a-bove, Where the glo-ri-fied shall for-ev-er sing, Of a Saviour's free and unbounded love.

REFRAIN.

Oh, may that crown . . . in heaven be mine, And I a-mong . . . the angels shine; Be thou, O Lord, . . . my daily guide, Let me ev-er in thy love a-bide.
Oh, may that joy . . . in heaven be
Oh, may that home . . . in heaven be

Used by permission of T. C. O'Kane, owner of Copyright.

The Fountain of Blessing.

E. E. Hewitt.   Jno. R. Sweney.

1. A-bun-dant sal-va-tion thro' Jesus I know; Rich streams of re-
   fresh-ing from Cal-va-ry flow: Be-liev-ing his word, with re-
   joic-ing I see The foun-tain of bless-ing is

2. "A-live ev-er-more! he's a Sa-viour indeed; His ful-ness sur-
   pass-ing my ut-termost need; His boun-ty is "roy-al," ex-
   ceed-ing my plea— The foun-tain of bless-ing is

3. There's strength in tempta-tion, the vic-t'ry to gain; There's sunshine in
   dark-ness, and comfort in pain; This "plenteous re-demption" in
   Je-sus is free— The foun-tain of bless-ing is

4. The brightening waves of the riv-er of peace, And joy, fresh and
   spark-ling, find happy increase: All hon-or and glo-ry, dear
   Sa-viour, to thee— The foun-tain of bless-ing is

CHORUS.

flow-ing for me! Flow-ing for me, now flow-ing for me; The foun-tain of bless-ing is flow-ing for me.

Copyright, 1889 by Jno. R. Sweney.

206. I Will Praise Him.

Mrs. H. E. Brown.   Eph. iii. 18, 19.   Wm. J. Kirkpatrick.

1. I will praise him, I will praise him, I will sing un-to the Lord;
2. I will praise him, I will praise him, Witness to his love for me;
3. I will praise him, I will praise him, I will sing un-to the Lord;
4. I will praise him, I will praise him, I will sing un-to the Lord;

For his plenteous, free compassion, Round the earth like floods outpoured;
How he chose, and sought, and found me, With his grace so full and free;
For the joy of his sal-vation Shin-ing from his ho-ly word;
Loud extol the roy-al bounty His full treas-u-ries afford;

Reaching ev-'ry tribe and nation, To the earth's remot-est line,
How he leads me on with blessing, Close-ly holds this hand of mine,
Am-ply freighted with his mer-cy Is each sa-cred page and line,
Half his goodness was not told me! Oh, what glo-ries in him shine!

Touching, cleansing, healing, saving,—Oh, the *breadth* of love divine!
Keeps me when I shrink and falter.—Oh, the *length* of love divine!
E-ven to the chief of sinners,—Oh, the *depth* of love divine!
I can nev-er, nev-er tell it, All the *height* of love divine!

I will praise him, I will praise him, Ev-er be his name adored;
I will praise him, I will praise him, Ev-er be

Copyright, 1881, by John J. Hood.

I Will Praise Him.—CONCLUDED.

5 I will praise him, I will praise him,—
Holy Ghost, my song indite,—
For the love that passeth knowledge,
Length and *breadth* and *depth* and *height*;

Sing, O earth! let every creature
Help this feeble tongue of mine
To declare a love so precious,
Endless, infinite, divine!—

Asking.

F. R. HAVERGAL. JNO. R. SWENEY.

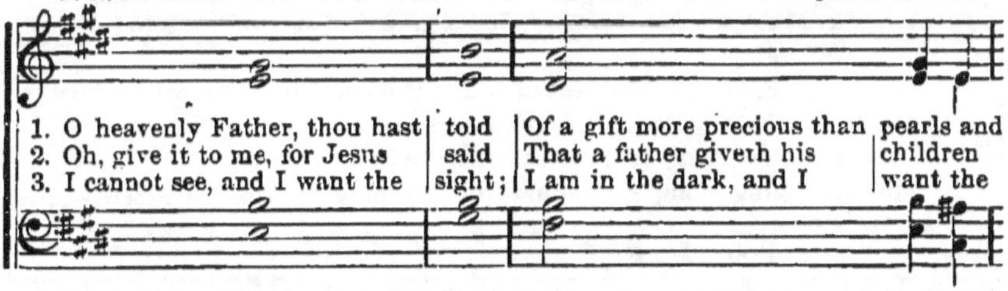

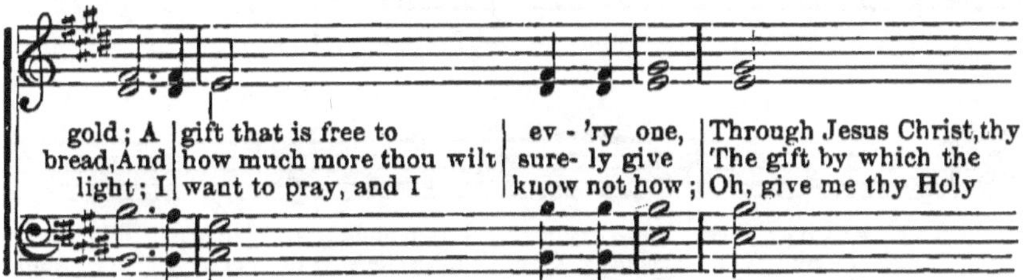

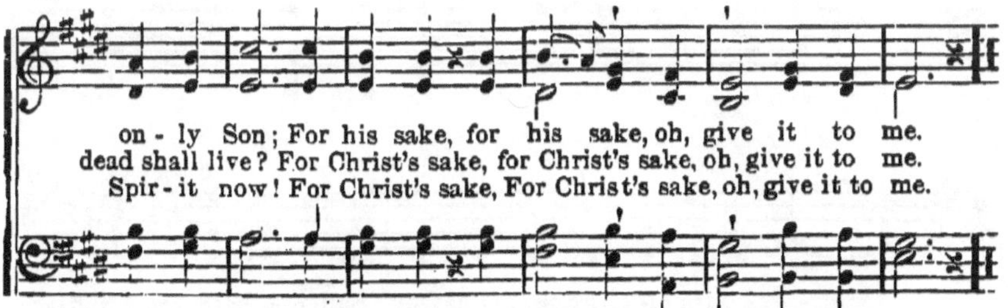

1. O heavenly Father, thou hast told Of a gift more precious than pearls and gold; A gift that is free to ev-'ry one, Through Jesus Christ, thy on-ly Son; For his sake, for his sake, oh, give it to me.
2. Oh, give it to me, for Jesus said That a father giveth his children bread, And how much more thou wilt sure-ly give The gift by which the dead shall live? For Christ's sake, for Christ's sake, oh, give it to me.
3. I cannot see, and I want the sight; I am in the dark, and I want the light; I want to pray, and I know not how; Oh, give me thy Holy Spir-it now! For Christ's sake, For Christ's sake, oh, give it to me.

4 Thou hast said it, I must be- | lieve,
It is only "ask" and I | shall receive;
If thou said it, it must be true,
And there's nothing else for | me to do!
For Christ's sake, oh, give it to me.

5 So I come and ask, because my | need
Is very great and | real indeed, [say.
On the strength of thy Word I | come and
Oh, let thy Word come | true to-day!
For Christ's sake, oh, give it to me!

Copyright, 1887, by John J. Hood.

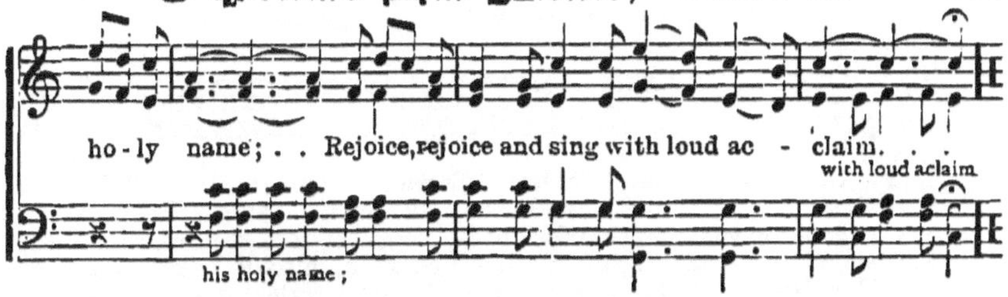

O Praise His Name,—CONCLUDED. 211

ho-ly name;.. Rejoice, rejoice and sing with loud ac - claim...
with loud aclaim.
his holy name;

Calling, Gently Calling.

"And the Lord came, and stood and called as at other times, Samuel, Samuel. Then Samuel answered, Speak; for thy servant heareth." 1 Sam. iii. 10.

Rev. J. M. Lyons. John J. Hood.

1. In the midnight si-lent watch-es, What a wondrous voice I hear!
2. Blessed Lord, O great Cre-a-tor, How I won-der can it be,

Charming accents sweet and ten-der, Mu-sic-like sal-ute mine ear.
He that built the star-ry man-sion Doth re-gard a child like me.

CHORUS.

Call-ing, gently calling. Wondrous accents, sweet and mild! Calling, for he

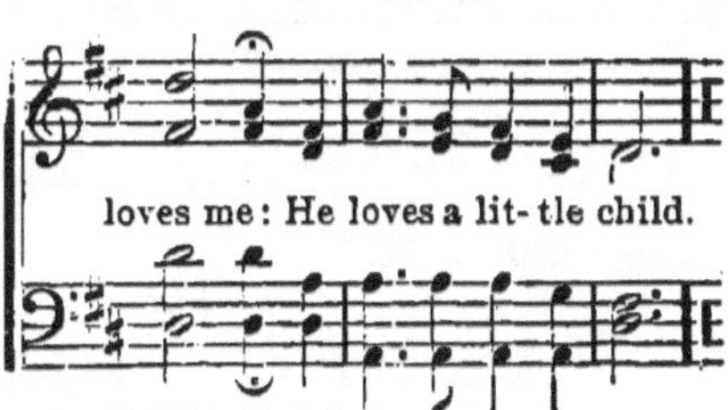

loves me: He loves a lit-tle child.

3 There again I hear thee calling,
In such tender accents near;
Here am I! oh, yes I listen:
Speak, and I will gladly hear.

4 Speak, O Lord, thy servant heareth;
Help thou me to understand;
Here I wait to do thy errands,
And obey, Lord, thy command.

Copyright, 1881, by John J. Hood.

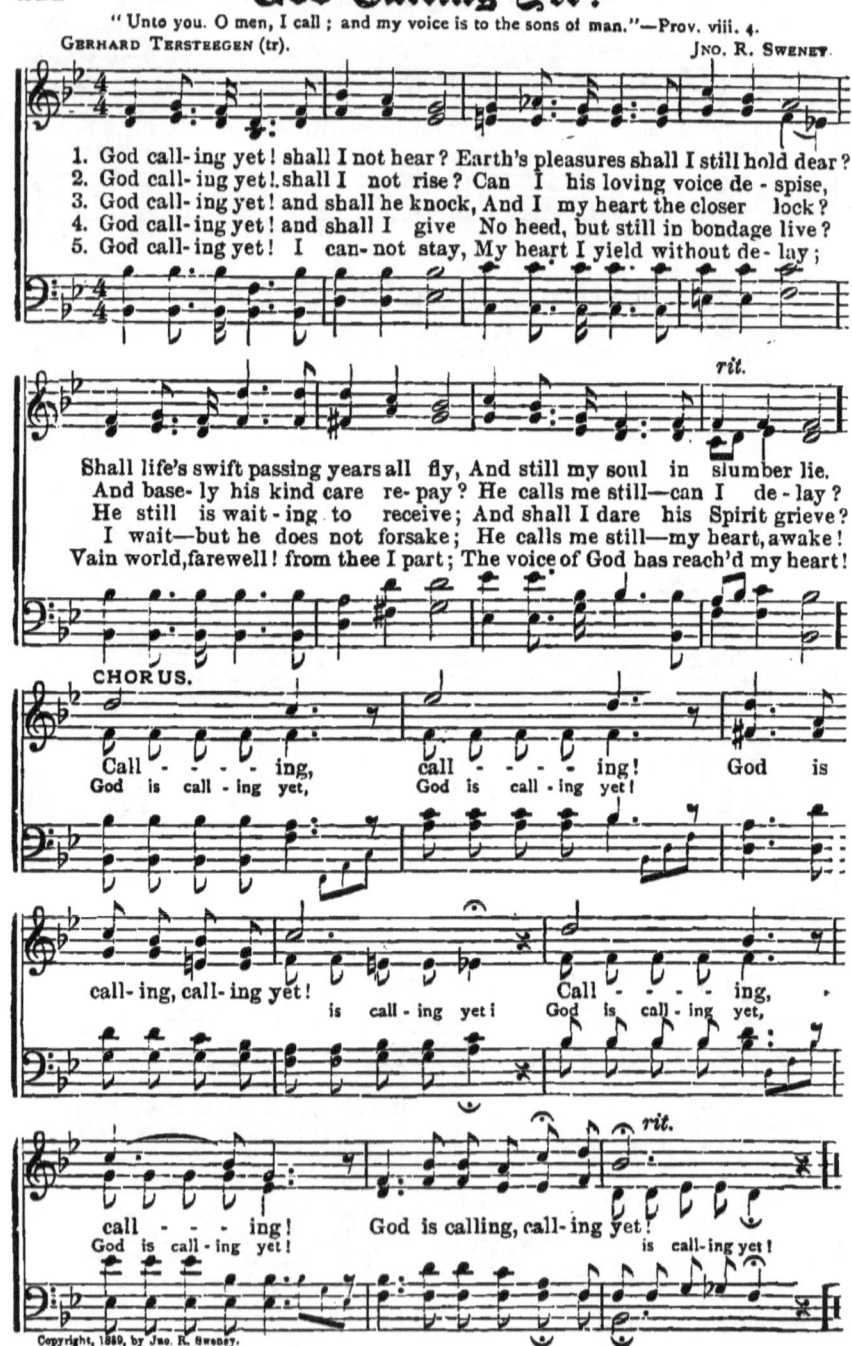

Scatter Seeds of Kindness. 213

Mrs. Albert Smith.   S. J. Vail. By per.

1. Let us gather up the sunbeams Lying all around our path; Let us keep the wheat and roses, Casting out the thorns and chaff. Let us find our sweetest comfort In the blessings of to-day, With a patient hand removing All the briars from the way. Then scatter seeds of kindness, Then scatter seeds of kindness, Then scatter seeds of kindness, For our reaping by and by.

2. Strange we never prize the music Till the sweet-voiced bird is flown! Strange that we should slight the violets Till the lovely flow'rs are gone! Strange that summer skies and sunshine Never seem one half so fair, As when winter's snowy pinions Shake the white down in the air.

3 If we knew the baby fingers,
   Pressed against the window-pane,
Would be cold and stiff to-morrow,—
   Never trouble us again, —
Would the bright eyes of our darling
   Catch the frown upon our brow?—
Would the prints of rosy fingers
   Vex us then as they do now?

4 Ah! those little ice-cold fingers,
   How they point the memories back
To the hasty words and actions
   Strewn around our backward track!
How these little hands remind us,
   As in snowy grace they lie,
Not to scatter thorns, but roses,
   For our reaping by and by.

Sing unto God.—CONCLUDED.

Now   let his courts   with ho - - - - ly rapture
Now let   his courts,   now let his courts,   Now let   his courts   with
Strong   is his love,   a - bid - - - - ing ev - er-
Strong is   his love,   strong is his love,   Strong is   his love,   a -
Sing   as ye fly   to do   your Sov'reign's
Sing as   ye fly,   sing as ye fly,   Sing as   ye fly   to

ring;   Wake,   wake a - gain   the
ho - ly rap- ture ring;   Wake, wake a - gain,   wake, wake, a - gain,
more;   Sing   un-to God,   and
bid - ing ev - er- more;   Sing un - to God,   sing un - to God,
will,   Sing   un - to God,   let
do your Sov'reigh's will,   Sing un - to God,   sing un - to God,

si - - - lent harp of Ju - - - - dah! Break   forth, ye
Wake, wake a - gain the harp, the si - lent harp of Ju-dah; Break forth, ye hills,
let   the voice of glad - - - ness Break   from our
Sing un - to God, and let the voice, the voice of gladness, Break from our hearts,
an - - - thems ev - er roll - - - - ing, Earth   and the
Sing un - to God, let an - thems, anthems ev - er roll - ing, Earth and the sky,

First four lines as Chorus.

hills,   and let . . . . the des - ert sing.   D.O.
break forth, ye hills,   Break forth, ye hills,   and   let the des- ert sing.
hearts   and spread . from shore to shore.
break from our hearts, Break from our hearts   and   spread from shore to shore.
sky   with joy . . . and gladness fill.
earth and the sky,   Earth and the sky   with   joy and gladness fill.

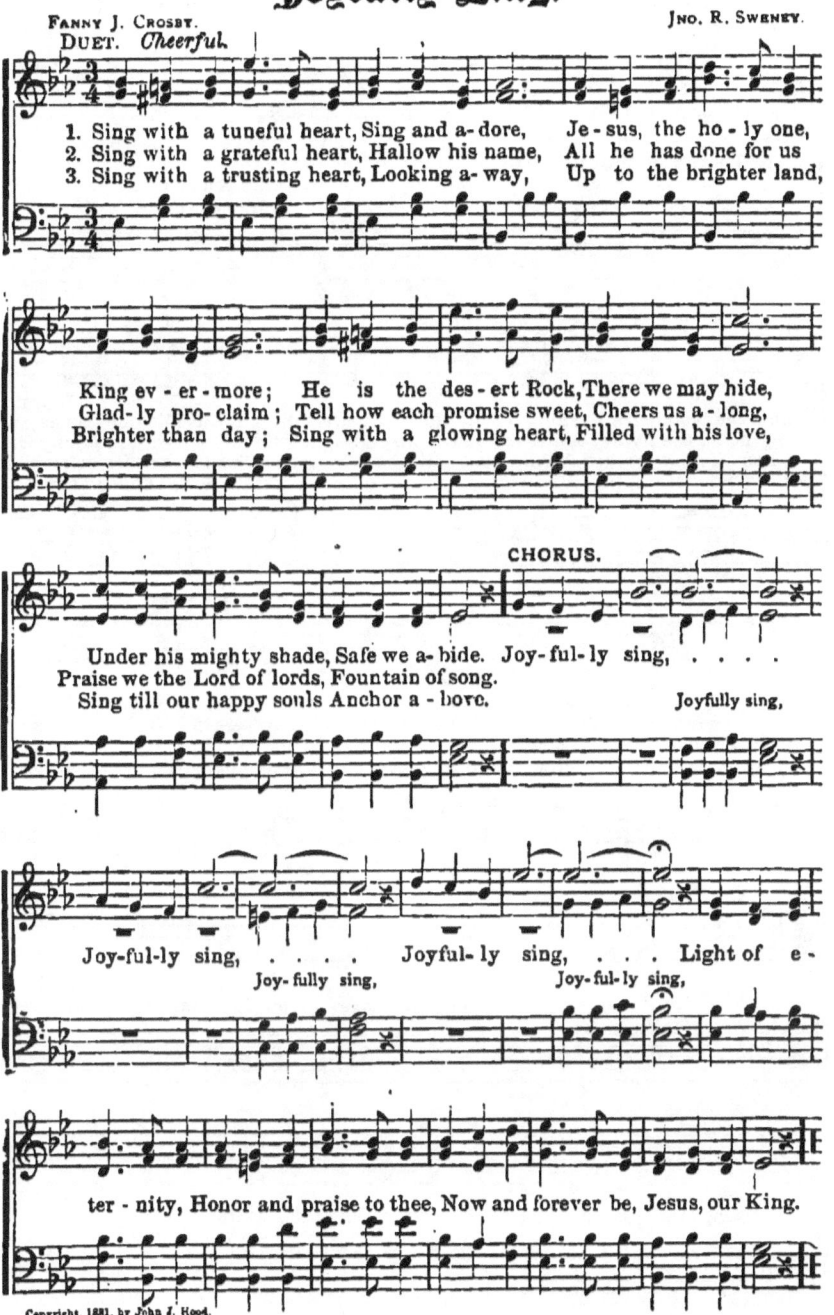

222. What a Gath'ring that will be.

J. H. K.   "Gather my saints together unto me."—Ps. l. 5   J. H. KURZENKNABE.

1. At the sounding of the trumpet, when the saints are gather'd home, We will greet each other by the crystal sea, With the friends and all the lov'd ones there a-waiting us to come, What a gath'ring of the faithful that will be!

2. When the angel of the Lord proclaims that time shall be no more, We shall gather, and the saved and ransom'd see. Then to meet again together, on the bright ce-lestial shore, What a gath'ring of the faithful that will be!

3. At the great and final judg-ment, when the hidden comes to light, When the Lord in all his glory we shall see; At the bidding of our Saviour, "Come, ye blessed to my right, What a gath'ring of the faithful that will be!

4. When the golden harps are sounding, and the angel bands proclaim, In tri-umphant strains the glorious jubilee; Then to meet and join to sing the song of Moses and the Lamb, What a gath'ring of the faithful that will be!

CHORUS.

What a gath - - - 'ring, gath - - 'ring. At the sounding of the glorious jubi-lee! What a gath - 'ring,
What a gath'ring of the loved ones when we'll meet with one an-oth-er, jubilee! What a gath'ring when the friends and all the

From "Song Treasury," by per.

"Come."—CONCLUDED.

Now the Day is Over.

"I will both lay me down in peace, and sleep."—Ps. iv. 8.

Rev. S. BARING GOULD.   J. BARNBY.

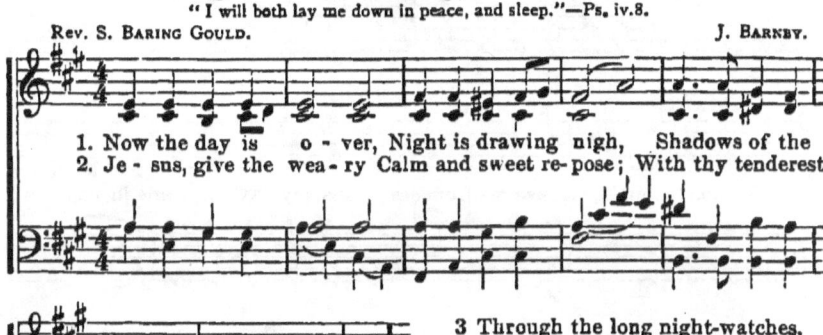

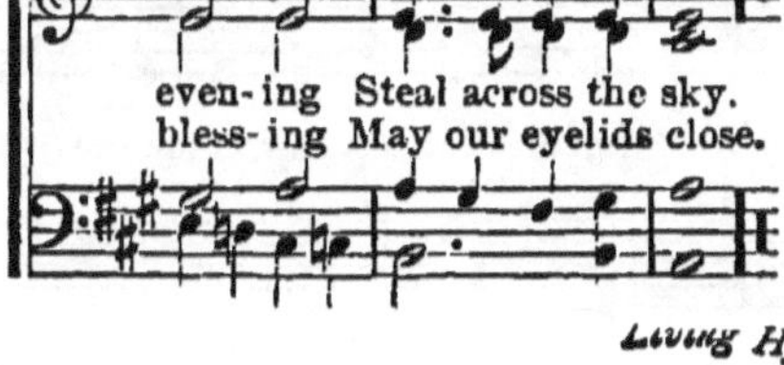

1. Now the day is o-ver, Night is drawing nigh, Shadows of the even-ing Steal across the sky.
2. Je-sus, give the wea-ry Calm and sweet re-pose; With thy tenderest bless-ing May our eyelids close.

3 Through the long night-watches,
   May thine angels spread
   Their white wings above me,
   Watching round my bed.

4 When the morning wakens
   Then may I arise,
   Pure, and fresh, and sinless
   In thy holy eyes.

Living Hymns—P

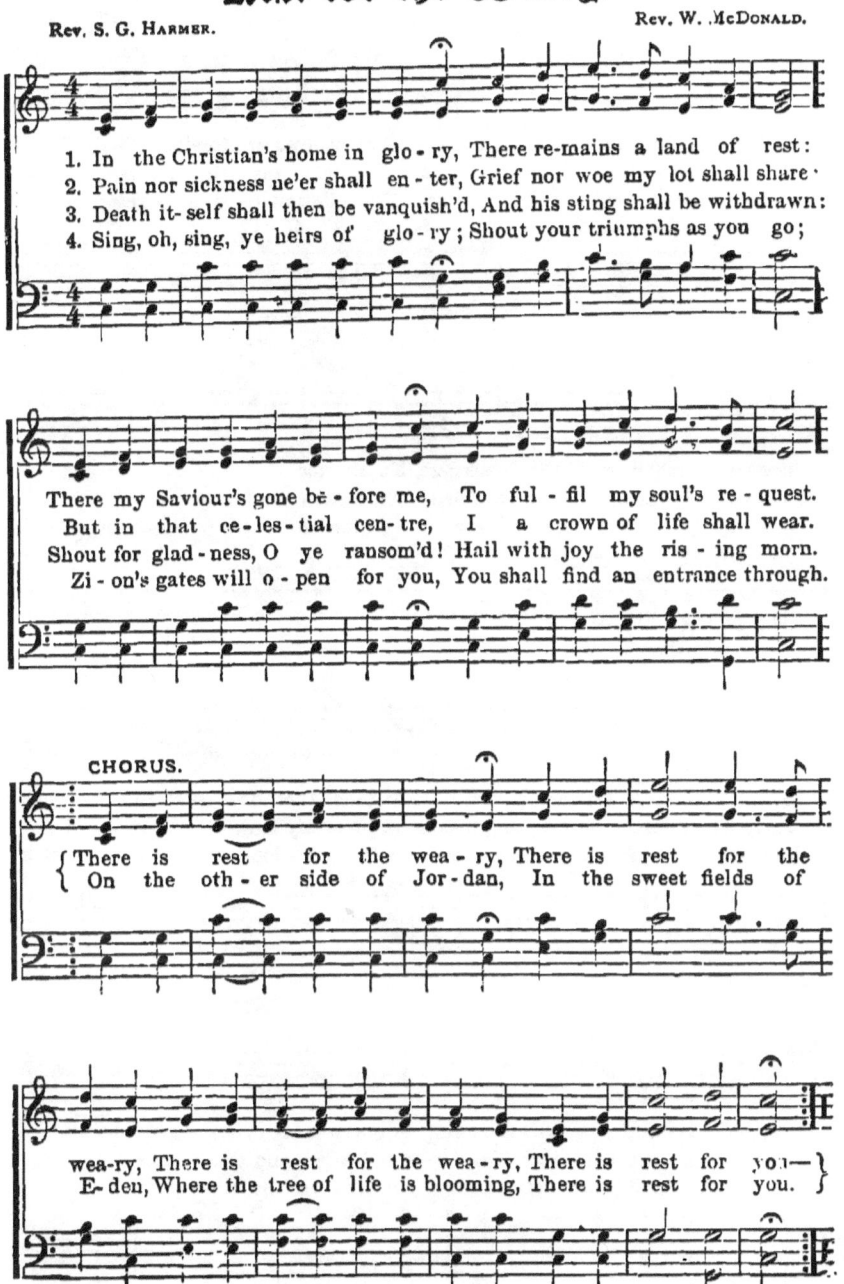

Master, the Tempest, etc.—CONCLUDED.

CHORUS.

The winds and the waves shall obey thy will, Peace, be still! Peace, be still! peace, be still! Whether the wrath of the storm-tossed sea, Or demons or men, or whatever it be, No waters can swallow the ship where lies The Master of ocean, and earth, and skies; They all so sweetly obey thy will, Peace, be still! Peace, be still! They all so sweetly obey thy will, Peace, peace, be still!

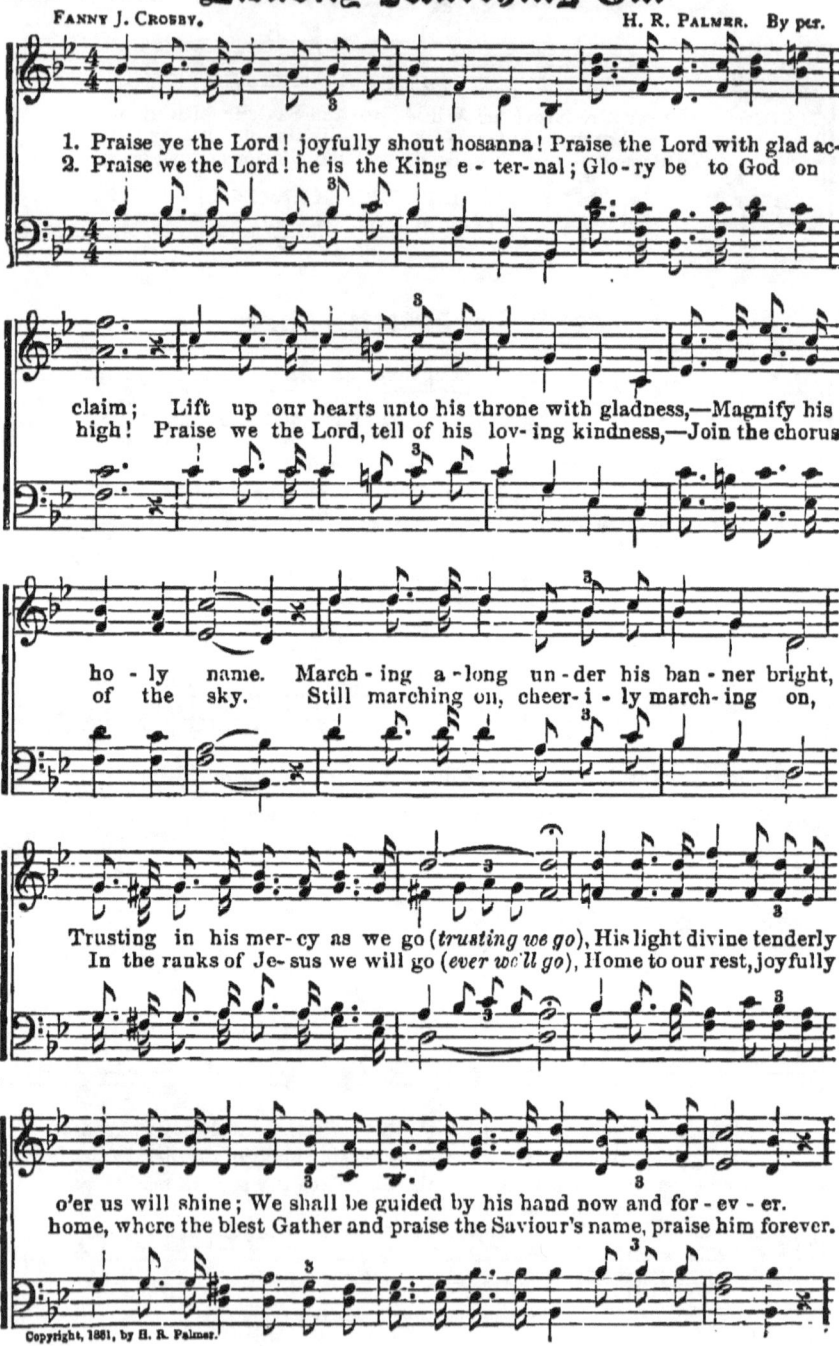

5 If I still hold closely to him,
   What hath he at last?
   "Sorrow vanquished, labor ended,
   Jordan past."

6 If I ask him to receive me,
   Will he say me nay?
   "Not till earth and not till heaven
   Pass away."

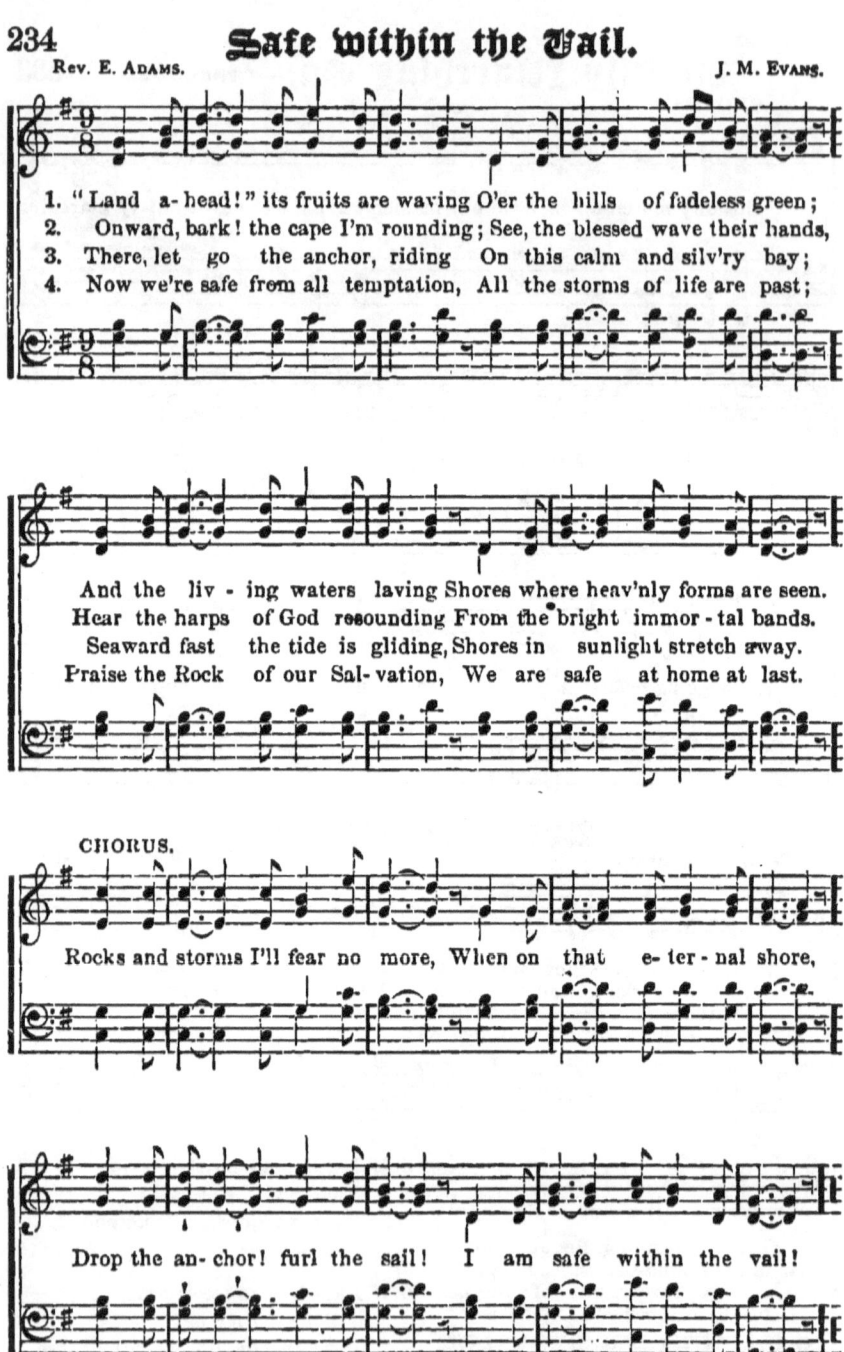

The Earth is the Lord's.—CONTINUED. 237

righteousness from the God of his sal-va-tion, He shall re-ceive the blessing from the Lord, And righteousness from the God of his sal-va-tion.

GIRLS or A CLASS.

This is the gen-er-a-tion of them that seek him, That seek thy face, O God of Jacob.

Adagio. **SCHOOL.** *Allegro.*

Lift up your heads, O ye gates, and be ye lift-ed up, ye ev-er-last-ing doors; And the King of glo-ry shall come in, the King of glo-ry

238 The Earth is the Lord's.—CONTINUED.

BOYS.
shall come in, The King of glo-ry shall come in. Who is this King of

SCHOOL.
glo-ry? Who is this King of glory? The Lord, the Lord strong and mighty, the

PRIMARY DEPT. or A CLASS.
Lord, the Lord might-y in bat-tle. Lift up your heads, O ye gates, Even lift them

up, ye ev-er-last-ing doors, And the King of glo-ry shall come in, the

BOYS.
King of glory shall come in, The King of glory shall come in. Who is this King of

The Lord shall Comfort Zion. 245

Isa. li. 3. Jno. R. Sweney.

Copyright, 1887, by John J. Hood.

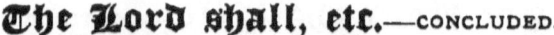

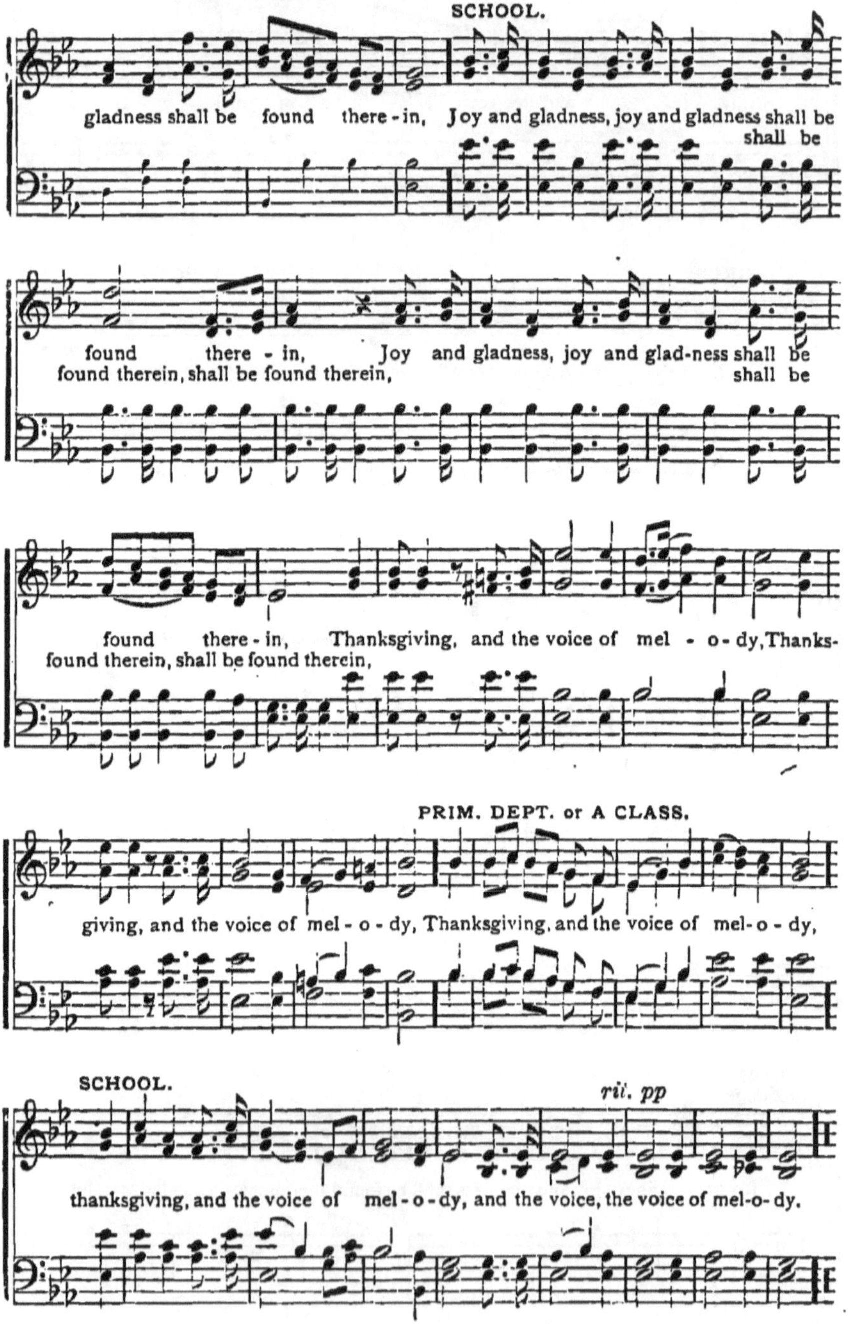
SCHOOL.
gladness shall be found there-in, Joy and gladness, joy and gladness shall be
shall be
found there - in, Joy and gladness, joy and glad-ness shall be
found therein, shall be found therein, shall be
found there - in, Thanksgiving, and the voice of mel - o - dy, Thanks-
found therein, shall be found therein,
PRIM. DEPT. or A CLASS.
giving, and the voice of mel - o - dy, Thanksgiving, and the voice of mel- o - dy,
SCHOOL.
rit. pp
thanksgiving, and the voice of mel - o - dy, and the voice, the voice of mel-o- dy.

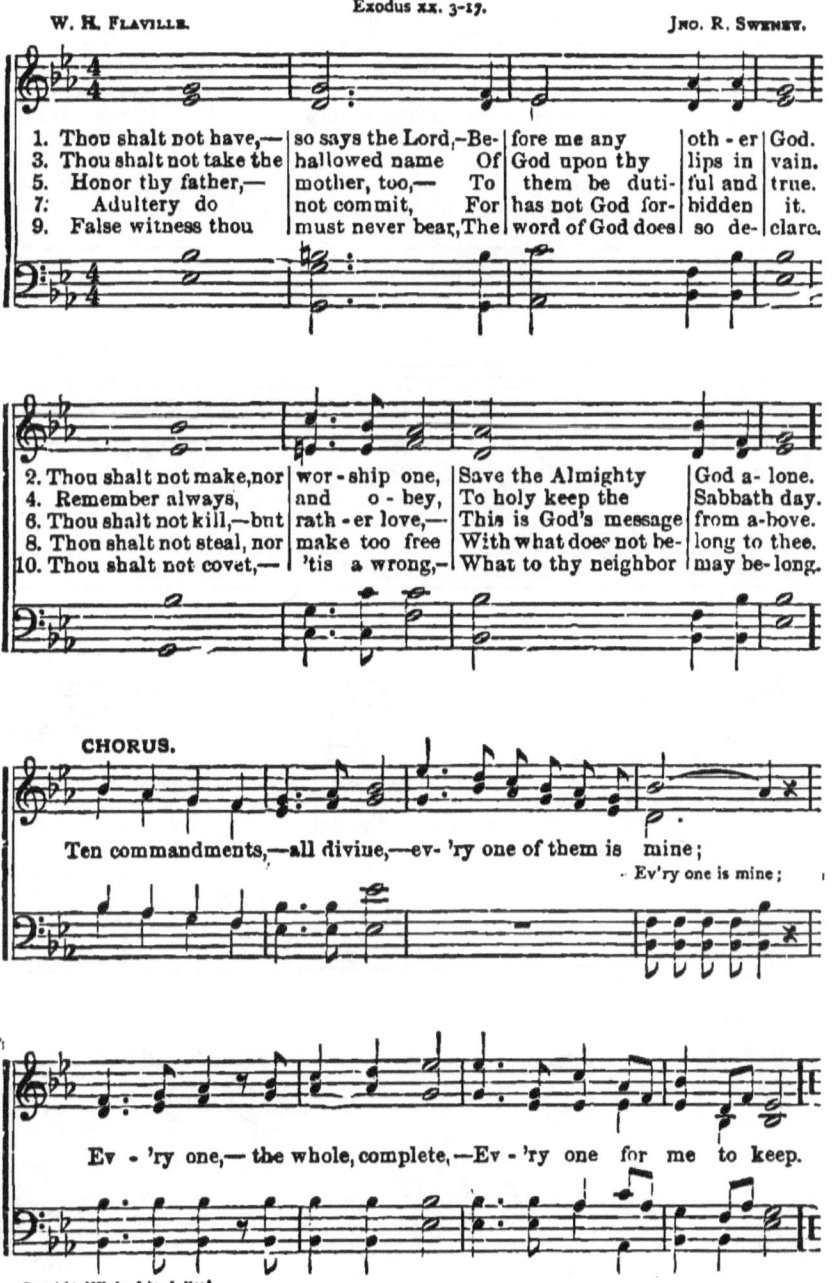

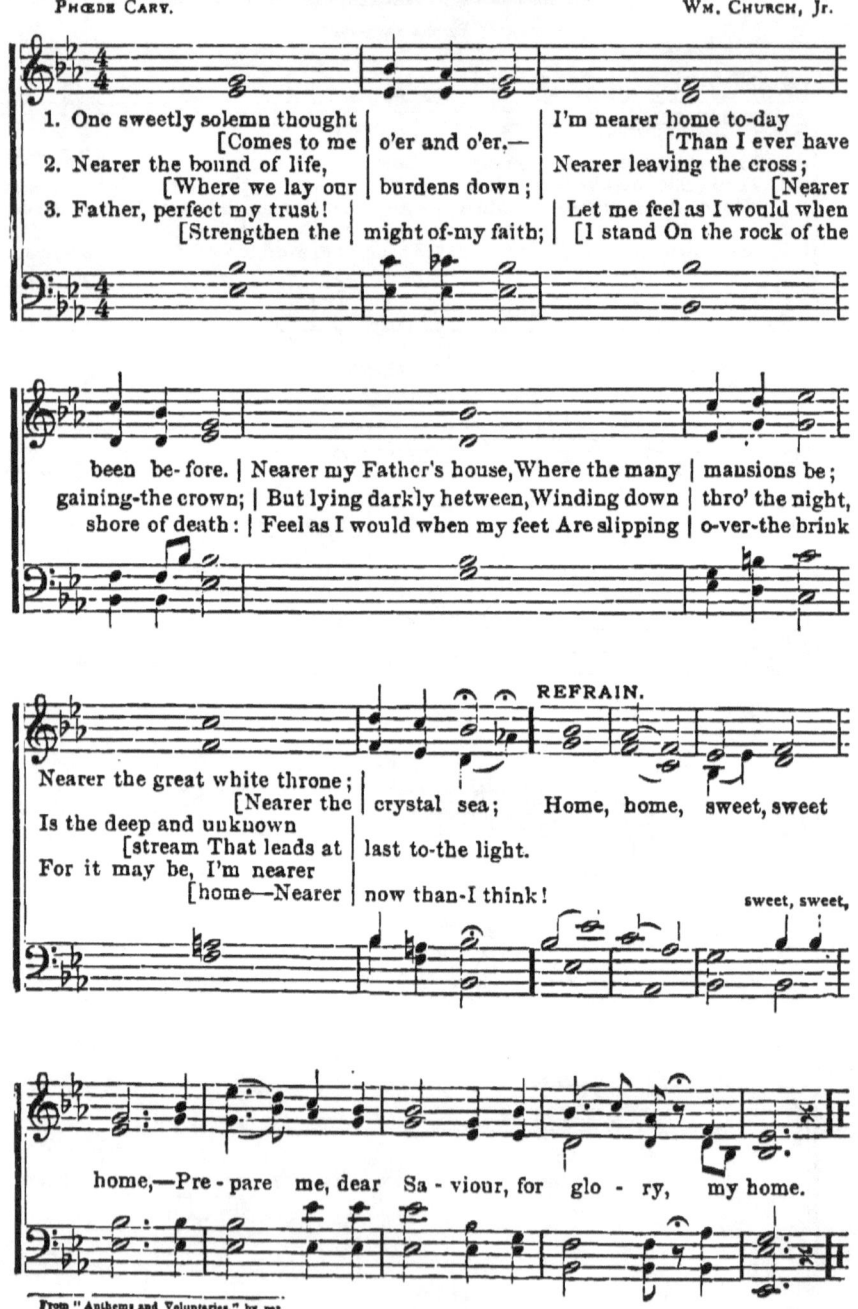

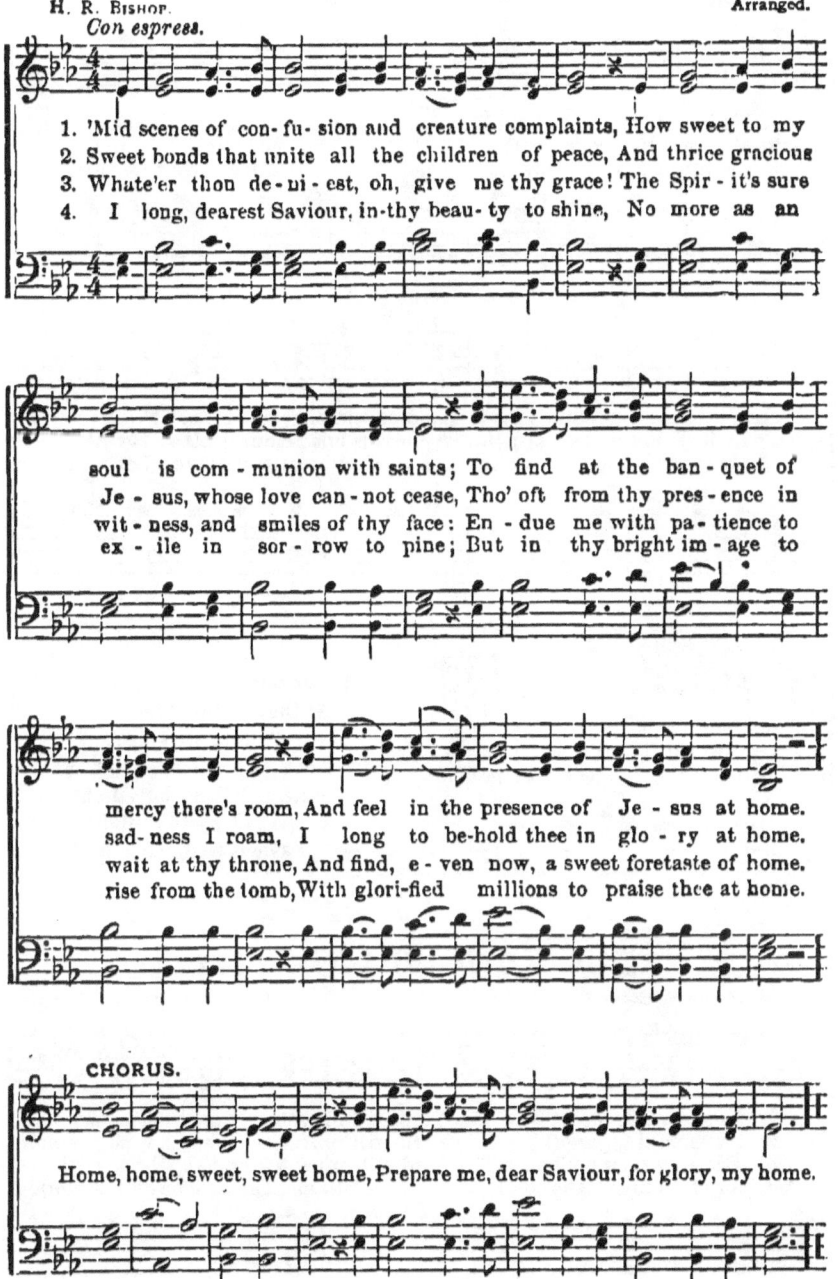

252. America.

S. F. SMITH.

1. My country! 'tis of thee, Sweet land of lib-er-ty, Of thee I sing:
2. My na-tive country, thee, Land of the no-ble, free, Thy name I love:
3. Let music swell the breeze, And ring from all the trees Sweet freedom's song:

Land where my father's died! Land of the pilgrims' pride! From ev-'ry
I love thy rocks and rills, Thy woods and templed hills: My heart with
Let mortal tongues a-wake; Let all that breathe partake; Let rocks their

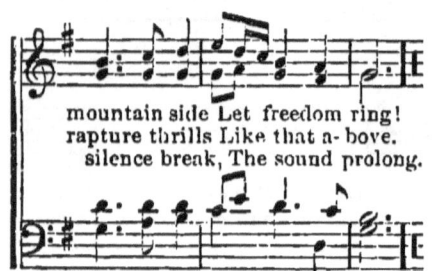

mountain side Let freedom ring!
rapture thrills Like that a-bove.
silence break, The sound prolong.

4 Our fathers' God! to thee,
Author of liberty,
 To thee we sing:
Long may our land be bright
With freedom's holy light;
Protect us by thy might,
 Great God, our King!

253. The Lord will Provide.

Mrs. M. A. W. COOK.   C. S. HARRINGTON. By per.

1. In some way or oth-er The Lord will provide; It may not be my way,
2. At some time or oth-er The Lord will provide; It may not be my time,
3. Despond then no longer, The Lord will provide; And this be the token—
4. March on, then, right boldly, The sea shall divide; The pathway made glorious,

The Lord will Provide.—CONCLUDED.

It may not be thy way, And yet in his own way, "The Lord will provide."
It may not be thy time, And yet in his own time, "The Lord will provide."
No word he hath spoken Was ev-er yet broken,—"The Lord will provide."
With shoutings victorious, We'll join in the chorus, "The Lord will provide."

254 ## Abide with Me.

H. F. Lyte. Tune, EVENTIDE. 10.

1. A-bide with me! Fast falls the e-ven-tide, The dark-ness deep-ens—Lord, with me a-bide! When oth-er help-ers fail and comforts flee, Help of the helpless, oh, a-bide with me!
2. Swift to its close ebbs out life's lit-tle day; Earth's joys grow dim, its glo-ries pass a-way; Change and de-cay in all around I see; O thou, who changest not, a-bide with me!
3. I need thy pres-ence ev-'ry pass-ing hour; What but thy grace can foil the tempter's pow'r? Who, like thy-self, my guide and stay can be? Thro' cloud and sunshine, Lord, abide with me!
4. I fear no foe, with thee at hand to bless; Ills have no weight, and tears no bit-ter-ness; Where is death's sting? where grave, thy vic-to-ry? I triumph still, if thou a-bide with me!
5. Hold thou thy cross be-fore my clos-ing eyes; Shine thro' the gloom and point me to the skies; Heaven's morning breaks, and earth's vain shadows flee; In life, in death, O Lord, a-bide with me!

255. The Altered Motto.

Rev. Theo Monod.   J. G. Robinson.

1. O the bitter ‖ shame and sorrow, ‖ That a time could ‖ ever be, ‖ When I let the ‖ Saviour's pity ‖ Plead in ‖ vain, and proudly answer'd, All of self and none of thee.
2. Yet he found me, ‖ I beheld him ‖ Bleeding on the ac-‖ cursed tree ‖ Heard him pray, for ‖ give them, Father, ‖ And my ‖ wistful heart said faintly, Some of self and some of thee.

3 Day by day his ‖ tender mercy, ‖
  Healing, helping, ‖ full and free, ‖
  Sweet, and strong, ‖ and, oh, so patient, ‖
  Brought me ‖ lower while I whispered,
  Less of self and more of thee.

4 Higher than the ‖ highest heaven, ‖
  Deeper than the ‖ deepest sea, ‖
  Lord, thy love ‖ at last has conquer'd, ‖
  Grant me ‖ now my soul's desire,
  None of self and all of thee.

Copyright, 1880, by John J. Hood.

---

256. Father, Whate'er.

Anne Steele.   Tune, NAOMI. C. M.

1. Father, whate'er of earthly bliss Thy sovereign will denies,
Accepted at thy throne of grace Let this petition rise.

2 Give me a calm, a thankful heart,
  From every murmur free;
  The blessings of thy grace impart,
  And make me live to thee.

3 Let the sweet hope that thou art mine
  My life and death attend;
  Thy presence through my journey shine,
  And crown my journey's end.

257. We'll Work till Jesus Comes.

Mrs. Elizabeth Mills.   Arr. by W. J. K., 1859.   Dr. Wm. Miller.

1. O land of rest for thee I sigh,
   When will the moment come,
   When I shall lay my armor by
   And dwell in peace at home?

   Cho.—We'll work till Jesus comes,
   We'll work till Jesus comes,
   We'll work till Jesus comes,
   And we'll be gather'd home.

2. No tranquil joys on earth I know,
   No peaceful sheltering dome,
   This world's a wilderness of woe,
   This world is not my home.

3. To Jesus Christ I fled for rest;
   He bade me cease to roam,
   And lean for succor on his breast,
   Till he conduct me home.

4. I sought at once my Saviour's side,
   No more my steps shall roam;
   With him I'll brave death's chilling tide,
   And reach my heavenly home.

258. Happy Land.

Old Melody.

2. Bright, in that happy land,
   Beams every eye;
   Kept by a Father's hand,
   Love cannot die.
   On, then, to glory run;
   Be a crown and kingdom won;
   And bright, above the sun,
   Reign evermore.

3. Come to that happy land,
   Come, come away;
   Why will you doubting stand?
   Why still delay?
   Oh, we shall happy be.
   When from sin and sorrow free;
   Lord, we shall dwell with thee,
   Blest evermore.

260. Beyond the Smiling.

H. LONAR.   W. A. TARBUTTON.

1. Beyond the smiling and the weeping, I shall be soon; Beyond the waking and the sleeping, Beyond the sowing and the reaping, I shall be soon.

Love, rest, and home! sweet home! Lord, tarry not, but come.

1 Beyond the smiling and the weeping,
   I shall be soon;
Beyond the waking and the sleeping,
Beyond the sowing and the reaping,
   I shall be soon.

2 Beyond the blooming and the fading,
   I shall be soon;
Beyond the shining and the shading,
Beyond the hoping and the dreading,
   I shall be soon.

3 Beyond the rising and the setting,
   I shall be soon;
Beyond the calming and the fretting,
Beyond remembering and forgetting,
   I shall be soon.

4 Beyond the parting and the meeting,
   I shall be soon;
Beyond the farewell and the greeting,
Beyond the pulse's fever beating,
   I shall be soon.

261. Gloria Patri.

C. NORRIS.

Glory be to the Father, and to the Son, And to the Holy Ghost; As it was in the beginning, is now, and ever shall be, World without end. A-men.

2 Have we trials and temptations?
  Is there trouble anywhere?
We should never be discouraged,
  Take it to the Lord in prayer.
Can we find a friend so faithful
  Who will all our sorrows share?
Jesus knows our every weakness,
  Take it to the Lord in prayer.

3 Are we weak and heavy laden,
  Cumbered with a load of care?—
Precious Saviour, still our refuge,—
  Take it to the Lord in prayer.
Do thy friends despise, forsake thee?
  Take it to the Lord in prayer;
In his arms he'll take and shield thee,
  Thou wilt find a solace there.

265. Toil on, Teachers.

Tune, SMYRNA. 8s & 7s. D.

1. Toil on, teachers, toil on boldly, Labor on and watch and pray;
Men may scoff and treat you coldly, Heed them not, go on your way;
Jesus is a loving Master; Cease not then his work to do;
Cleave to him still closer, faster, He will own and honor you.

2. Toil on, teachers! toil on ever, Constantly, unflinching toil;
Faint ye not, and weary never, Labor on in ev'ry soil;
Listless souls one day may waken, Buried seeds spring up and grow,
Sin's stout bulwarks may be shaken, Hardened hearts may be brought low.

3. Toil on, teachers! earnest, steady, Sowing well the seed of truth;
Always willing, cheerful, ready, Watching, praying for your youth;
Patient, firm and persevering, Leaning on the promise sure;
Prayer will surely gain a hearing, Faithful to the end endure.

266. Saviour, like a Shepherd Lead Us.

1 Saviour, like a shepherd lead us,
  Much we need thy tenderest care;
In thy pleasant pastures feed us,
  For our use thy folds prepare:
Blessed Jesus, blessed Jesus,
  Thou hast bought us, thine we are.

2 We are thine, do thou befriend us,
  Be the guardian of our way;
Keep thy flock, from sin defend us,
  Seek us when we go astray:
Blessed Jesus, blessed Jesus,
  Hear thy children when they pray.

3 Thou hast promised to receive us,
  Poor and sinful though we be;
Thou hast mercy to relieve us,
  Grace to cleanse, and power to free:
Blessed Jesus, blessed Jesus,
  Let us ever turn to thee.

267. Jesus, I my Cross have Taken.

HENRY F. LYTE. Tune, ELLESDIE. 8, 7, d.

1. Jesus, I my cross have taken, All to leave and follow thee;
Naked, poor, despised, forsaken, Thou, from hence, my all shalt be:
Perish ev-'ry fond ambition, All I've sought and hoped, and known;
Yet how rich is my condition, God and heaven are still my own!

2 Let the world despise and leave me,
They have left my Saviour, too;
Human hearts and looks deceive me;
Thou art not, like man, untrue;
And, while thou shalt smile upon me,
God of wisdom, love, and might,
Foes may hate, and friends may shun me;
Show thy face, and all is bright.

3 Go, then, earthly fame and treasure!
Come, disaster, scorn, and pain!
In thy service, pain is pleasure;
With thy favor, loss is gain.
I have called thee, "Abba, Father;"
I have stayed my heart on thee;
Storms may howl, and clouds may gather,
All must work for good to me.

4 Man may trouble and distress me,
'Twill but drive me to thy breast;
Life with trials hard may press me,
Heaven will bring me sweeter rest.
O 'tis not in grief to harm me,
While thy love is left to me;
O 'twere not in joy to charm me,
Were that joy unmixed with thee.

5 Know, my soul, thy full salvation;
Rise o'er sin, and fear, and care;
Joy to find in every station
Something still to do or bear.

Think what Spirit dwells within thee;
What a Father's smile is thine;
What a Saviour died to win thee:
Child of heaven, shouldst thou repine?

6 Haste thee on from grace to glory,
Armed by faith, and winged by prayer;
Heaven's eternal day's before thee,
God's own hand shall guide thee there.
Soon shall close thy earthly mission,
Swift shall pass thy pilgrim days,
Hope shall change to glad fruition,
Faith to sight, and prayer to praise.

268. Gently Lead Us.

1 Gently, Lord, oh, gently lead us
Through this lonely vale of tears,
Through the changes thou'st decreed us,
Till our last great change appears;
When temptation's darts assail us,
When in devious paths we stray,
Let thy goodness never fail us,
Lead us in thy perfect way.

2 In the hour of pain and anguish,
In the hour when death draws near,
Suffer not our hearts to languish,
Suffer not our souls to fear;
And when mortal life is ended,
Bid us in thine arms to rest,
Till by angel bands attended
We awake among the blest.

—THOS. HASTINGS.

269. Revive us again.

Wm. P. Mackay.   J. J. Husband.

1. We praise thee, O God! for the Son of thy love,
For Jesus who died and is now gone above.

REFRAIN.
Hal-le-lujah! thine the glory; Halle-lujah! a-men! Revive us a-gain.

2 We praise thee, O God! for thy Spirit of light,
Who has shown us our Saviour and scattered our night.

3 All glory and praise to the Lamb that was slain,
Who has borne all our sins, and has cleansed every stain.

4 All glory and praise to the God of all grace,
Who has bought us, and sought us, and guided our ways.

270. While Jesus Whispers to You.

Will. E. Witter.   H. R. Palmer.

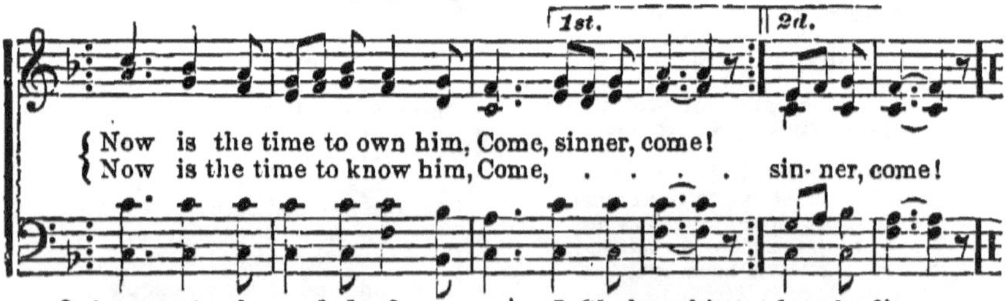

1. { While Jesus whispers to you, Come, sinner, come!
   { While we are praying for you, Come, . . . sin-ner, come!

   { Now is the time to own him, Come, sinner, come!
   { Now is the time to know him, Come, . . . sin-ner, come!

2 Are you too heavy laden?
Come, sinner, come!
Jesus will bear your burden,
Come, sinner, come!
Jesus will not deceive you,
Come, sinner, come!
Jesus can now redeem you,
Come, sinner, come!

3 Oh, hear his tender pleading,
Come, sinner, come!
Come and receive the blessing,
Come, sinner, come!
While Jesus whispers to you,
Come, sinner, come!
While we are praying for you,
Come, sinner, come!

Copyright, 1879, by H. R. Palmer.

271. I am Coming to the Cross.

Rev. Wm. McDonald. — John vi. 37. — Wm. G. Fischer. By per

1. I am com-ing to the cross; I am poor, and weak, and blind;
2. Long my heart has sighed for thee, Long has e-vil dwelt within;
3. Here I give my all to thee, Friends, and time, and earthly store;

CHO.—I am trust-ing, Lord, in thee, Blest Lamb of Cal-va-ry;
D. C.

I am count-ing all but dross, I shall full sal-va-tion find.
Je-sus sweet-ly speaks to me,— "I will cleanse you from all sin."
Soul and bo-dy thine to be,— Whol-ly thine for ev-er-more.

Humbly at thy cross I bow, Save me, Je-sus, save me now.

4 In thy promises I trust,
   Now I feel the blood applied:
  I am prostrate in the dust,
   I with Christ am crucified.

5 Jesus comes! he fills my soul!
   Perfected in him I am;
  I am every whit made whole;
   Glory, glory to the Lamb.

272. Happy Day.

P. Doddridge. — English Melody.

1. { O happy day, that fixed my choice On thee, my Saviour and my God!
    Well may this glowing heart rejoice, And tell its raptures all abroad. } Happy day, happy day,
   When Jesus washed my sins away!
{ He taught me how to watch and pray,
   And live rejoicing ev'ry day.

2 O happy bond, that seals my vows
   To him who merits all my love!
  Let cheerful anthems fill his house,
   While to that sacred shrine I move.

3 'Tis done! the great transaction's done!
   I am my Lord's, and he is mine:
  He drew me, and I followed on,
   Charmed to confess that voice divine.

4 Now rest, my long-divided heart;
   Fixed on this blissful center, rest;
  Nor ever from thy Lord depart;
   With him of every good possessed.

5 High heav'n that heard the solemn vow,
   That vow renewed shall daily hear,
  Till in life's latest hour I bow,
   And bless in death a bond so dear.

273. My Jesus, as Thou wilt.

BENJAMIN SCHMOLKA. Tr. by Miss J. BORTHWICK.   Tune, JEWETT. 6s.

1. My Jesus, as thou wilt: O may thy will be mine; In-to thy hand of love I would my all re-sign. Thro' sor-row or thro' joy, Conduct me as thine own, And help me still to say, "My Lord, thy will be done."

2. My Jesus, as thou wilt: Tho' seen thro' many-a tear, Let not my star of hope Grow dim or dis-ap-pear. Since thou on earth hast wept And sorrowed oft alone, If I must weep with thee, My Lord, thy will be done.

3. My Jesus, as thou wilt: All shall be well for me; Each changing fu-ture scene I gladly trust with thee. Straight to my home a-bove, I trav-el calmly on, And sing in life or death, "My Lord, thy will be done."

274. Holy, holy, holy.

REGINALD HEBER.   Tune, NICEA. 11, 12, 10.

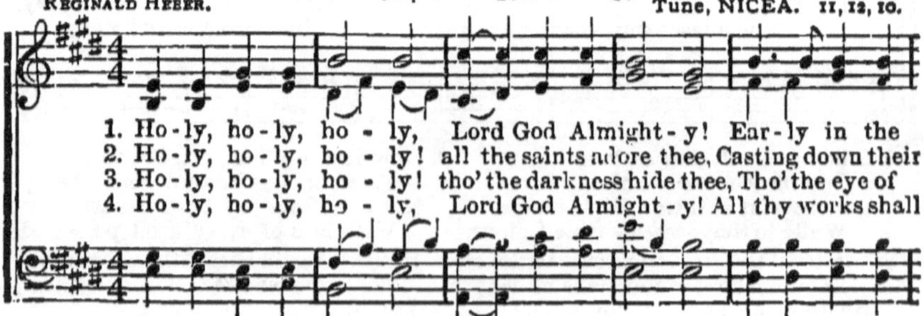

1. Holy, holy, holy, Lord God Almight-y! Early in the
2. Holy, holy, holy! all the saints adore thee, Casting down their
3. Holy, holy, holy! tho' the darkness hide thee, Tho' the eye of
4. Holy, holy, holy, Lord God Almight-y! All thy works shall

Holy, holy, holy.—CONCLUDED.

morn - ing our song shall rise to thee; Ho-ly, ho-ly, ho-ly,
gold-en crowns around the glas-sy sea; Cher-u-bim and seraphim
sin-ful man thy glo-ry may not see; On-ly thou art ho-ly!
praise thy name, in earth, and sky, and sea; Ho-ly, ho-ly, ho-ly.

mer-ci-ful and might-y, God in Three Persons, blessed Trin-i-ty!
falling down before thee, Which wert, and art, and evermore shalt be.
there is none be-side thee, Per-fect in power, in love, and pur-i-ty.
mer-ci-ful and might-y, God in Three Persons, blessed Trin-i-ty!

275 **Rock of Ages.** Tune, TOPLADY. 7.

1 Rock of a-ges, cleft for me, Let me hide myself in thee;
D. C.—Be of sin the double cure,—Cleanse me from its guilt and pow'r.

Let the wa-ter and the blood From thy wounded side which flowed,

2 Not the labor of my hands,
Can fulfil the law's demands;
Could my zeal no respite know,
Could my tears forever flow,
All for sin could not atone,—
Thou must save, and thou alone.

3 Nothing in my hand I bring;
Simply to thy cross I cling;
Naked, come to thee for dress,

Helpless, look to thee for grace,—
Vile, I to the fountain fly,
Wash me, Saviour, or I die.

4 While I draw this fleeting breath,
When my heart-strings break in death,
When I soar to worlds unknown,
See thee on thy judgement-throne,—
Rock of ages, cleft for me,
Let me hide myself in thee.

276. Sun of My Soul.

JOHN KEBLER. Tune, HURSLEY. L. M.

1. Sun of my soul, thou Saviour dear, It is not night if thou be near:
O may no earthborn cloud a-rise To hide thee from thy servant's eyes.

2. When the soft dews of kindly sleep My wearied eye-lids gently steep,
Be my last thought, how sweet to rest Forever on my Saviour's breast.

3 Abide with me from morn till eve,
For without thee I cannot live;
Abide with me when night is nigh,
For without thee I dare not die.

4 If some poor wandering child of thine
Hath spurned to-day the voice divine,
Now, Lord, the gracious work begin;
Let him no more lie down in sin.

5 Watch by the sick; enrich the poor
With blessings from thy boundless store;
Be every mourner's sleep to-night,
Like infant's slumbers, pure and light.

6 Come near and bless us when we wake,
Ere through the world our way we take;
Till in the ocean of thy love,
We lose ourselves in heaven above.

277. Sweet is the Work.

1 Sweet is the work, my God, my King,
To praise thy name, give thanks and sing,
To show thy love by morning light,
And talk of all thy truth at night.

2 Sweet is the day of sacred rest,
No mortal cares shall seize my breast;
Oh! may my heart in tune be found,
Like David's harp of solemn sound.

3 My heart shall triumph in my Lord,
And bless his works and bless his word;
Thy works of grace, how bright they shine!
How deep thy counsels! how divine!

278. Jesus, Engrave it.

1 Jesus, engrave it on my heart,
That thou the one thing needful art;
I could from all things parted be,
But never, never, Lord, from thee.

2 Needful art thou to make me live;
Needful art thou all grace to give;
Needful to guide me, lest I stray;
Needful to help me every day.

3 Needful is thy most precious blood;
Needful is thy correcting rod;
Needful is thine indulgent care,
Needful thine all-prevailing prayer.

4 Needful art thou to be my stay
Through all life's dark and thorny way;
Nor less in death thou'lt needful be,
When I yield up my soul to thee.

279. Before Jehovah's.

Tune, OLD HUNDRED. L. M.

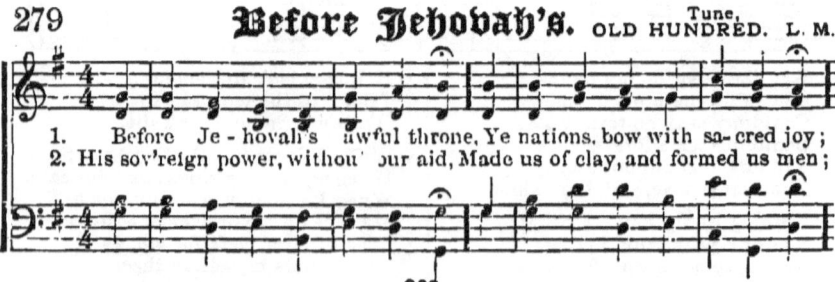

1. Before Je-hovah's awful throne, Ye nations, bow with sacred joy;
2. His sov'reign power, without our aid, Made us of clay, and formed us men;

Before Jehovah's.—CONCLUDED.

Know that the Lord is God a-lone—He can create, and he destroy.
And when, like wand'ring sheep, we strayed, He brought us to his fold again.

3 We are thy people, we thy care,
  Our souls and all our mortal frame:
What lasting honors shall we rear,
  Almighty Maker, to thy name!

4 We'll crowd thy gates with thankful songs,
  High as the heavens our voices raise,
And earth, with her ten thousand tongues,
  Shall fill thy courts with sounding
  [praise.

280 O Thou to Whose.

Tr. by J. Wesley. Tune. STONEFIELD. L. M.

1. O thou, to whose all-searching sight
   The darkness shineth as the light, Search, prove my heart, it pants for thee; O burst these bonds, and set it free.

2. Wash out its stains, refine its dross, Nail my affections to the cross; Hallow each thought; let all within Be clean, as thou, my Lord, art clean.

3 If in this darksome wild I stray,
  Be thou my light, be thou my way:
No foes, no violence I fear,
No fraud, while thou, my God, art near.

4 When rising floods my soul o'erflow,
  When sinks my heart in waves of woe,
Jesus, thy timely aid impart,
And raise my head, and cheer my heart.

5 Saviour, where'er thy steps I see,
  Dauntless, untired, I follow thee;
O let thy hand support me still,
And lead me to thy holy hill.

6 If rough and thorny be the way,
  My strength proportion to my day;
Till toil, and grief, and pain shall cease,
Where all is calm, and joy, and peace.

281. Blow ye the Trumpet.

Tune LENOX, H. M.

1. Blow ye the trumpet, blow, The gladly solemn sound! Let all the nations know, To earth's re-motest bound, The year of ju-bi-lee is come! The year of ju-bi-lee is come, Return, ye ransomed sinners, home.

2. Jesus, our great High Priest, Hath full atonement made: Ye weary spirits, rest: Ye mournful souls, be glad: The year of ju-bi-lee is come!

3 Extol the Lamb of God,
    The all-atoning Lamb;
Redemption in his blood
    Throughout the world proclaim:
The year of jubilee is come!
Return, ye ransomed sinners, home.

4 Ye slaves of sin and hell,
    Your liberty receive,
And safe in Jesus dwell,
    And blest in Jesus live:
The year of jubilee is come!
Return, ye ransomed sinners, home.

5 Ye who have sold for naught
    Your heritage above,
Shall have it back unbought,
    The gift of Jesus' love:
The year of jubilee is come!
Return, ye ransomed sinners, home.

6 The gospel trumpet hear,
    The news of heavenly grace;
And, saved from earth, appear
    Before your Saviour's face:
The year of jubilee is come!
Return, ye ransomed sinners, home.

282. Come, every pious heart.

1 Come, every pious heart,
    That loves the Saviour's name,
Your noblest powers exert
    To celebrate his fame;
Tell all above, and all below,
The debt of love to him you owe.

2 He left his starry crown,
    And laid his robes aside,
On wings of love came down,
    And wept, and bled, and died;
What he endured, oh, who can tell,
To save our souls from death and hell?

3 From the dark grave he rose,
    The mansions of the dead,
And thence his mighty foes
    In glorious triumph led;
Up through the sky the conqueror rode,
And reigns on high, the Saviour God.

4 Jesus, we ne'er can pay
    The debt we owe thy love;
Yet tell us how we may
    Our gratitude approve;
Our hearts, our all to thee we give,—
The gift, though small, thou wilt receive.

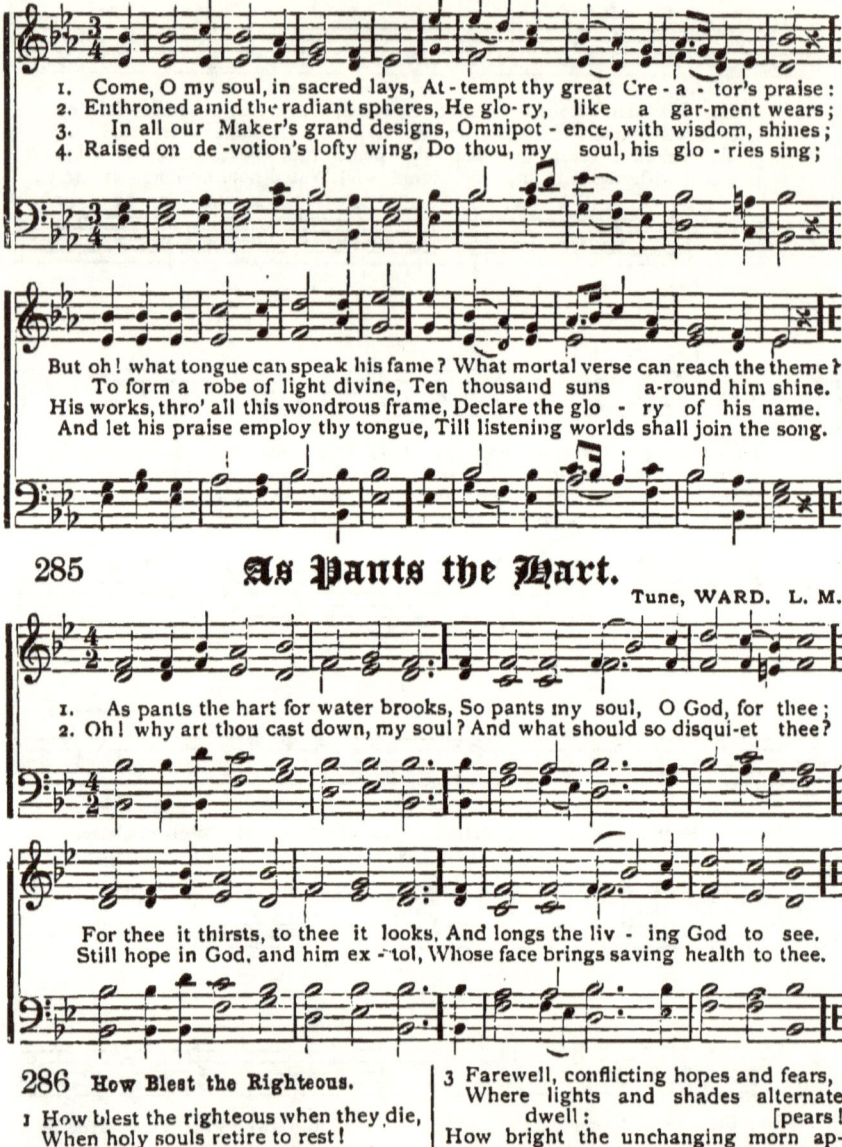

284. Come, O my Soul.
THOMAS BLACKLOCK.   Tune, LUTON. L. M.

1. Come, O my soul, in sacred lays, Attempt thy great Creator's praise:
   But oh! what tongue can speak his fame? What mortal verse can reach the theme?
2. Enthroned amid the radiant spheres, He glory, like a garment wears;
   To form a robe of light divine, Ten thousand suns a-round him shine.
3. In all our Maker's grand designs, Omnipotence, with wisdom, shines;
   His works, thro' all this wondrous frame, Declare the glory of his name.
4. Raised on devotion's lofty wing, Do thou, my soul, his glories sing;
   And let his praise employ thy tongue, Till listening worlds shall join the song.

285. As Pants the Hart.
Tune, WARD. L. M.

1. As pants the hart for water brooks, So pants my soul, O God, for thee;
   For thee it thirsts, to thee it looks, And longs the living God to see.
2. Oh! why art thou cast down, my soul? And what should so disquiet thee?
   Still hope in God, and him extol, Whose face brings saving health to thee.

286. How Blest the Righteous.

1 How blest the righteous when they die,
    When holy souls retire to rest!
How mildly beams the closing eye!
    How gently heaves the expiring breast!

2 So fades a summer cloud away;
    So sinks the gale when storms are o'er;
So gently shuts the eye of day;
    So dies a wave along the shore.

3 Farewell, conflicting hopes and fears,
    Where lights and shades alternate
        dwell: [pears!
How bright the unchanging morn ap-
    Farewell, inconstant world, farewell!

4 Life's duty done, as sinks the clay,
    Light from its load the spirit flies;
While heaven and earth combine to say,
    "How blest the righteous when he
        dies!"

Forest. L. M.

287 O that my load of sin were gone. L.M.

1 O that my load of sin were gone!
O that I could at last submit
At Jesus' feet to lay it down—
To lay my soul at Jesus' feet!

2 Rest for my soul I long to find:
Saviour of all, if mine thou art,
Give me thy meek and lowly mind,
And stamp thine image on my heart.

3 Break off the yoke of inbred sin,
And fully set my spirit free;
I cannot rest till pure within,
Till I am wholly lost in thee.

4 Fain would I learn of thee, my God,
Thy light and easy burden prove,
The cross all stained with hallowed blood,
The labor of thy dying love.

5 I would, but thou must give the power;
My heart from every sin release;
Bring near, bring near the joyful hour,
And fill me with thy perfect peace.
—CHAS. WESLEY.

288 Lord, I am Thine. L.M.

1 Lord, I am thine, entirely thine,
Purchased and saved by blood divine;
With full consent thine would I be,
And own thy sovereign right in me.

2 Thine would I live, thine would I die;
Be thine through all eternity;
The vow is past, beyond repeal,
And now I set the solemn seal.

3 Here, at that cross where flows the blood
That bought my guilty soul for God,
Thee, my new Master now I call,
And consecrate to thee my all.

4 Do thou assist a feeble worm
The great engagement to perform;
Thy grace can full assistance lend,
And on that grace I dare depend.
—SAMUEL DAVIES.

289 I thirst, Thou wounded Lamb of God. L.M.

1 I thirst, thou wounded Lamb of God,
To wash me in thy cleansing blood;
To dwell within thy wounds; then pain
Is sweet, and life or death is gain.

2 Take my poor heart, and let it be
Forever closed to all but thee:
Seal thou my breast, and let me wear
That pledge of love forever there.

3 How blest are they who still abide
Close sheltered in thy bleeding side!
Who thence their life and strength derive,
And by thee move, and in thee live.

4 What are our works but sin and death,
Till thou thy quickening Spirit breathe?
Thou giv'st the power thy grace to move;
O wondrous grace! O wondrous love!

5 How can it be, thou heavenly King,
That thou shouldst us to glory bring?
Make slaves the partners of thy throne,
Decked with a never-fading crown?

6 Hence our hearts melt, our eyes o'erflow,
Our words are lost, nor will we know,
Nor will we think of aught beside,
"My Lord, my Love is crucified."
—NICOLAUS L. ZINZENDORF.

290 While Life Prolongs.

1 While life prolongs its precious light
  Mercy is found, and peace is given,
But soon, ah! soon, approaching night
  Shall blot out every hope of heaven.

2 While God invites, how blest the day,
  How sweet the Gospel's charming sound;
Come, sinners, haste, oh, haste away,
  While yet a pardoning God is found.

3 Soon, borne on time's most rapid wing,
  Shall death command you to the grave:
Before his bar your spirits bring,
  And none be found to hear or save.

4 In that lone land of deep despair,
  No Sabbath's heavenly light shall rise—
No God regard your bitter prayer,
  No Saviour call you to the skies.

291 Just as I am.

1 Just as I am, without one plea,
  But that thy blood was shed for me,
And that thou bids't me come to thee,
  O Lamb of God, I come! I come!

2 Just as I am, and waiting not
  To rid my soul of one dark blot, [spot,
To thee, whose blood can cleanse each
  O Lamb of God, I come! I come!

3 Just as I am, though tossed about
  With many a conflict, many a doubt,
Fightings within and fears without,
  O Lamb of God, I come! I come!

4 Just as I am—poor, wretched, blind;
  Sight, riches, healing of the mind,
Yea, all I need, in thee to find,
  O Lamb of God, I come! I come!

5 Just as I am—thou wilt receive,
  Wilt welcome, pardon, cleanse, relieve,
Because thy promise I believe,
  O Lamb of God, I come! I come!

6 Just as I am—thy love unknown
  Hath broken every barrier down;
Now, to be thine, yea, thine alone,
  O Lamb of God, I come! I come!

292 Come, Holy Spirit.

1 Come, Holy Spirit, calm my mind,
  And fit me to approach my God;
Remove each vain, each worldly thought,
  And lead me to thy blest abode.

2 Hast thou imparted to my soul
  A living spark of holy fire?
Oh! kindle now the sacred flame,
  Make me to burn with pure desire.

3 A brighter faith and hope impart,
  And let me now my Saviour see;
Oh! soothe and cheer my burdened heart,
  And bid my spirit rest in thee.

293 When I Survey.

1 When I survey the wondrous cross,
  On which the Prince of Glory died,
My richest gain I count but loss,
  And pour contempt on all my pride.

2 Forbid it, Lord, that I should boast,
  Save in the death of Christ, my God;
All the vain things that charm me most,
  I sacrifice them to his blood.

3 See, from his head, his hands, his feet,
  Sorrow and love flow mingled down;
Did e'er such love and sorrow meet,
  Or thorns compose so rich a crown?

4 His dying crimson, like a robe,
  Spreads o'er his body on the tree,
Then am I dead to all the globe,
  And all the globe is dead to me.

5 Were the whole realm of nature mine,
  That were a present far too small;
Love so amazing, so divine,
  Demands my soul, my life, my all.

294. Go, Labor On.

H. BONAR. Tune, MISSIONARY CHANT. L. M.

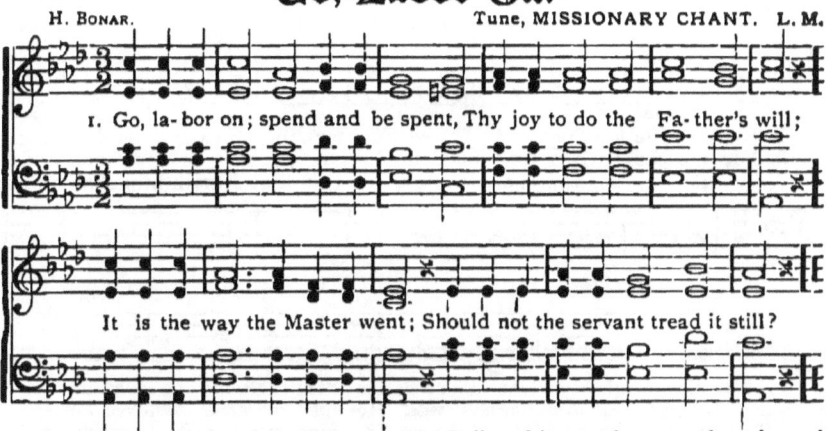

1. Go, labor on; spend and be spent, Thy joy to do the Father's will;
It is the way the Master went; Should not the servant tread it still?

2 Go, labor on; 'tis not for naught;
Thine earthly loss is heavenly gain;
Men heed thee, love thee, praise thee not;
The Master praises,—what are men?

3 Go, labor on; your hands are weak;
Your knees are faint, your soul cast down;
Yet falter not; the prize you seek
Is near,—a kingdom and a crown!

4 Toil on, faint not; keep watch, and pray!
Be wise the erring soul to win;
Go forth into the world's highway;
Compel the wanderer to come in.

5 Toil on, and in thy toil rejoice;
For toil comes rest, for exile home;
Soon shalt thou hear the Bridegroom's voice,
The midnight peal, "Behold, I come!"

295. Awake, my Soul.

P. DODDRIDGE. Tune, CHRISTMAS. C. M.

1. Awake, my soul, stretch ev'ry nerve, And press with vigor on; A heavenly race demands thy zeal, And an immortal crown, And an immortal crown.

2 A cloud of witnesses around
Hold thee in full survey;
Forget the steps already trod,
And onward urge thy way.

3 'Tis God's all-animating voice
That calls thee from on high;
'Tis his own hand presents the prize
To thine aspiring eye:—

4 That prize, with peerless glories bright,
Which shall new luster boast,
When victors' wreaths and monarchs' gems
Shall blend in common dust.

5 Blest Saviour, introduced by thee,
Have I my race begun;
And, crowned with victory, at thy feet
I'll lay my honors down.

Living Hymns-8

296. He Loved Me So.

E. O. E.
God so loved the world.—John iii 16.
E. O. Excell.

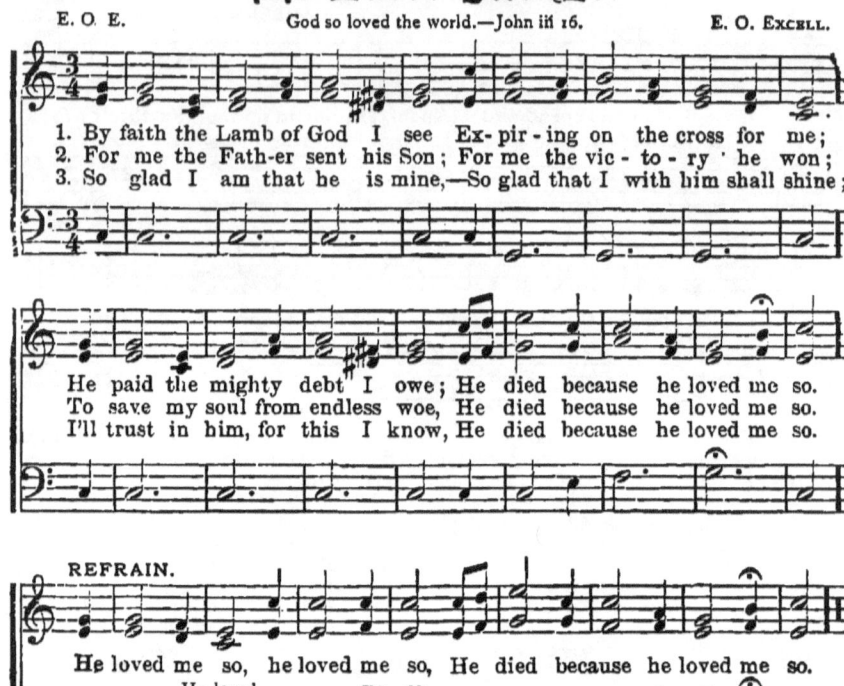

1. By faith the Lamb of God I see Ex-pir-ing on the cross for me;
2. For me the Father sent his Son; For me the vic-to-ry he won;
3. So glad I am that he is mine,—So glad that I with him shall shine;

He paid the mighty debt I owe; He died because he loved me so.
To save my soul from endless woe, He died because he loved me so.
I'll trust in him, for this I know, He died because he loved me so.

REFRAIN.
He loved me so, he loved me so, He died because he loved me so.

4 O Lamb of God, that made me free,
I consecrate my all to thee:
My all,—for this I surely know,
He died because he loved me so.

5 And when my Lord shall bid me come
To join the loved ones 'round the throne,
I'll sing, as through the gates I go,
He died because he loved me so.

Copyright, 1880, by John J. Hood.

297. Give me the Wings of Faith.

Rev. I. Watts.
Arr. by Walter Kittredge.
Melody by per. of O. Ditson Co.

SOLO.

1. Give me the wings of faith to rise Within the vail, and see The
2. Once they were mourners here below, And pour'd out cries and tears; They
3. I ask them whence their victory came: They with u-nit-ed breath A-

saints a-bove, how great their joys, How bright their glo-ries be.
wres-tled hard, as we do now, With sins, and doubts and fears.
scribe their con-quest to the Lamb, Their tri-umph to his death.

2 He thy strength in weakness,
    Will thy refuge be;
  Cast on him thy burden,
    He will care for thee.
3 Come, in faith believing,
    To his will resigned;

Ask, and he will give thee;
  Seek, and thou shalt find.
4 See the door of Mercy,
    Wouldst thou enter there?
  Knock, and he will open;
    Lo! the key is prayer.

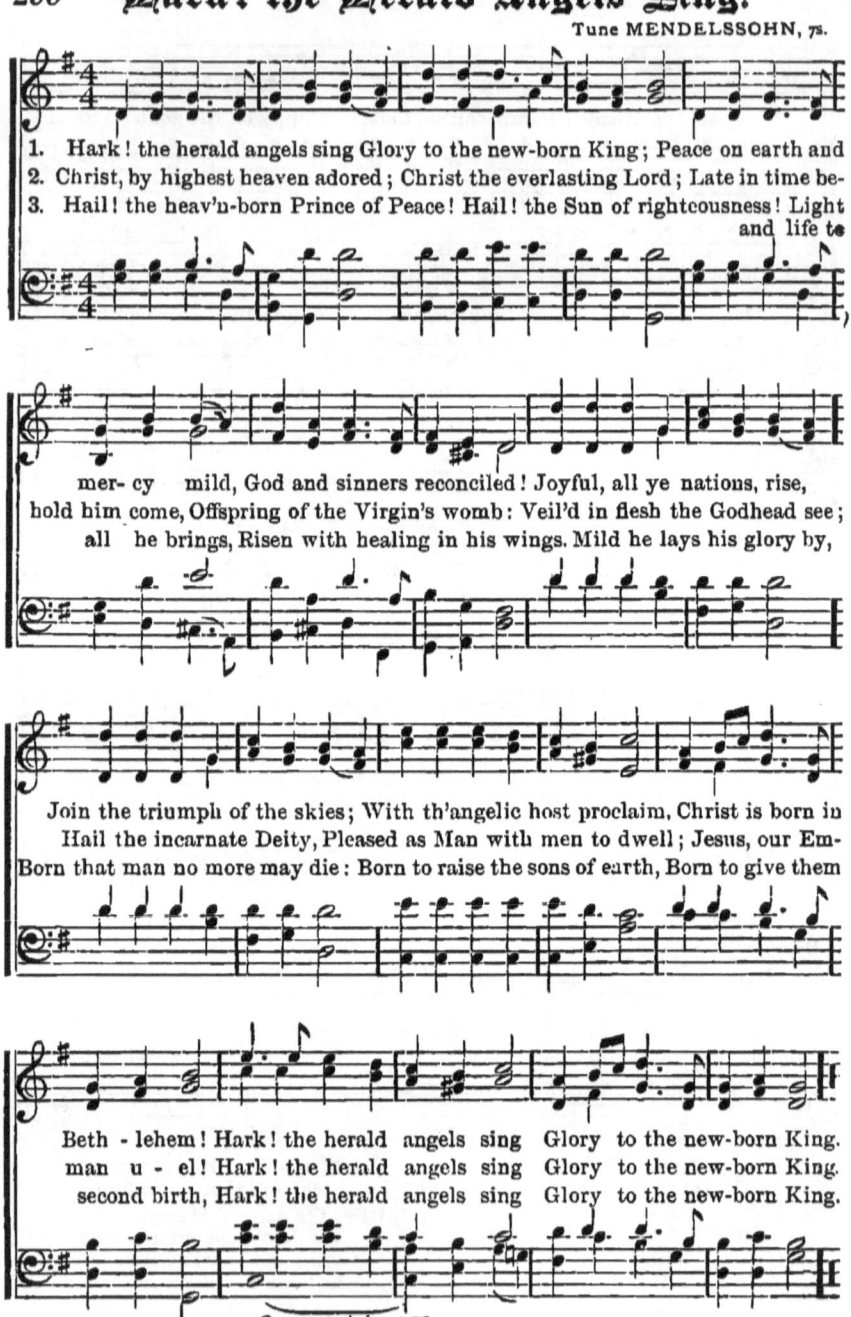

Missionary Hymn.

L. Mason.

300 *From Greenland's icy.*

1 From Greenland's icy mountains,
  From India's coral strand,
Where Afric's sunny fountains
  Roll down their golden sand,
From many an ancient river,
  From many a palmy plain,
They call us to deliver
  Their land from error's chain.

2 What though the spicy breezes
  Blow soft o'er Ceylon's isle,
Though every prospect pleases,
  And only man is vile;
In vain with lavish kindness
  The gifts of God are strewn,
The heathen, in their blindness,
  Bow down to wood and stone.

3 Shall we, whose souls are lighted
  With wisdom from on high,
Shall we, to men benighted,
  The lamp of life deny?
Salvation! oh, salvation!
  The joyful sound proclaim,
Till earth's remotest nation
  Has learned Messiah's name.

4 Waft, waft, ye winds, his story,
  And you, ye waters, roll,
Till, like a sea of glory,
  It spreads from pole to pole;
Till o'er our ransomed nature,
  The Lamb for sinners slain,
Redeemer, King, Creator,
  In bliss returns to reign.

301 *Hail to the Lord's Anointed.*

1 Hail to the Lord's Anointed!
  Great David's greater Son!
Hail in the time appointed,
  His reign on earth begun!
He comes to break oppression,
  To set the captive free,—
To take away transgression,
  And rule in equity.

2 He shall come down like showers
  Upon the fruitful earth,
And love and joy, like flowers,
  Spring in his path to birth:
Before him on the mountains
  Shall peace, the herald, go;
And righteousness, in fountains,
  From hill to valley flow.

3 For him shall prayer unceasing
  And daily vows ascend;
His kingdom still increasing,
  A kingdom without end;
The tide of time shall never
  His covenant remove;
His name shall stand forever,
  That name to us is—Love.

Bera. L. M.

J. E. GOULD.

302   Asleep in Jesus!

1 Asleep in Jesus! blessed sleep,
From which none ever wakes to weep;
A calm and undisturbed repose,
Unbroken by the last of foes.

2 Asleep in Jesus! oh, how sweet
To be for such a slumber meet!
With holy confidence to sing,
That death hath lost its venomed sting.

3 Asleep in Jesus! peaceful rest!
Whose waking is supremely blest;
No fear, no woe, shall dim that hour,
Which manifests the Saviour's power.

4 Asleep in Jesus! oh, for me
May such a blissful refuge be!
Securely shall my ashes lie,
And wait the summons from on high.

303   What Sinners Value I Resign;
Tune, Park Street.

1 What sinners value I resign;
Lord, 'tis enough that thou art mine;
I shall behold thy blissful face,
And stand complete in righteousness.

2 This life's a dream—an empty show;
But the bright world to which I go
Hath joys substantial and sincere;
When shall I wake and find me there?

3 Oh, glorious hour!—oh, blest abode!
I shall be near and like my God;
And flesh and sin no more control
The sacred pleasures of the soul.

3 My flesh shall slumber in the ground,
Till the last trumpet's joyful sound:
Then burst the chains with sweet surprise,
And in my Saviour's image rise.

304   From every Stormy Wind.

1 From every stormy wind that blows,
From every swelling tide of woes,
There is a calm, a sure retreat;
'Tis found beneath the mercy-seat.

2 There is a place where Jesus sheds
The oil of gladness on our heads—
A place than all besides more sweet;
It is the blood-bought mercy-seat.

3 There is a scene where spirits blend,
Where friend holds fellowship with friend;
Though sundered far, by faith they meet
Around one common mercy-seat.

4 There, there on eagle wings we soar,
And time and sense seem all no more,
And heaven comes down our souls to greet,
And glory crowns the mercy-seat.

305   Jesus shall Reign.
Tune, Park Street.

1 Jesus shall reign where'er the sun
Does its successive journeys run;
His kingdom stretch from shore to shore,
Till moons shall wax and wane no more.

2 For him shall endless prayer be made,
And endless praises crown his head;
His name, like sweet perfume, shall rise
With every morning sacrifice.

3 People and realms of every tongue
Dwell on his love with sweetest song,
And infant voices shall proclaim
Their early blessings on his name.

4 Let every creature rise and bring
Peculiar honors to our King;
Angels descend with songs again,
And earth repeat the loud Amen.

306   Lo! Round the Throne.

MARY L. DUNCAN.   Tune, PARK STREET. L. M.

1. Lo! round the throne, a glorious band, The saints in countless myriads stand; Of ev-'ry tongue redeemed to God, Arrayed in garments washed in blood, Arrayed in garments washed in blood.

2 Through tribulation great they came;
They bore the cross, despised the shame;
But now from all their labors rest,
In God's eternal glory blest.

3 They see the Saviour face to face;
They sing the triumph of his grace;
And day and night, with ceaseless praise,
To him their loud hosannas raise.

4 O may we tread the sacred road
That holy saints and martyrs trod;
Wage to the end the glorious strife,
And win, like them, a crown of life!

307   Now to the Lord.

1 Now to the Lord a noble song:
Awake, my soul, awake, my tongue;
Hosanna to the eternal name,
And all his boundless love proclaim.

2 See where it shines in Jesus' face,
The brightest image of his grace;
God, in the person of his Son,
Has all his mightiest works outdone.

3 The spacious earth and spreading flood
Proclaim the wise and powerful God;
And thy rich glories from afar
Sparkle in every rolling star.

4 Grace! 'tis a sweet, a charming theme,
My thoughts rejoice at Jesus name;
Ye angels, dwell upon the sound,
Ye heavens, reflect it to the ground.

5 Oh! may I reach that happy place,
Where he unveils his lovely face,
Where all his beauties you behold,
And sing his name to harps of gold.
—ISAAC WATTS

308   Soon may the last glad song.

1 Soon may the last glad song arise,
Through all the millions of the skies;
That song of triumph which records
That all the earth is now the Lord's.

2 Let thrones, and powers, and kingdoms be
Obedient, mighty God, to thee; [be
And over land, and stream, and main,
Now wave the scepter of thy reign.

3 O let that glorious anthem swell;
Let host to host the triumph tell,
Till not one rebel heart remains,
But over all the Saviour reigns.
—Mrs. VOKE.

309. Heaven is My Home.

SCOTCH MELODY.

1. I'm but a stranger here, Heav'n is my home;
   Earth is a desert drear, Heav'n is my home;
   Danger and sorrow stand round me on ev'ry hand; Heav'n is my Fatherland, Heav'n is my home.

2. What tho' the tempest rage? Heav'n is my home;
   Short is my pilgrimage, Heav'n is my home;
   Time's cold and wintry blast soon will be o-verpast; I shall reach home at last; Heav'n is my home.

3 Peace! O my troubled soul,
  Heav'n is my home;
  I soon shall reach the goal;
  Heav'n is my home;
  Swiftly the race I'll run,
  Yield up my crown to none;
  Forward! the prize is won;
  Heav'n is my home.

4 There, at my Saviour's side,
  Heav'n is my home;
  I shall be glorified;
  Heav'n is my home;
  There are the good and blest,
  Those I loved most and best,
  There, too, I soon shall rest,
  Heav'n is my home.

310. Nearer, My God! to Thee.

1 Nearer, my God! to thee,
  Nearer to thee!
  E'en though it be a cross
  That raiseth me!
  Still all my song shall be,
  Nearer, my God! to thee,
  Nearer to thee!

2 Though like the wanderer,
  The sun gone down,
  Darkness be over me,
  My rest a stone,
  Yet in my dreams I'd be
  Nearer, my God! to thee,
  Nearer to thee!

3 There let the way appear,
  Steps unto heaven;
  All that thou sendest me,
  In mercy given;
  Angels to beckon me
  Nearer, my God! to thee,
  Nearer to thee!

4 Then, with my waking thoughts
  Bright with thy praise,
  Out of my stony griefs
  Bethel I'll raise;
  So by my woes to be
  Nearer, my God! to thee,
  Nearer to thee!

5 Or if, on joyful wing
  Cleaving the sky,
  Sun, moon and stars forgot,
  Upward I fly,
  Still all my song shall be,
  Nearer, my God! to thee,
  Nearer to thee!

311 How do Thy Mercies.

C. Wesley. — Tune, FEDERAL STREET. L. M.

1. How do thy mercies close me round! Forever be thy name adored!
I blush in all things to abound; The servant is above his Lord.

2. Inured to poverty and pain, A suff'ring life my Master led;
The Son of God, the Son of Man, He had not where to lay his head.

3 But lo! a place he hath prepared
For me, whom watchful angels keep;
Yea, he himself becomes my guard;
He smooths my bed, and gives me sleep.

4 Jesus protects; my fears, be gone;
What can the Rock of Ages move?
Safe in thy arms I lay me down,
Thine everlasting arms of love.

5 While thou art intimately nigh,
Who, who shall violate my rest?
Sin, earth, and hell I now defy:
I lean upon my Saviour's breast.

6 I rest beneath the Almighty's shade;
My griefs expire, my troubles cease;
Thou, Lord, on whom my soul is stayed,
Wilt keep me still in perfect peace.

312 Jesus, and Shall it Ever Be.

1 Jesus, and shall it ever be,
A mortal man ashamed of thee?
Ashamed of thee whom angels praise,
Whose glories shine through endless days!

2 Ashamed of Jesus, that dear friend
On whom my hopes of heaven depend!
No, when I blush, be this my shame,
That I no more revere his name.

3 Ashamed of Jesus! yes, I may,
When I've no guilt to wash away,
No tear to wipe, no good to crave,
No fears to quell, no soul to save.

4 Till then—nor is my boasting vain—
Till then, I boast a Saviour slain;
And oh, may this my glory be,
That Christ is not ashamed of me!

313 Come Hither, All Ye Weary Souls.

1 Come hither, all ye weary souls,
Ye heavy-laden sinners, come;
I'll give you rest from all your toils,
And raise you to my heavenly home.

2 They shall find rest that learn of me;
I'm of a meek and lowly mind;
But passion rages like the sea,
And pride is restless as the wind.

3 Blest is the man whose shoulders take
My yoke, and bear it with delight;
My yoke is easy to his neck,
My grace shall make the burden light.

4 Jesus, we come at thy command,
With faith, and hope, and humble zeal,
Resign our spirits to thy hand,
To mould and guide us at thy will.

314 My Gracious Lord!

1 My gracious Lord! I own thy right
To every service I can pay;
And call it my supreme delight
To hear thy dictates and obey.

2 What is my being but for thee,
Its sure support, its noblest end,
Thine ever-smiling face to see,
And serve the cause of such a friend?

3 'Tis to my Saviour I would live,
To him who for my ransom died;
Nor could untainted Eden give
Such bliss as blossoms at his side.

4 His work my hoary age shall bless,
When youthful vigor is no more,
And my last hour of life confess
His dying love, his saving power.

315 When Thou, my Righteous.

Tune, MERIBAH. C. P. M.

1 **When** thou, my righteous Judge, shalt come
  To take thy ransomed people home,
    Shall I among them stand?
  Shall such a worthless worm as I,
  Who sometimes am afraid to die,
    Be found at thy right hand?

2 I love to meet among them now,
  Before thy feet with them to bow,
    Though vilest of them all;
  But, can I bear the piercing thought!
  What if my name should be left out
    When thou for them shalt call?

3 O Lord, prevent it by thy grace—
  Be thou my only hiding place,
    In this, the accepted day;
  Thy pardoning voice, oh, let me hear,
  To still my unbelieving fear,
    Nor let me fall, I pray.

4 Among thy saints let me be found,
  Whene'er the archangel's trump shall sound,
    To see thy smiling face;
  Then loudest of the throng I'll sing,
  While heaven's resounding mansions ring
    With shouts of sovereign grace.

316 I would not Live Alway.

Tune, FREDERICK. 11s.

1. I would not live al-way; I ask not to stay Where storm aft-er
2. I would not live al-way; no, welcome the tomb: Since Je-sus hath
3. Who, who would live alway a-way from his God, A-way from yon
4. Where saints of all a-ges in har-mo-ny meet, Their Saviour and

I would not Live Alway.—CONCLUDED.

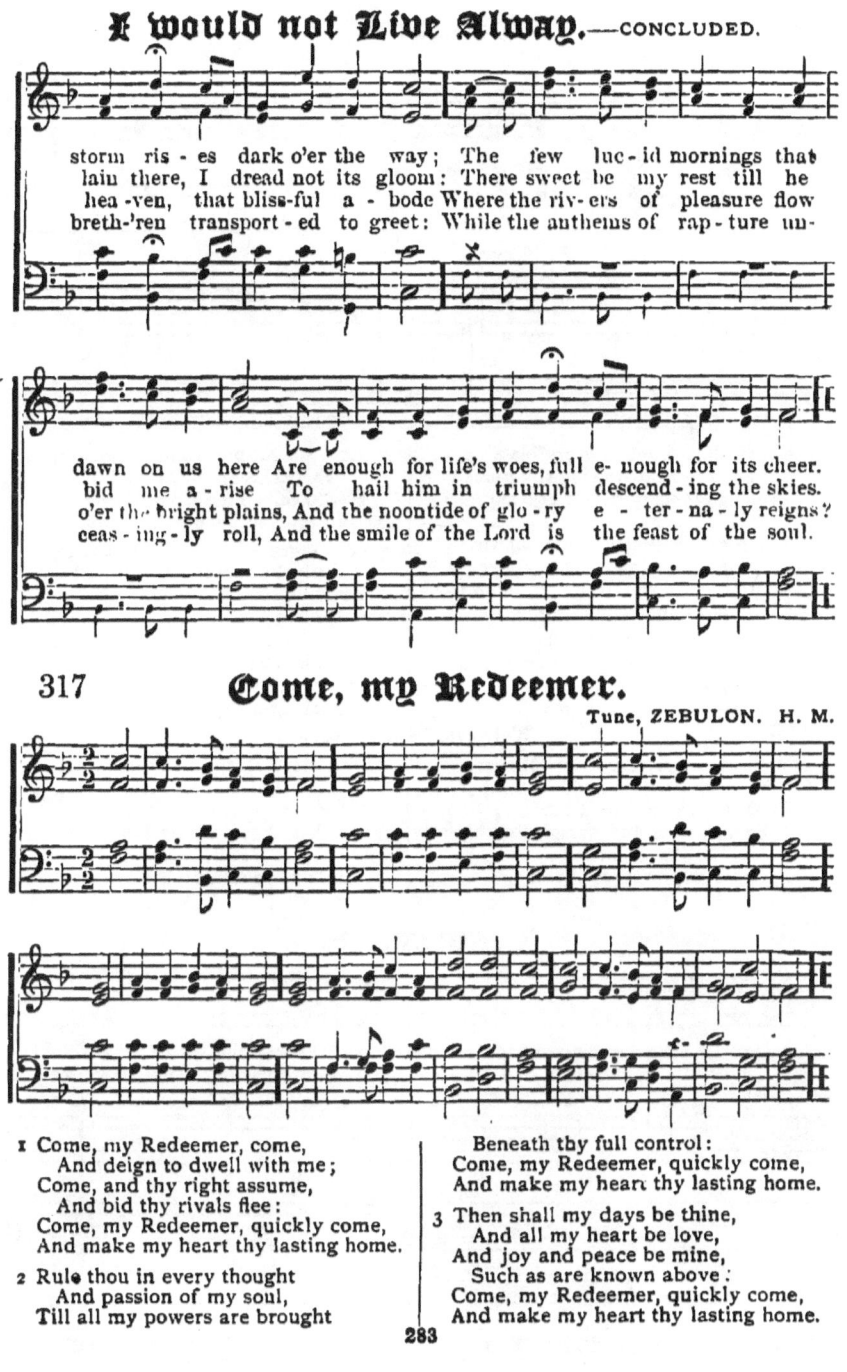

storm ris-es dark o'er the way; The few luc-id mornings that
lain there, I dread not its gloom: There sweet be my rest till he
hea-ven, that bliss-ful a-bode Where the riv-ers of pleasure flow
breth-'ren transport-ed to greet: While the anthems of rap-ture un-

dawn on us here Are enough for life's woes, full e-nough for its cheer.
bid me a-rise To hail him in triumph descend-ing the skies.
o'er the bright plains, And the noontide of glo-ry e-ter-na-ly reigns?
ceas-ing-ly roll, And the smile of the Lord is the feast of the soul.

317 Come, my Redeemer.
Tune, ZEBULON. H. M.

1 Come, my Redeemer, come,
   And deign to dwell with me;
Come, and thy right assume,
   And bid thy rivals flee:
Come, my Redeemer, quickly come,
And make my heart thy lasting home.

2 Rule thou in every thought
   And passion of my soul,
Till all my powers are brought
   Beneath thy full control:
Come, my Redeemer, quickly come,
And make my heart thy lasting home.

3 Then shall my days be thine,
   And all my heart be love,
And joy and peace be mine,
   Such as are known above:
Come, my Redeemer, quickly come,
And make my heart thy lasting home.

Nettleton. 8, 7.

1 Come, thou fount of every blessing,
  Tune my heart to sing thy grace;
Streams of mercy, never ceasing,
  Call for songs of loudest praise.
Teach me some melodious sonnet,
  Sung by flaming tongues above;
Praise the mount! I'm fixed upon it,
  Mount of God's unchanging love!

2 Here I'll raise my Ebenezer;
  Hither by thy help I'm come;
And I hope, by thy good pleasure,
  Safely to arrive at home.
Jesus sought me when a stranger,
  Wandering from the fold of God;
He, to rescue me from danger,
  Interposed his precious blood.

3 Oh, to grace how great a debtor
  Daily I'm constrained to be!
Let thy goodness, like a fetter,
  Bind my wand'ring heart to thee.
Prone to wander, Lord, I feel it,—
  Prone to leave the God I love,—
Here's my heart; oh, take and seal it,
  Seal it for thy courts above.

319 Welcome, Dear Redeemer.

1 Welcome, welcome, dear Redeemer,
  Welcome to this heart of mine;
Lord, I make a full surrender,
  Every power and thought be thine;
    Thine entirely,
  Through eternal ages thine.

2 Known to all to be thy mansion,
  Earth and hell will disappear;
Or in vain attempt possession,
  When they find the Lord is near;
    Shout, O Zion!
  Shout, ye saints! the Lord is here.

Vespers. 8, 7.

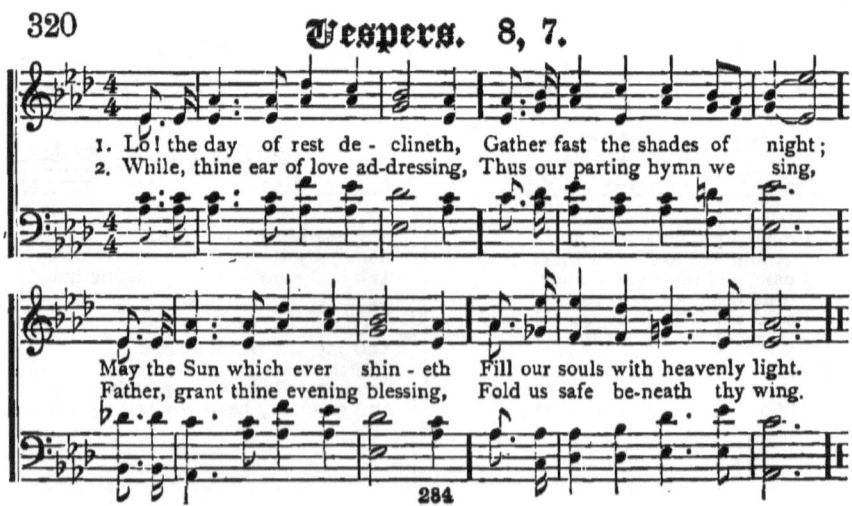

1. Lo! the day of rest declineth, Gather fast the shades of night;
   May the Sun which ever shineth Fill our souls with heavenly light.
2. While, thine ear of love addressing, Thus our parting hymn we sing,
   Father, grant thine evening blessing, Fold us safe beneath thy wing.

Sicily. 8, 7, 4.

321   Lord, Dismiss Us.

1 Lord, dismiss us with thy blessing,
   Fill our hearts with joy and peace;
Let us each, thy love possessing,
   Triumph in redeeming grace;
     Oh, refresh us,
Traveling through this wilderness.

2 Thanks we give, and adoration,
   For thy gospel's joyful sound;
May the fruits of thy salvation
   In our hearts and lives abound;
     May thy presence
With us evermore be found.

3 So, whene'er the signal's given,
   Us from earth to call away,
Borne on angel's wings to heaven,
   Glad to leave our cumbrous clay,
     May we, ready,
Rise and reign in endless day.

322   Saviour! Visit Thy Plantation.

1 Saviour! visit thy plantation;
   Grant us, Lord, a gracious rain;
All will come to desolation,
   Unless thou return again.

Cho.—Lord revive us, Lord revive us,
   All our help must come from thee.

2 Keep no longer at a distance;
   Shine upon us from on high,
Lest, for want of thy assistance,
   Every plant should droop and die.

3 Let our mutual love be fervent,
   Make us prevalent in prayers;
Let each one esteemed thy servant
   Shun the world's enticing snares.

4 Break the tempter's fatal power:
   Turn the stony heart to flesh,
And begin, from this good hour,
   To revive thy work afresh.

323   May the Grace of Christ.

1 May the grace of Christ our Saviour,
   And the Father's boundless love,
With the Holy Spirit's favor,
   Rest upon us from above!

2 Thus may we abide in union
   With each other and the Lord;
And posess, in sweet communion,
   Joys which earth cannot afford.

324   We have Come to Worship Jesus.
Tune Vespers.

1 We have come to worship Jesus,
   And in adoration bow
Low before our gracious Saviour,
   Who vouchsafes to hear us now.

2 Jesus, Friend of earth-bound sinners,
   Wash away our every stain;
May our hearts to thee be opened,
   So that thou may'st in them reign.

3 May we find thy great salvation,
   And our souls be filled with love;
May thy Kingdom here, Lord Jesus,
   Soon be like to heav'n above.

4 Prayers ascend, like incense rising,
   For new pardon, grace, and peace;
May thy Spirit's influence brighten
   All our lives,—our faith increase.

5 May the wisdom of thy gospel
   Comfort for all times afford;
And may we be waiting, ready
   At thy coming, dearest Lord
                 H S. Jones.

325. O Day of Rest and Gladness.

C. Wordsworth.
Tune, MENDEBRAS. 7, 6.

1. O day of rest and gladness, O day of joy and light,
O balm of care and sadness, Most beautiful, most bright;
On thee, the high and lowly, Through ages joined in tune,
Sing "Holy, holy, holy," To the great God Triune.

2. On thee, at the creation, The light first had its birth;
On thee, for our salvation, Christ rose from depths of earth;
On thee our Lord, victorious, The Spirit sent from heaven;
And thus on thee, most glorious, A triple light was given.

3 To-day on weary nations
The heavenly manna falls;
To holy convocations
The silver trumpet calls,
Where gospel light is glowing
With pure and radiant beams,
And living water flowing
With soul-refreshing streams.

4 New graces ever gaining,
From this our day of rest,
We reach the rest remaining
To spirits of the blest;
To Holy Ghost be praises,
To Father and to Son;
The Church her voice upraises
To thee, blest Three in One.

326. Now be the Gospel Banner.

1 Now be the gospel banner
In every land unfurled,
And be the shout, Hosanna!
Re-echoed through the world;
Till every isle and nation,
Till every tribe and tongue,
Receive the great salvation,
And join the happy throng.

2 What though the embattled legions
Of earth and hell combine,
His arm throughout their regions
Shall soon resplendent shine;
Ride on, O Lord, victorious.
Immanuel, Prince of Peace,
Thy triumph shall be glorious,
Thy empire still increase.

3 Yes, thou shalt reign forever,
O Jesus, King of kings;
Thy light, thy love, thy favor,
Each ransomed captive sings:
The isles for thee are waiting,
The deserts learn thy praise;
The hills and valleys greeting,
The song responsive raise.

327 The Morning Light.

SAMUEL F. SMITH.   Tune, WEBB. 7, 6.

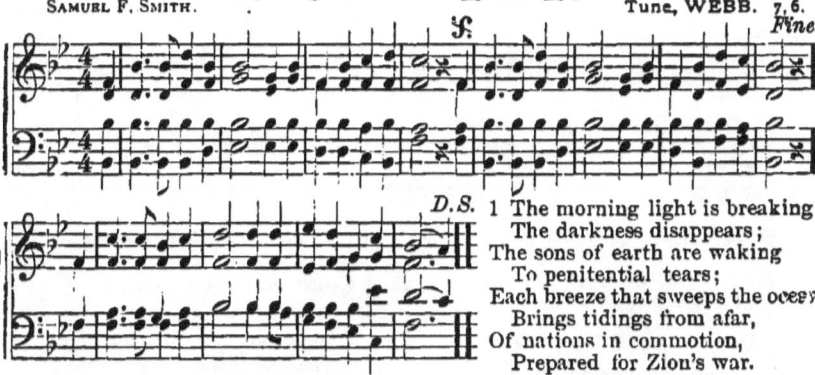

D.S. 1 The morning light is breaking:
The darkness disappears;
The sons of earth are waking
To penitential tears;
Each breeze that sweeps the ocean
Brings tidings from afar,
Of nations in commotion,
Prepared for Zion's war.

2 See heathen nations bending
Before the God we love,
And thousand hearts ascending
In gratitude above;
While sinners, now confessing,
The gospel call obey,
And seek the Saviour's blessing,
A nation in a day.

3 Blest river of salvation,
Pursue thine onward way;
Flow thou to every nation,
Nor in thy richness stay:
Stay not till all the lowly
Triumphant reach their home;
Stay not till all the holy
Proclaim, "The Lord is come!"

328   Geo. Duffield, Jr.   Stand up, stand up for Jesus.   Tune above.

1 STAND up, stand up for Jesus,
Ye soldiers of the cross;
Lift high his royal banner,
It must not suffer loss;
From victory unto victory
His army shall he lead
Till every foe is vanquished
And Christ is Lord indeed.

2 Stand up, stand up for Jesus,
The trumpet call obey;
Forth to the mighty conflict,
In this his glorious day:
"Ye that are men, now serve him,"
Against unnumbered foes:
Your courage rise with danger,
And strength to strength oppose.

3 Stand up, stand up for Jesus,
Stand in his strength alone;
The arm of flesh will fail you;
Ye dare not trust your own:
Put on the gospel armor,
Each piece put on with prayer;
Where duty calls, or danger,
Be never wanting there.

4 Stand up, stand up for Jesus,
The strife will not be long;
This day the noise of battle,
The next the victor's song:
To him that overcometh,
A crown of life shall be;
He with the King of glory
Shall reign eternally.

329   When, His Salvation Bringing.

1 When, his salvation bringing,
To Zion Jesus came,
The children all stood singing
Hosannas to his name.
Nor did their zeal offend him,
For as he rode along,
He let them still attend him,
And smiled to hear their song.

2 And since the Lord retaineth
His love for children still;
Though now as King he reigneth
On Zion's heavenly hill,
We'll flock around his banner,
Who sits upon the throne;
And cry aloud "Hosanna
To David's royal Son!"

3 For should we fail proclaiming
Our great Redeemer's praise:
The stones, our silence shaming
Might well hosannas raise.
But shall we only render
The tribute of our words?
No! while our hearts are tender,
They, too, shall be the Lord's.

Boylston. S. M.

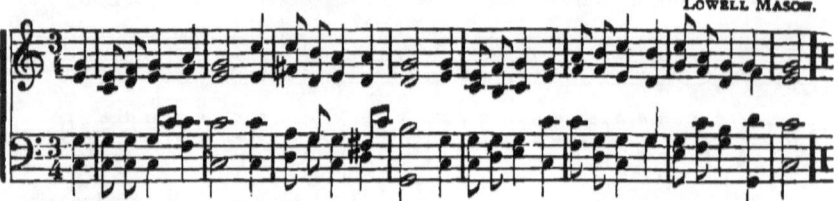

LOWELL MASON.

330 Lord, God, the Holy Ghost.

1 LORD, God, the Holy Ghost!
In this accepted hour,
As on the day of Pentecost,
Descend in all thy power.

2 We meet with one accord
In our appointed place,
And wait the promise of our Lord,—
The Spirit of all grace.

3 Like mighty, rushing wind
Upon the waves beneath,
Move with one impulse every mind;
One soul, one feeling breathe.

4 The young, the old, inspire
With wisdom from above; [fire,
And give us hearts and tongues of
To pray, and praise, and love.

5 Spirit of light! explore,
And chase our gloom away,
With luster shining more and more,
Unto the perfect day.

331 Come, Holy Spirit, come.

1 COME, Holy Spirit, come,
With energy divine,
And on this poor, benighted soul
With beams of mercy shine.

2 From the celestial hills
Light, life, and joy dispense;
And may I daily, hourly, feel
Thy quickening influence.

3 O melt this frozen heart,
This stubborn will subdue;
Each evil passion overcome,
And form me all anew.

4 The profit will be mine,
But thine shall be the praise;
Cheerful to thee will I devote
The remnant of my days.

332 The Day is Past and Gone.

1 The day is past and gone,
The evening shades appear!
Oh! may we all remember well
The night of death draws near.

2 We lay our garments by,
Upon our beds to rest;
So death shall soon disrobe us all
Of what we here possessed.

3 Lord, keep us safe this night,
Secure from all our fears;
May angels guard us while we sleep,
Till morning light appears.

333 Lord Teach Us how to Pray.

1 Lord, teach us how to pray,
And give us hearts to ask;
Or all we think, or do, or say,
Will be a tiresome task.

2 Thy Holy Spirit send,
Our bosoms to inspire;
Then shall our praise to thee ascend
With pure and warm desire.

3 Jesus, our great High Priest,
Present our prayers above;
And spread abroad o'er all thou seest
The mantle of thy love.

4 Teach us to find our bliss
In earnest, fervent prayer,
For where we pray our Saviour is,
And bliss is only there.

334 A Charge to Keep I Have.

1 A charge to keep I have,
A God to glorify;
A never-dying soul to save,
And fit it for the sky.

2 To serve the present age,
My calling to fulfill,—
Oh, may it all my powers engage
To do my Master's will.

3 Arm me with jealous care,
As in thy sight to live;
And oh, thy servant, Lord, prepare,
A strict account to give.

4 Help me to watch and pray,
And on thyself rely,
Assured, if I my trust betray,
I shall forever die.

335   I love Thy kingdom.

1 I LOVE thy kingdom, Lord,
   The house of thine abode,
The Church our blest Redeemer saved
   With his own precious blood.

2 I love thy Church, O God!
   Her walls before thee stand,
Dear as the apple of thine eye,
   And graven on thy hand.

3 For her my tears shall fall,
   For her my prayers ascend :
To her my cares and toils be given,
   Till toils and cares shall end.

4 Beyond my highest joy
   I prize her heavenly ways,
Her sweet communion, solemn vows,
   Her hymns of love and praise.

5 Sure as thy truth shall last,
   To Zion shall be given
The brightest glories earth can yield,
   And brighter bliss of heaven.

336   Grace!

1 GRACE! 'tis a charming sound,
   Harmonious to the ear;
Heaven with the echo shall resound,
   And all the earth shall hear.

2 Grace first contrived a way
   To save rebellious man ;
And all the steps that grace display,
   Which drew the wondrous plan.

3 Grace taught my roving feet
   To tread the heavenly road;
And new supplies each hour I meet,
   While pressing on to God.

4 Grace all the work shall crown
   Through everlasting days;
It lays in heaven the topmost stone,
   And well deserves our praise.

Living Hymns—T

337   Stand up, and bless.

1 STAND up, and bless the Lord,
   Ye people of his choice ;
Stand up, and bless the Lord your God,
   With heart, and soul, and voice.

2 Though high above all praise,
   Above all blessing high,
Who would not fear his holy name,
   And laud, and magnify?

3 O for the living flame
   From his own altar brought,
To touch our lips, our souls inspire,
   And wing to heaven our thought!

4 God is our strength and song,
   And his salvation ours;
Then be his love in Christ proclaimed
   With all our ransomed powers.

5 Stand up, and bless the Lord ;
   The Lord your God adore ;
Stand up, and bless his glorious name,
   Henceforth, forevermore.

338   Purity of heart.

1 BLEST are the pure in heart,
   For they shall see our God ;
The secret of the Lord is theirs ;
   Their soul is his abode.

2 Still to the lowly soul
   He doth himself impart,
And for his temple and his throne
   Selects the pure in heart.

3 Lord, we thy presence seek,
   May ours this blessing be ;
O give the pure and lowly heart,—
   A temple meet for thee.

339   Doxology. S. M.

To God, the Father, Son,
   And Spirit, One in Three,
Be glory, as it was, is now,
   And shall forever be.

340 Safely through Another Week.

JOHN NEWTON.   Arr. by LOWELL MASON.

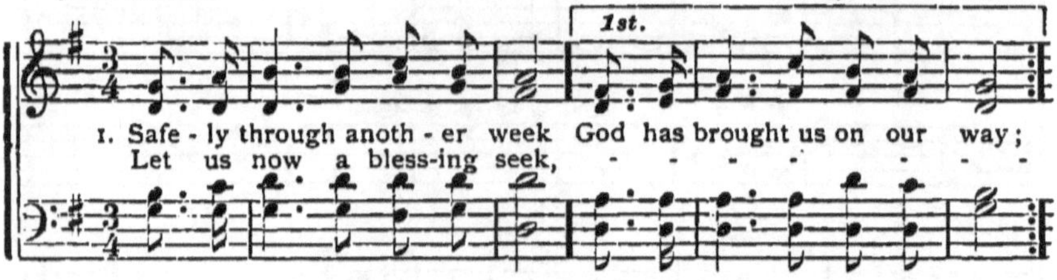

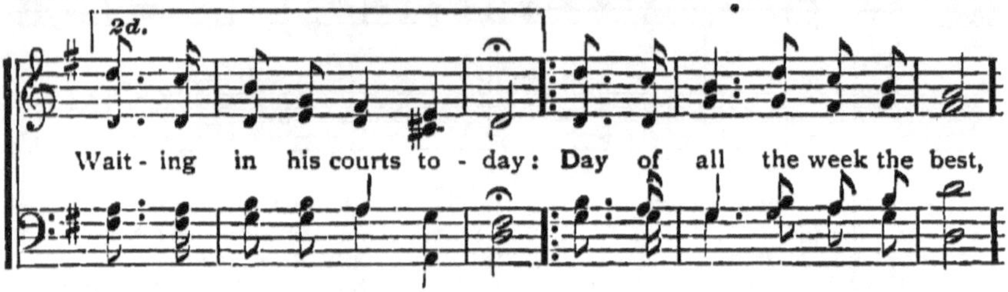

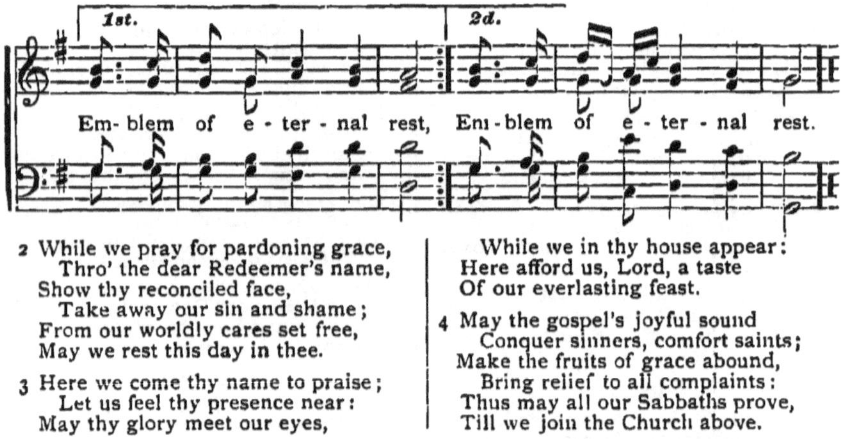

1. Safe - ly through anoth - er week God has brought us on our way;
Let us now a bless-ing seek,
Wait - ing in his courts to - day: Day of all the week the best,
Em - blem of e - ter - nal rest, Em - blem of e - ter - nal rest.

2 While we pray for pardoning grace,
   Thro' the dear Redeemer's name,
Show thy reconciled face,
   Take away our sin and shame;
From our worldly cares set free,
May we rest this day in thee.

3 Here we come thy name to praise;
   Let us feel thy presence near:
May thy glory meet our eyes,

While we in thy house appear:
Here afford us, Lord, a taste
Of our everlasting feast.

4 May the gospel's joyful sound
   Conquer sinners, comfort saints;
Make the fruits of grace abound,
   Bring relief to all complaints:
Thus may all our Sabbaths prove,
Till we join the Church above.

341 Hasten, Lord, the Glorious Time.

HARRIET AUBER.   Tune, ELTHAM. 7, 6 l.

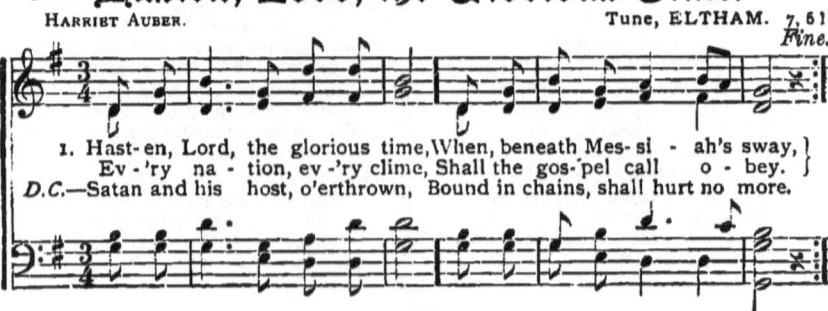

1. Hast-en, Lord, the glorious time, When, beneath Mes-si - ah's sway,
Ev-'ry na - tion, ev-'ry clime, Shall the gos-pel call o - bey.
D.C.—Satan and his host, o'erthrown, Bound in chains, shall hurt no more.

Hasten, Lord, etc.—CONCLUDED.

Mightiest kings his power shall own, Heathen tribes his name adore;

2 Then shall wars and tumults cease;
Then be banished grief and pain;
Righteousness, and joy, and peace,
Undisturbed, shall ever reign.

Bless we, then, our gracious Lord;
Ever praise his glorious name;
All his mighty acts record,
All his wondrous love proclaim.

Amsterdam. 7s & 6s D.

342 Rise, My Soul.

1 Rise, my soul, and stretch thy wings,
  Thy better portion trace;
Rise from transitory things,
  Toward's heaven, thy native place.
Sun and moon and stars decay;
  Time shall soon this earth remove;
Rise, my soul, and haste away,
  To seats prepared above.

2 Rivers to the ocean run,
  Nor stay in all their course;
Fire ascending seeks the sun;
  Both speed them to their source;
So a soul that's born of God
  Pants to view his glorious face,
Upward tends to his abode,
  To rest in his embrace.

3 Cease, ye pilgrims, cease to mourn;
  Press onward to the prize;
Soon our Saviour will return,
  Triumphant in the skies.

Yet a season, and you know
  Happy entrance will be given;
All our sorrows left below,
  And earth exchanged for heaven.

343 Time is Winging us Away.

1 Time is winging us away
  To our eternal home;
Life is but a winter's day,
  A journey to the tomb:
Youth and vigor soon will flee,
  Blooming beauty lose its charms;
All that's mortal soon will be
  Enclosed in death's cold arms.

2 Time is winging us away
  To our eternal home;
Life is but a winter's day,
  A journey to the tomb:
But the Christian shall enjoy
  Health and beauty soon above;
Far beyond the world's alloy,
  Secure in Jesus' love.

344. Jesus, the Name.

C. Wesley. Tune, CORONATION. C. M.

1. Jesus! the name high over all, In hell, or earth, or sky;
Angels and men before it fall, And devils fear and fly.

2. Jesus! the name to sinners dear, The name to sinners given;
It scatters all their guilty fear; It turns their hell to heaven.

3 Jesus the prisoner's fetters breaks,
  And bruises Satan's head;
Power into strengthless souls he speaks,
  And life into the dead.

4 O that the world might taste and see
  The riches of his grace!
The arms of love that compass me
  Would all mankind embrace.

5 His only righteousness I show
  His saving truth proclaim:
'Tis all my business here below,
  To cry, "Behold the Lamb!"

6 Happy, if with my latest breath
  I may but gasp his name;
Preach him to all, and cry in death,
  "Behold, behold the Lamb!"

345. Crown Him Lord of All.
C. M.

1 All hail the power of Jesus' name!
  Let angels prostrate fall;
Bring forth the royal diadem,
  And crown him Lord of all.

2 Crown him, ye morning stars of light,
  Who fixed this earthly ball;
Now hail the strength of Israel's might,
  And crown him Lord of all.

3 Ye chosen seed of Israel's race,
  Ye ransomed from the fall,
Hail him who saves you by his grace,
  And crown him Lord of all.

4 Sinners, whose love can ne'er forget
  The wormwood and the gall,
Go, spread your trophies at his feet.
  And crown him Lord of all.

5 Let every kindred, every tribe,
  On this terrestrial ball,
To him all majesty ascribe,
  And crown him Lord of all.

6 O that with yonder sacred throng
  We at his feet may fall!
We'll join the everlasting song,
  And crown him Lord of all.

Antioch. C. M.

346   O for a thousand tongues.

1 O FOR a thousand tongues, to sing
My great Redeemer's praise;
The glories of my God and King,
The triumphs of his grace!

2 My gracious Master and my God,
Assist me to proclaim,
To spread through all the earth abroad,
The honors of thy name.

3 Jesus! the name that charms our fears,
That bids our sorrows cease;
'Tis music in the sinner's ears,
'Tis life, and health, and peace.

4 He breaks the power of canceled sin,
He sets the prisoner free;
His blood can make the foulest clean;
His blood availed for me.

5 He speaks, and, listening to his voice,
New life the dead receive;
The mournful, broken hearts rejoice;
The humble poor believe.

6 Hear him, ye deaf; his praise, ye dumb,
Your loosened tongues employ;
Ye blind, behold your Saviour come;
And leap, ye lame, for joy.

347   Joy to the world!

1 Joy to the world! the Lord is come;
Let earth receive her King;
Let every heart prepare him room,
And heaven and nature sing.

2 Joy to the world! the Saviour reigns;
Let men their songs employ;
While fields and floods, rocks, hills and
Repeat the sounding joy.   [plains,

3 No more let sin and sorrow grow,
Nor thorns infest the ground;
He comes to make his blessings flow
Far as the curse is found.

4 He rules the world with truth and grace,
And makes the nations prove
The glories of his righteousness,
And wonders of his love.

348   The Lord's Prayer.

Reverently.

1. Our Father which art in heaven, hallowed | be thy | name, || Thy kingdom come
thy will be done in | earth, as-it | is in | heaven.

2. Give us this day our | daily | bread, || And forgive us our trespasses, as we for-
give | them that | trespass a- | gainst us.

3. And lead us not into temptation, but deliver | us from | evil; || For thine is the
kingdom, and the power and the | glory for- | ever and | ever. || A- | men.

349. Jerusalem the Golden.

BERNARD OF CLUNY. Tr. by J. M. NEALE.
Tune, EWING. 7, 6.

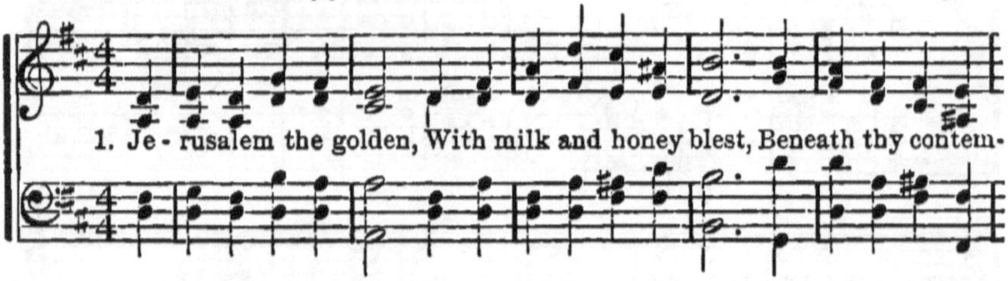

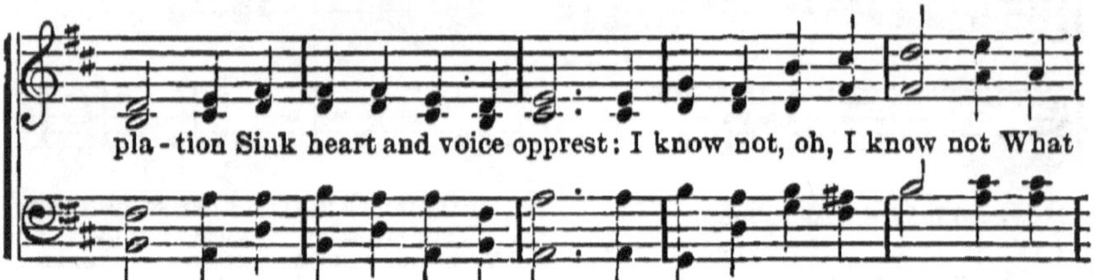

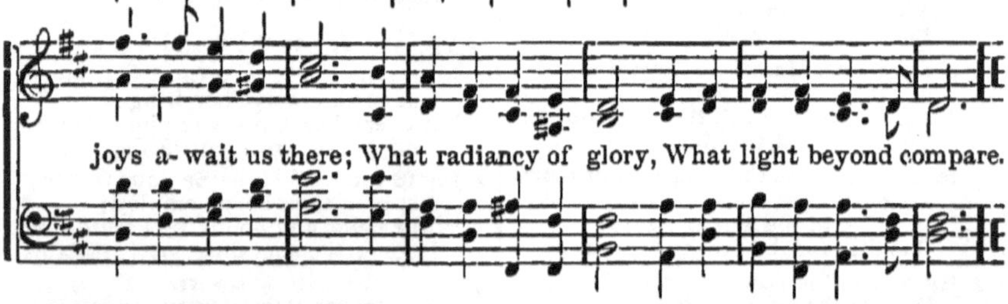

1. Je-rusalem the golden, With milk and honey blest, Beneath thy contem-pla-tion Sink heart and voice opprest; I know not, oh, I know not What joys a-wait us there; What radiancy of glory, What light beyond compare.

2 They stand, those halls of Zion,
    All jubilant with song,
  And bright with many an angel,
    And all the martyr throng:
  The Prince is ever in them,
    The daylight is serene;
  The pastures of the blessed
    Are decked in glorious sheen.

3 There is the throne of David;
    And there, from care released,
  The song of them that triumph,
    The shout of them that feast;
  And they who, with their Leader,
    Have conquered in the fight,
  Forever and forever
    Are clad in robes of white.

4 O sweet and blessed country,
    The home of God's elect!
  O sweet and blessed country
    That eager hearts expect!
  Jesus, in mercy bring us
    To that dear land of rest;
  Who art, with God the Father,
    And Spirit, ever blest.

350. Love Divine.

CHARLES WESLEY.
Tune, LOVE DIVINE. 8, 7, d.

1. Love di-vine, all love ex-cel-ling, Joy of heaven, to earth come down!

Love Divine.—CONCLUDED.

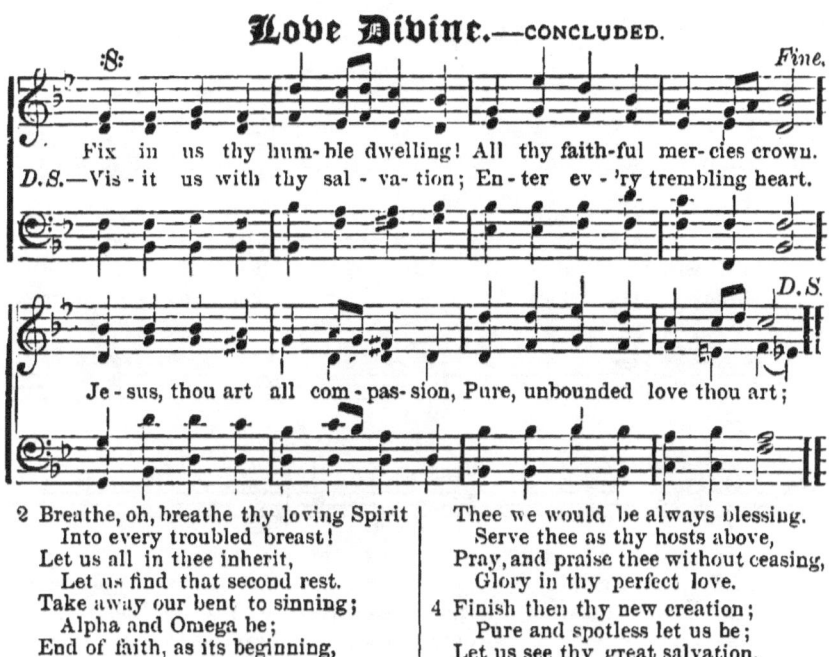

Fix in us thy hum-ble dwelling! All thy faith-ful mer-cies crown.
D.S.—Vis-it us with thy sal-va-tion; En-ter ev-'ry trembling heart.

Je-sus, thou art all com-pas-sion, Pure, unbounded love thou art;

2 Breathe, oh, breathe thy loving Spirit
  Into every troubled breast!
Let us all in thee inherit,
  Let us find that second rest.
Take away our bent to sinning;
  Alpha and Omega be;
End of faith, as its beginning,
  Set our hearts at liberty.

3 Come, almighty to deliver,
  Let us all thy life receive;
Suddenly return, and never,
  Never more thy temples leave;

Thee we would be always blessing.
  Serve thee as thy hosts above,
Pray, and praise thee without ceasing,
  Glory in thy perfect love.

4 Finish then thy new creation;
  Pure and spotless let us be;
Let us see thy great salvation,
  Perfectly restored in thee:
Changed from glory into glory,
  Till in heaven we take our place,
Till we cast our crowns before thee,
  Lost in wonder, love, and praise.

---

351 Num. vi. 24-26. **The Lord Bless Thee.** W. J. K.

A blessing for use in closing Sabbath-school, or other service, in the absence of a minister.

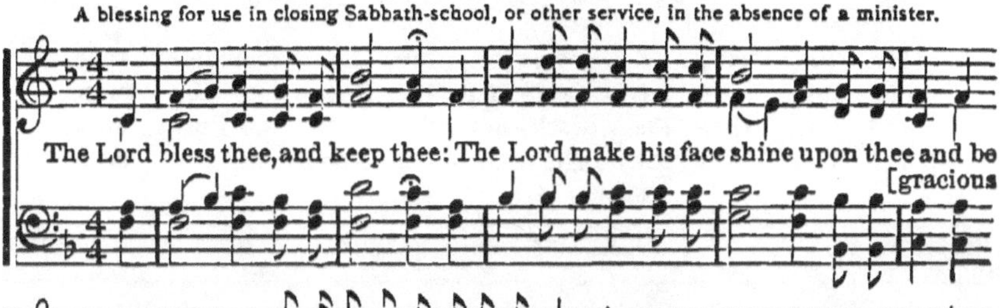

The Lord bless thee, and keep thee: The Lord make his face shine upon thee and be [gracious

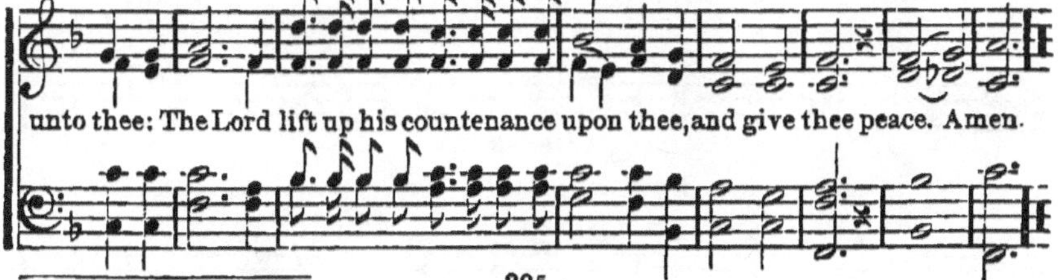

unto thee: The Lord lift up his countenance upon thee, and give thee peace. Amen.

Copyright, 1891, by John J. Hood.

Stockwell. 8s, 7s.

353 Yes, for Me, for Me He Careth.

1 Yes, for me, for me he careth
With a brother's tender care;
Yes, with me, with me he shareth
Every burden, every fear.

2 Yes, for me he standeth pleading
At the mercy-seat above,
Ever for me interceeding,
Constant in untiring love.

3 Yes, in me abroad he shedeth
Joys unearthly, love and light;
And to cover me he spreadeth
His paternal wing of might.

4 Yes, in me, in me he dwelleth,
I in him, and he in me;
And my empty soul he filleth
Here and through eternity.

5 Thus I wait for his returning,
Singing all the way to heaven;
Such the joyful song of morning,
Such the tranquil song of even.

354 Tarry With Me, O, My Saviour.

1 Tarry with me, O my Saviour!
For the day is passing by;
See! the shades of evening gather,
And the night is drawing nigh.

2 Deeper, deeper grow the shadows,
Paler now the glowing west,
Swift the night of death advances;
Shall it be the night of rest?

3 Lonely seems the vale of shadow;
Sinks my heart with troubled fear;
Give me faith for clearer vision,
Speak thou, Lord! in words of cheer.

4 Let me hear thy voice behind me,
Calming all these wild alarms;
Let me, underneath my weakness,
Feel the everlasting arms.

5 Feeble, trembling, fainting, dying,
Lord! I cast myself on thee;
Tarry with me through the darkness;
While I sleep still watch by me.

6 Tarry with me, O my Saviour!
Lay my head upon thy breast
Till the morning; then awake me—
Morning of eternal rest.

355 My Hope is Built.

1 My hope is built on nothing less,
Than Jesus' blood and righteousness;
I dare not trust the sweetest frame,
But wholly lean on Jesus' name.

CHO.—On Christ the solid Rock I stand:
All other ground is sinking sand,
All other ground is sinking sand.

2 When darkness veils his lovely face,
I rest on his unchanging grace;
In every high and stormy gale,
My anchor holds within the vail.

3 His oath, his covenant, his blood,
Support me in the whelming flood;
When all around my soul gives way,
He then is all my hope and stay.

4 When he shall come with trumpet sound,
O, may I then in him be found;
Drest in his righteousness alone,
Faultless to stand before the throne!

Goshen.

356. How Sweet is the Sabbath.

1 How sweet is the Sabbath, the morning of rest, [best;
The day of the week which I surely love
The morning my Saviour arose from the tomb,
And took from the grave all its terror and gloom.

2 Oh, let me be thoughtful and prayerful to-day,
And not spend a minute in trifling or play;
Remembering these seasons were graciously given
To teach me to seek and prepare me for heaven.

3 In the house of my God, in his presence and fear, [cere;
When I worship to-day, may it all be sin-
In the school when I learn, may I do it with care,
And be grateful to those who watch over me there.

4 Instruct me, my Saviour, a child though I be,
I am not too young to be noticed by thee;
Renew all my heart, keep me firm in thy ways,
I would love thee, and serve thee, and give thee the praise.

357. Begone, Unbelief.

1 Begone, unbelief, my Saviour is near,
And for my relief he will surely appear;
By prayer let me wrestle, and he will perform;
With Christ in the vessel, I smile at the storm.

2 Though dark be my way, thou, Lord! art my guide;
'Tis mine to obey, 'tis thine to provide;
Though cisterns be broken and creatures all fail,
The word thou hast spoken shall surely prevail.

3 Since all that I meet shall work for my good,
The bitter is sweet, the medicine food:
Though painful at present, 'twill cease before long,
And then oh, how pleasant the conqueror's song!

358. Delay Not.

1 Delay not, delay not, O sinner, draw near,
The waters of life are now flowing for thee;
No price is demanded, the Saviour is here;
Redemption is purchased, salvation is free.

2 Delay not, delay not; why longer abuse
The love and compassion of Jesus thy God? [fuse
A fountain is opened; how canst thou re-
To wash and be cleansed in his pardoning blood?

3 Delay not, delay not; the Spirit of grace
Long grieved and resisted, may take his sad flight,
And leave thee in darkness to finish thy race,
To sink in the vale of eternity's night.

5 "E'en down to old age all my people shall prove [love;
My sovereign, eternal, unchangeable
And when hoary hairs shall their temples adorn, [be borne.
Like lambs they shall still in my bosom

6 "The soul that on Jesus hath leaned for repose,
I will not, I will not desert to his foes;
That soul, though all hell should endeavor to shake,
I'll **never**, no never, no never forsake!"

360. Come, my Soul.

JOHN NEWTON. Tune, HENDON. 7.

1. Come, my soul, thy suit prepare,
Jesus loves to answer prayer;
He himself invites thee near,
Bids thee ask him, waits to hear.

2. Lord, I come to thee for rest;
Take possession of my breast;
There thy blood-bought right maintain,
And without a rival reign.

3 While I am a pilgrim here.
Let thy love my spirit cheer;
As my guide, my guard, my friend,
Lead me to my journey's end.

5 Show me what I have to do;
Every hour my strength renew;
Let me live a life of faith,
Let me die thy people's death.

361 Children of the Heavenly King.

1 Children of the heavenly King,
As we journey we will sing,—
Sing our Saviour's worthy praise,
Glorious in his works and ways.

2 We are traveling home to God,
In the way the fathers trod;
They are happy now, and we
Soon their happiness shall see.

3 O ye mourning souls, be glad,
Christ our advocate is made;
Us to save our flesh assumes,
Brother to our souls becomes.

4 Shout, ye little flock, and blest,
Soon we'll enter into rest;
There our seat is now prepared,
There our Kingdom and reward.

5 Lord, submissive make us go,
Gladly leaving all below;
Only thou our leader be,
And we still will follow thee.

362 Hark, My Soul.

1 Hark, my soul, it is the Lord;
'Tis thy Saviour, hear his word;
Jesus speaks, and speaks to thee,
"Say, poor sinner, lovest thou me?"

2 "I delivered thee when bound,
And, when wounded, healed thy wound;
Sought thee wandering, set thee right,
Turned thy darkness into light.

3 Can a woman's tender care
Cease toward the child she bare?
Yes, she may forgetful be,
Yet will I remember thee.

4 Mine is an unchanging love,
Higher than the heights above,
Deeper than the depths beneath,
Free and faithful, strong as death.

5 Thou shalt see my glory soon,
When the work of grace is done;
Partner of my throne shalt be;
Say, poor sinner, lovest thou me?"

6 Lord, it is my chief complaint,
That my love is weak and faint;
Yet I love thee and adore,
Oh, for grace to love thee more!

363. Yield not to Temptation.

H. R. PALMER. By per.

1. Yield not to tempta-tion, For yielding is sin, Each victr'y will help you some oth-er to win; Fight manfully onward, Dark passions sub-due,
2. Shun e-vil companions, Bad language disdain, God's name hold in rev'rence, nor take it in vain; Be thoughtful and earnest, Kind-hearted and true,
3. To him that o'ercometh God giveth a crown, Thro' faith we will conquer, though often cast down; He who is our Saviour, Our strength will renew,

CHORUS.
Look ev-er to Je-sus, He'll car-ry you through. Ask the Saviour to help you, Comfort, strengthen, and keep you, He is willing to aid you, He will carry you through.

364 Lo! the Stone is Rolled Away.

1 Lo! the stone is rolled away,
Death yields up his mighty prey;
Jesus, rising from the tomb,
Scatters all its fearful gloom.

2 Praise him in the noblest songs,
From ten thousand thousand tongues
Every note with rapture swell,
And the Saviour's triumph tell.

3 Let Immanuel be adored—
Ransom, Mediator, Lord!
To creation's utmost bound,
Let the eternal praise resound.

365 Wait, my Soul, Upon the Lord.

1 Wait, my soul, upon the Lord,
To his gracious promise flee,
Laying hold upon this word,
"As thy days, thy strength shall be."

2 If the sorrows of thy case
Seem peculiar still to thee,
God has promised needful grace,—
"As thy days, thy strength shall be."

3 Days of trial, days of grief,
In succession thou mayst see;
This is still my sweet relief,—
"As thy days, thy strength shall be."

Ariel. C. P. M. Arr. by Lowell Mason.

366   O Love Divine.

1 O LOVE divine, how sweet thou art!
  When shall I find my willing heart
    All taken up by thee?
  I thirst, I faint, I die to prove
  The greatness of redeeming love,
    The love of Christ to me.

2 Stronger his love than death or hell!
  Its riches are unsearchable;
    The first-born sons of light
  Desire in vain its depths to see;
  They cannot reach the mystery,
    The length, the breadth, the height.

3 God only knows the love of God;
  O that it now were shed abroad
    In this poor stony heart!
  For love I sigh, for love I pine;
  This only portion, Lord, be mine;
    Be mine this better part.

4 O that I could forever sit
  With Mary at the Master's feet!
    Be this my happy choice;
  My only care, delight, and bliss,
  My joy, my heaven on earth, be this,
    To hear the Bridegroom's voice.

5 O that I could, with favored John,
  Recline my weary head upon
    The dear Redeemer's breast!
  From care, and sin, and sorrow free,
  Give me, O Lord, to find in thee
    My everlasting rest.

367   O could I Speak.

1 O COULD I speak the matchless worth,
  O could I sound the glories forth,
    Which in my Saviour shine,
  I'd soar and touch the heavenly strings,
  And vie with Gabriel while he sings
    In notes almost divine.

2 I'd sing the precious blood he spilt,
  My ransom from the dreadful guilt
    Of sin, and wrath divine;
  I'd sing his glorious righteousness,
  In which all-perfect, heavenly dress
    My soul shall ever shine.

3 I'd sing the characters he bears,
  And all the forms of love he wears,
    Exalted on his throne;
  In loftiest songs of sweetest praise,
  I would to everlasting days
    Make all his glories known.

4 Well, the delightful day will come
  When my dear Lord will bring me home,
    And I shall see his face;
  Then with my Saviour, Brother, Friend,
  A blest eternity I'll spend,
    Triumphant in his grace.

Avon. C. M.

C. Wesley.

368 *I will Remember Thee.*

1 According to thy gracious word,
　In meek humility,
This will I do, my dying Lord,
　I will remember thee.

2 Thy body, broken for my sake,
　My bread from heaven shall be;
Thy testamental cup I take,
　And thus remember thee.

3 Gethsemane can I forget?
　Or there thy conflict see,
Thine agony and bloody sweat,
　And not remember thee?

4 When to the cross I turn mine eyes,
　And rest on Calvary,
O Lamb of God, my sacrifice,
　I must remember thee.—

5 Remember thee and all thy pains,
　And all thy love to me;
Yea, while a breath, a pulse remains,
　Will I remember thee.

369 *Jesus, I Love.*

1 Jesus, I love thy charming name,
　'Tis music to mine ear;
Fain would I sound it out so loud
　That earth and heaven should hear.

2 Yes, thou art precious to my soul,
　My joy, my hope, my trust;
Jewels, to thee, are gaudy toys,
　And gold is sordid dust.

3 All my capacious powers can wish
　In thee most richly meet;
Nor to mine eyes is light so dear,
　Nor friendship half so sweet.

4 Thy grace still dwells upon my heart,
　And sheds its fragrance there,
The noblest balm of all its wounds,
　The cordial of its care.

370 *Alas! and Did My Saviour Bleed.*

1 Alas! and did my Saviour bleed,
　And did my Sovereign die?
Would he devote that sacred head
　For such a worm as I?

2 Was it for crimes that I had done,
　He groaned upon the tree?
Amazing pity! grace unknown!
　And love beyond degree!

3 Well might the sun in darkness hide,
　And shut his glories in,
When God, the mighty Maker, died
　For man, the creature's, sin.

4 Thus might I hide my blushing face,
　While his dear cross appears,
Dissolve my heart in thankfulness,
　And melt my eyes to tears.

5 But drops of grief can ne'er repay
　The debt of love I owe;
Here, Lord, I give myself away,
　'Tis all that I can do.

371 *Come, Humble Sinner.*

1 Come, humble sinner, in whose breast
　A thousand thoughts revolve,—
Come with your guilt and fear oppressed
　And make this last resolve:

2 "I'll go to Jesus, though my sin
　High as a mountain rose;
I know his courts, I'll enter in,
　Whatever may oppose.

3 Perhaps he will admit my plea,
　Perhaps will hear my prayer;
But if I perish, I will pray,
　And perish only there.

4 I can but perish if I go,
　I am resolved to try;
For if I stay away, I know
　I must forever die."

372   Come, Said Jesus.

1 Come, said Jesus' sacred voice,
Come, and make my path your choice,
I will guide you to your home;
Weary pilgrim, hither come.

2 Thou who, houseless, sole, forlorn,
Long hast borne the proud world's scorn,
Long hast roamed the barren waste,
Weary pilgrim, hither haste.

3 Ye who, tossed on beds of pain,
Seek for ease, but seek in vain;
Ye, by fiercer anguish torn,
In remorse for guilt who mourn;

4 Hither come, for here is found
Balm that flows for every wound,
Peace that ever shall endure,
Rest eternal, sacred, sure.

373   As the Twilight Shadows.

1 As the twilight shadows fall,
  Let us, in the closing day,
Mark the solemn hour when all
  Earthly things shall fade away.

2 In the grave to which we haste,
  No repentance can be found;
Shall we then our moments waste
  While we stand on trial-ground?

3 Ere the coming of that night,
  (When its coming who can say?)
Let us do with all our might,
  Strive and labor, watch and pray.

4 Lord, do thou thy grace impart;
  Penitence and faith bestow!
Come and sanctify each heart,
  Let us thy salvation know.

5 That when waning years have fled,
  And these scenes have passed away,
Rising with the summoned dead,
  We may wake to endless day.

374   Gentle Jesus.

1 Gentle Jesus, meek and mild,
Look upon a little child;
Pity my simplicity,
Suffer me to come to thee.

2 Fain I would to thee be brought;
Gracious God, forbid it not;
Give me, O my God, a place
In the kingdom of thy grace!

3 Put thy hands upon my head,
Let me in thine arms be stayed;
Let me lean upon thy breast,
Lull me there, O Lord, to rest.

4 Fain I would be as thou art;
Give me thy obedient heart;
Thou art pitiful and kind;
Let me have thy loving mind.

375   Depth of Mercy!

1 Depth of mercy! can there be
Mercy still reserved for me?
Can my God his wrath forbear,—
Me, the chief of sinners, spare?

2 I have long withstood his grace;
Long provoked him to his face;
Would not hearken to his calls;
Grieved him by a thousand falls.

3 Now incline me to repent;
Let me now my sins lament;
Now my foul revolt deplore,
Weep, believe, and sin no more.

4 Kindled his relentings are;
Me he now delights to spare;
Cries, 'how can I give thee up?'
Lets the lifted thunder drop.

5 There for me the Saviour stands,
Shows his wounds, and spreads his [hands
God is love! I know, I feel;
Jesus weeps, and loves me still.

Pleyel's Hymn. 7s.

IGNACE PLEYEL.

376 Gracious Spirit, love divine.

1 GRACIOUS Spirit, love divine,
 Let thy light within me shine!
 All my guilty fears remove;
 Fill me with thy heavenly love.

2 Speak thy pardoning grace to me;
 Set the burdened sinner free;
 Lead me to the Lamb of God;
 Wash me in his precious blood.

3 Life and peace to me impart;
 Seal salvation on my heart;
 Breathe thyself into my breast,
 Earnest of immortal rest.

4 Let me never from thee stray;
 Keep me in the narrow way;
 Fill my soul with joy divine;
 Keep me, Lord, forever thine.

377 Hasten, Sinner, to be Wise.

1 Hasten, sinner, to be wise;
 Stay not for the morrow's sun:
 Wisdom if you still despise,
 Harder is it to be won.

2 Hasten mercy to implore,
 Stay not for the morrow's sun,
 Lest thy season should be o'er,
 Ere this evening's course be run.

3 Hasten, sinner, to return,
 Stay not for the morrow's sun,
 Lest thy lamp should cease to burn
 Ere salvation's work is done.

4 Hasten, sinner, to be blest,
 Stay not for the morrow's sun,
 Lest perdition thee arrest,
 Ere the morrow is begun.

378 Holy Ghost, with light divine.

1 HOLY GHOST, with light divine,
 Shine upon this heart of mine;
 Chase the shades of night away,
 Turn my darkness into day.

2 Holy Ghost, with power divine,
 Cleanse this guilty heart of mine;
 Long hath sin, without control,
 Held dominion o'er my soul.

3 Holy Ghost, with joy divine,
 Cheer this saddened heart of mine;
 Bid my many woes depart,
 Heal my wounded, bleeding heart.

4 Holy Spirit, all divine,
 Dwell within this heart of mine;
 Cast down every idol-throne,
 Reign supreme—and reign alone.

379 Ere Another Sabbath's Close.

1 Ere another Sabbath's close,
 Ere again we seek repose,
 Lord! our song ascends to thee;
 At thy feet we bow the knee.

2 For the mercies of the day,
 For this rest upon our way,
 Thanks to thee alone be given,
 Lord of earth, and King of heaven!

3 Whilst this thorny path we tread,
 May thy love our footsteps lead,
 When our journey here is past,
 May we rest with thee at last.

4 Let these earthly Sabbaths prove
 Foretastes of our joys above;
 While their steps thy pilgrims bend
 To the rest which knows no end.

THOMAS HASTINGS. **Zion.** 8, 7, 4.

380 Guide Me, O Thou Great.

1 Guide me, O thou great Jehovah,
  Pilgrim through this barren land:
I am weak, but thou art mighty;
  Hold me with thy powerful hand:
    Bread of heaven,
  Feed me till I want no more.

2 Open now the crystal fountain,
  Whence the healing streams do flow;
Let the fiery, cloudy pillar,
  Lead me all my journey through:
    Strong Deliverer,
  Be thou still my strength and shield.

3 When I tread the verge of Jordan,
  Bid my anxious fears subside;
Bear me through the swelling current;
  Land me safe on Canaan's side·
    Songs of praises
  I will ever sing to thee.

381 Where We oft Met in Gladness.

1 Where we oft have met in gladness,
    On the holy Sabbath day,
  Now we gather in our sadness,
    Mourning over one away:
      Tears are falling
    On this holy Sabbath day.

2 One we loved has left our number,—
    In the narrow dwelling laid;
  There to rest in dreamless slumber,
    Till the trump that wakes the dead:
      When the angel
    From their slumbers wakes the dead.

3 But while we in sadness gather,
    Mourning thus for one away,
  Lo, the angels say, "Another
    Joins our holy song to-day!"
      Weep no longer;
    Join with them the sacred lay.

4 Let our grief, then, turn to gladness,
    As we praise the saving love,
  Which o'er every shade of sadness
    Sheds the light of joys above:
      Grief dispelling
    By the light of joys above.

382 On the Mountain's Top.

1 On the mountain's top appearing,
    Lo! the sacred herald stands,
  Welcome news to Zion bearing—
    Zion long in hostile lands;
      Mourning captive!
    God himself will loose thy bands.

2 Has thy night been long and mournful,
    All thy friends unfaithful proved?
  Have thy foes been proud and scornful,
    By thy sighs and tears unmoved?
      Cease thy mourning;
    Zion still is well beloved.

3 God, thy God, will now restore thee,
    He himself appears thy friend;
  All thy foes shall flee before thee,
    Here their boasts and triumphs end;
      Great deliverance
    Zion's King will quickly send.

4 Peace and joy shall now attend thee,
    All thy warfare now is past,
  God, thy Saviour, shall defend thee,
    Peace and joy are come at last;
      All thy conflicts
    End in everlasting rest.

383 May the Grace.   8 & 7.

1 May the grace of Christ our Saviour,
    And the Father's boundless love,
  With the Holy Spirit's favor,
    Rest upon us from above!

2 Thus may we abide in union
    With each other and the Lord;
  And possess, in sweet communion,
    Joys which earth cannot afford.

384. One There Is.

JOHN NEWTON. Tune, WILMOT. 8s & 7s.

1. One there is above all others Well deserves the name of Friend;
   His is love beyond a brother's, Costly, free, and knows no end.
2. Which of all our friends to save us Could or would have shed his blood?
   But this Saviour died, to have us Reconciled in him to God.
3. When he lived on earth, abased, Friend of Sinners was his name;
   Now, above all glory raised, He rejoices in the same.
4. Oh, for grace our hearts to soften! Teach us, Lord! at length to love;
   We alas! forget too often What a Friend we have above.

385. Sweet the Moments.

Tune, DORRNANCE. 8s & 7s.

1. Sweet the moments, rich in blessing,
   Which before the cross I spend,—
   Life and health, and peace posessing,
   From the sinners dying Friend.

2 Here I'll sit forever viewing
   Mercy stream in streams of blood;
   Precious drops, my soul bedewing,
   Plead and claim my peace with God.

3 Truly blessed is this station,
   Low before his cross to lie,—
   While I see divine compassion
   Floating in his languid eye.

4 Here it is I find my heaven,
   While upon the cross I gaze;
   Love I much? I'm much forgiven,—
   I'm a miracle of grace.

5 Love and grief my heart dividing,
   With my tears his feet I bathe;
   Constant still in faith abiding,
   Life deriving from his death.

386. Jesus, Lover of My Soul.

CHARLES WESLEY.
JNO R. SWENEY.

SOLO.

1. Jesus, lover of my soul! Let me to thy bosom fly,
2. Other refuge have I none; Hangs my helpless soul on thee:
3. Plenteous grace with thee is found, Grace to cover all my sin:

While the nearer waters roll, While the tempest still is high!
Leave, oh, leave me not alone, Still support and comfort me:
Let the healing streams abound; Make and keep me pure within.

CHORUS.

Hide me, O my Saviour, hide, Till the storm of life is past;
All my trust on thee is stayed, All my help from thee I bring;
Thou of life the fountain art, Freely let me take of thee:

Safe into the haven guide, Oh, receive my soul at last!
Cover my defenceless head With the shadow of thy wing!
Spring thou up within my heart, Rise to all eternity.

From "Anthems and Voluntaries," by per.

387. Watchman, Tell us of the Night.

Sir JOHN BOWRING. Tune, WATCHMAN. 7s, d.

1. Watchman, tell us of the night, What its signs of promise are;
Traveler, o'er yon mountain's height See that glo-ry-beam-ing star!
Watchman, does its beauteous ray Aught of hope or joy for-tell?
Traveler, yes; it brings the day, Prom-ised day of Is-ra-el.

2 Watchman, tell us of the night;
  Higher yet that star ascends.
Traveler, blessedness and light,
  Peace and truth, its course portends!
Watchman, will its beams alone
  Gild the spot that gave them birth?
Traveler, ages are its own,
  See, it bursts o'er all the earth!

3 Watchman, tell us of the night,
  For the morning seems to dawn.
Traveler, darkness takes its flight;
  Doubt and terror are withdrawn.
Watchman, let thy wandering cease;
  Hie thee to thy quiet home!
Traveler, lo! the Prince of Peace,
  Lo! the Son of God is come!

---

388. People of the Living God.

1 People of the living God,
  I have sought the world around,
Paths of sin and sorrow trod,
  Peace and comfort nowhere found.
Now to you my spirit turns—
  Turns, a fugitive unblest;
Brethren, where your altar burns,
  Oh, receive me into rest.

2 Lonely I no longer roam,
  Like the cloud, the wind, the wave;
Where you dwell shall be my home,
  Where you die shall be my grave.
Mine the God whom you adore,
  Your Redeemer shall be mine;
Earth can fill my heart no more,
  Every idol I resign.

3 Tell me not of gain or loss,
  Ease, enjoyment, pomp and power;
Welcome poverty and cross,
  Shame, reproach, affliction's hour.
"Follow me!" I know thy voice!
  Jesus, Lord! thy steps I see:
Now I take thy yoke by choice;
  Light thy burden now on me.

Zerah. C. M.

Dr. L. Mason.

389 Come, ye that love.

1 COME, ye that love the Saviour's name,
  And joy to make it known,
  The Sovereign of your hearts proclaim,
  And bow before his throne.

2 Behold your Lord, your Master crowned
  With glories all divine;
  And tell the wondering nations round
  How bright those glories shine.

3 When, in his earthly courts, we view
  The glories of our King,
  We long to love as angels do,
  And wish like them to sing.

4 And shall we long and wish in vain?
  Lord, teach our songs to rise:
  Thy love can animate the strain,
  And bid it reach the skies.

390 What glory gilds.

1 WHAT glory gilds the sacred page!
  Majestic, like the sun,
  It gives a light to every age;
  It gives, but borrows none.

2 The power that gave it still supplies
  The gracious light and heat;
  Its truths upon the nations rise;
  They rise, but never set.

3 Lord, everlasting thanks be thine
  For such a bright display,
  As makes a world of darkness shine
  With beams of heavenly day.

4 My soul rejoices to pursue
  The steps of him I love,
  Till glory breaks upon my view
  In brighter worlds above.

391 The Prince of Peace.

1 To us a Child of hope is born,
  To us a Son is given;
  Him shall the tribes of earth obey,
  Him, all the hosts of heaven.

2 His name shall be the Prince of Peace,
  Forevermore adored;
  The Wonderful, the Counselor,
  The great and mighty Lord.

3 His power, increasing, still shall spread;
  His reign no end shall know;
  Justice shall guard his throne above,
  And peace abound below.

4 To us a Child of hope is born,
  To us a Son is given;
  The Wonderful, the Counselor,
  The mighty Lord of heaven.

392 The joyful sound.

1 SALVATION! O the joyful sound
  What pleasure to our ears!
  A sovereign balm for every wound,
  A cordial for our fears.

2 Salvation! let the echo fly
  The spacious earth around,
  While all the armies of the sky
  Conspire to raise the sound.

3 Salvation! O thou bleeding Lamb!
  To thee the praise belongs:
  Salvation shall inspire our hearts,
  And dwell upon our tongues.

393 Doxology. C. M.

To Father, Son, and Holy Ghost,
The God whom we adore,
Be glory, as it was, is now,
And shall be evermore.

Arlington. C. M.

394 *Through all the Changing.*

1 Through all the changing scenes of life,
  In trouble and in joy,
  The praises of my God shall still
  My heart and tongue employ.

2 My soul shall make her boast in him,
  And celebrate his fame;
  Come, magnify the Lord with me,
  With me exalt his name.

3 The hosts of God encamp around
  The dwellings of the just;
  Deliverance he affords to all
  Who on his succor trust.

4 Oh! make but trial of his love;
  Experience will will decide
  How blest they are, and only they,
  Who in his truth confide.

395 *This is the Day.*

1 This is the day the Lord hath made,
  He calls the hours his own—
  Let heaven rejoice, let earth be glad,
  And praise surround his throne.

2 To-day he rose and left the dead,
  And Satan's empire fell;
  To-day the saints his triumphs spread,
  And all his wonders tell.

3 Hosanna to the anointed King,
  To David's holy Son!
  Help us, O Lord! descend and bring
  Salvation from thy throne.

4 Blest be the Lord, who comes to men,
  With messages of grace,
  Who comes, in God his Father's name,
  To save our sinful race.

5 Hosanna in the highest strains
  The church on earth can raise;
  The highest heavens, in which he reigns,
  Shall give him nobler praise.

396 *Am I a Soldier of the Cross*

1 Am I a soldier of the cross,
  A follower of the Lamb,
  And shall I fear to own his cause,
  Or blush to speak his name?

2 Must I be carried to the skies
  On flowery beds of ease,
  While others fight to win the prize,
  And sail through bloody seas?

3 Are there no foes for me to face?
  Must I not stem the flood?
  Is this vile world a friend to grace,
  To help me on to God?

4 Sure I must fight if I would reign—
  Increase my courage, Lord:
  I'll bear the toil, endure the pain,
  Supported by thy word.

397 *Beneath Moriah's Rocky Side.*

1 Beneath Moriah's rocky side
  A gentle fountain springs:
  Silent and soft its waters glide,
  Like the peace the Spirit brings.

2 The thirsty Arab stoops to drink
  Of the cool and quiet wave—
  And the thirsty spirit stops to think
  Of Him who came to save.

3 Siloam is the fountain's name:
  It means *One sent of God;*
  And thus the holy Saviour's name
  It gently spreads abroad.

4 Oh, grant that I, like this sweet well
  May Jesus' image bear,
  And spend my life, my all, to tell
  How full his mercies are.

Balerma. C. M.

398 *How Happy is the Youth.*

1 How happy is the youth who hears
  Instruction's warning voice,
  And who celestial wisdom makes
  His early, only choice.

2 For she has treasure greater far
  Than east or west unfold;
  And her rewards more precious are
  Than all their stores of gold.

3 She guides the young with innocence
  In pleasure's path to tread;
  A crown of glory she bestows
  Upon the hoary head.

4 According as her labors rise,
  So her rewards increase;
  Her ways are ways of pleasantness,
  And all her paths are peace.

399 *Oh, for a Heart to Praise.*

1 Oh, for a heart to praise my God,
  A heart from sin set free;—
  A heart that always feels thy blood,
  So freely shed for me.

2 A heart resigned, submissive, meek,
  My great Redeemer's throne,
  Where only Christ is heard to speak,
  Where Jesus reigns alone!

3 Oh, for a lowly, contrite heart,
  Believing, true and clean;
  Which neither life, nor death can part,
  From him that dwells within;

4 A heart in every thought renewed,
  And full of love divine,
  Perfect, and right, and pure, and good,
  A copy, Lord, of thine!

400 Remember Me. C. M.

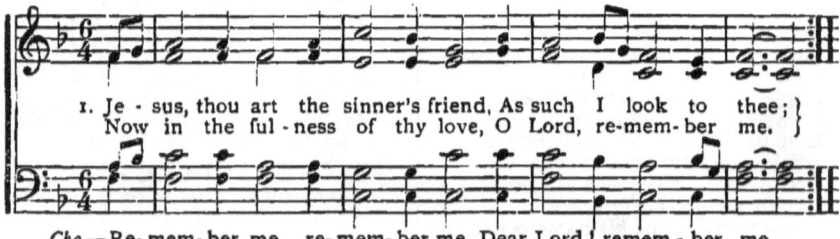

Cho.—Re-mem-ber me, re-mem-ber me, Dear Lord! remem-ber me.

2 Remember thy pure word of grace,
  Remember Calvary;
  Remember all thy dying groans,
  And then remember me.

3 Lord! I am guilty—I am vile,
  But thy salvation's free;
  Then, in thine all-abounding grace,
  Dear Lord! remember me.

Dundee. C. M.

401 How Sweet and Awful.

1 How sweet and awful is the place,
    With Christ within the doors;
While everlasting love displays
    The choicest of her stores.

2 While all our hearts, and all our songs,
    Join to admire the feast,
Each of us cries, with thankful tongues,
    "Lord, why was I a guest?"

3 "Why was I made to hear thy voice,
    And enter while there's room,
When thousands make a wretched choice,
    And rather starve than come.

4 "'Twas the same love that spread the
    That sweetly forced me in;   [feast,
Else we had still refused to taste,
    And perished in our sin.

402 How Oft, Alas!

1 How oft, alas! this wretched heart
    Has wandered from the Lord;
How oft my roving thoughts depart,
    Forgetful of his word

2 Yet sovereign mercy calls, "Return;"
    Dear Lord, and may I come?
My vile ingratitude I mourn,
    Oh, take the wanderer home.

3 Almighty grace, thy healing power
    How glorious, how divine,
That can to life and bliss restore
    So vile a heart as mine.

4 Thy pardoning love, so free, so sweet,
    Dear Saviour, I adore;
Oh, keep me at thy sacred feet,
    And let me rove no more.

403 O God, Our Help.

1 O God, our help in ages past
    Our hope for years to come,
Our shelter from the stormy blast,
    And our eternal home.

2 Before the hills in order stood,
    Or earth received her frame,
From everlasting thou art God,
    To endless years the same.

3 A thousand ages in thy sight
    Are like an evening gone,
Short as the watch that ends the night
    Before the rising dawn.

4 Time, like an ever-rolling stream,
    Bears all its sons away;
They fly, forgotten—as a dream
    Dies at the opening day.

404 The Lord Jehovah unto all.

1 The Lord Jehovah unto all
    His goodness doth declare,
And over all his mighty works
    His tender mercies are.

2 Thy kingdom shall for ever stand,
    Thy reign through ages all;
God raiseth all that are bowed down,
    Upholdeth all that fall.

3 The eyes of all things wait on thee,
    Thou Giver of all good!
And thou in season due dost give
    To every one his food.

4 My mouth the praises of the Lord
    To publish shall not cease;
Let all flesh join his holy name
    Forevermore to bless.

405 In the Cross of Christ.

Sir J. Bowring. Tune, RATHBUN. 8,7

1. In the cross of Christ I glory, Tow'ring o'er the wrecks of time; All the light of sa-cred sto-ry, Gathers round its head sublime.

2 When the woes of life o'ertake me,
Hopes deceive, and fears annoy,
Never shall the cross forsake me;
Lo! it glows with peace and joy.

3 When the sun of bliss is beaming
Light and love upon my way,
From the cross the radiance streaming
Adds more lustre to the day.

4 Bane and blessing, pain and pleasure,
By the cross are sanctified;
Peace is there, that knows no measure,
Joys that through all time abide.

5 In the cross of Christ I glory,
Towering o'er the wrecks of time;
All the light of sacred story
Gathers round its head sublime.

406 The Tranquil Hours. S. M.

Mrs. J. C. Yule. Jno. R. Sweney.

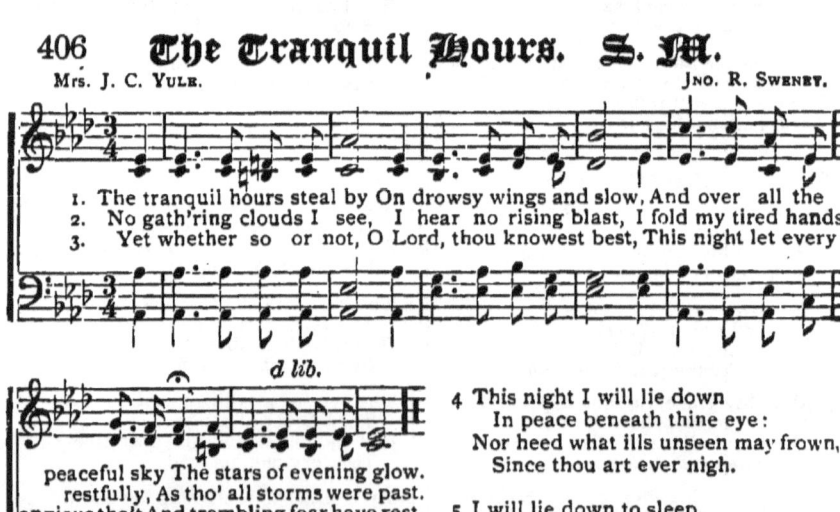

1. The tranquil hours steal by On drowsy wings and slow, And over all the peaceful sky The stars of evening glow.
2. No gath'ring clouds I see, I hear no rising blast, I fold my tired hands restfully, As tho' all storms were past.
3. Yet whether so or not, O Lord, thou knowest best, This night let every anxious tho't And trembling fear have rest.

4 This night I will lie down
In peace beneath thine eye;
Nor heed what ills unseen may frown,
Since thou art ever nigh.

5 I will lie down to sleep,
From every terror free;
Nor wake to tremble or to weep,
Secure, O Lord, in thee!

Copyright, 1889, by John J. Hood.

Siloam. C. M.

407 Approach, My Soul.

1 Approach, my soul, the mercy-seat,
  Where Jesus answers prayer;
There humbly fall before his feet,
  For none can perish there.

2 Thy promise is my only plea,
  With this I venture nigh;
Thou callest hardened souls to thee,
  And such, O Lord, am I.

3 Bowed down beneath a load of sin,
  By Satan sorely pressed,
By wars without and fears within,
  I come to thee for rest.

4 Be thou my shield and hiding place,
  That, sheltered near thy side,
I may my fierce accuser face,
  And tell him thou hast died.

5 O wondrous love! to bleed and die,
  To bear the cross and shame,
That guilty sinners, such as I,
  Might plead thy gracious name.

408 By Cool Siloam's Shady Rill.

1 By cool Siloam's shady rill
  How sweet the lily grows!
How sweet the breath, beneath the hill,
  Of Sharon's dewy rose.

2 Lo! such a child whose early feet
  The paths of peace have trod,
Whose sacred heart, with influence sweet,
  Is upward drawn to God.

3 By cool Siloam's shady rill
  The lily must decay;
The rose that blooms beneath the hill
  Must shortly fade away.

4 O Thou who givest life and breath,
  We ask thy grace alone,
In childhood, manhood, age and death,
  To keep us still thine own.

409 When the Worn Spirit.

1 When the worn spirit wants repose,
  And sighs her God to seek,
How sweet to hail the evening's close
  That ends the weary week!

2 How sweet to hail the early dawn
  That opens on the sight,
When first the soul-reviving morn
  Beams its new rays of light!

3 Sweet day, thine hours too soon will cease;
  Yet while they gently roll,
Breathe, Holy Spirit, source of peace,
  A Sabbath o'er my soul.

4 When will my pilgrimage be done,
  The world's long week be o'er,
That Sabbath dawn which needs no sun,
  That day which fades no more?

410 Of Thy Love. 8, 7, 4.

Of thy love some gracious taken
  Grant us, Lord, before we go;
Bless thy word which has been spoken,
  Life and peace on all bestow!
When we join the world again,
  Let our hearts with thee remain;
    Oh, direct us
    And protect us,
Till we gain the heavenly shore.

411. I Waited for The Lord.

Tune, PETERBOROUGH. C. M.

1. I waited for the Lord, my God, And patiently did bear,
At length to me he did incline, My voice and cry to hear.
2. He took me from a fearful pit, And from the miry clay,
And on a rock he set my feet, Establishing my way.
3. He put a new song in my mouth, Our God to magnify;
Many shall see it, and shall fear, And on the Lord rely.

412. There is an Hour.

Tune, WOODLAND. C. M.

1. There is an hour of peaceful rest To mourning wander'rs giv'n, There is a joy for souls distress'd, A balm for every wounded breast,'Tis found above, in heav'n
2. There is a home for weary souls, By sin and sorrow driv'n, When toss'd on life's tempestuous shoals, Where storms arise and ocean rolls, And all is drear but heav'n

3 There faith lifts up the tearless eye,
  To brighter prospects given;
And views the tempest passing by,
The evening shadows quickly fly,
  And all serene in heaven.

4 There fragrant flow'rs immortal bloom,
  And joys supreme are given;
There rays divine disperse the gloom;
Beyond the confines of the tomb
  Appears the dawn of heaven.

413

Tr. by CASWALL. Tune, EVAN. C. M.

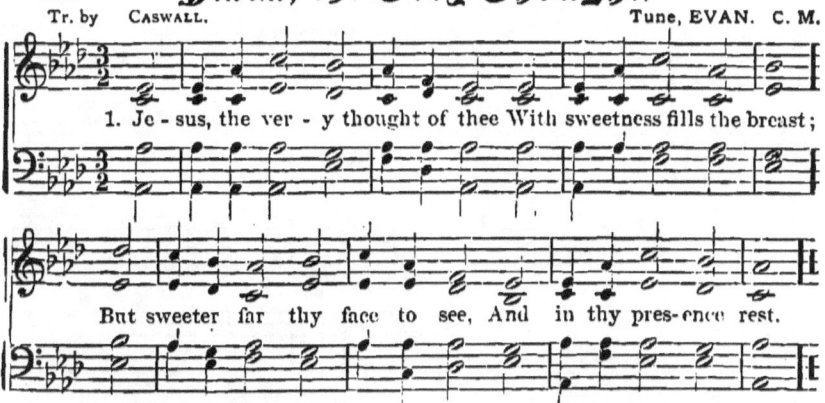

1. Jesus, the very thought of thee With sweetness fills the breast;
But sweeter far thy face to see, And in thy presence rest.

2 No voice can sing, no heart can frame,
  Nor can the memory find
A sweeter sound than Jesus' name,
  The Saviour of mankind.

3 O Hope of every contrite heart,
  O Joy of all the meek,
To those who ask, how kind thou art!
  How good, to those who seek!

4 But what to those who find? Ah, this
  Nor tongue nor pen can show:
The love of Jesus, what it is,
  None but his loved ones know.

5 Jesus, our only joy be thou,
  As thou our prize wilt be;
In thee be all our glory now,
  And through eternity.

414 Calm me, my God.

1 Calm me, my God, and keep me calm:
  Let thine outstretched wing
Be like the shade of Elim's palm,
  Beside her desert spring.

2 Yes, keep me calm, though loud and rude
  The sounds my ear that greet—
Calm in the closet's solitude,
  Calm in the bustling street,—

3 Calm in the hour of buoyant health,
  Calm in the hour of pain:
Calm in my poverty or wealth,
  Calm in my loss or gain,—

4 Calm in the sufferance of wrong,
  Like him who bore my shame;
Calm 'mid the threatening, taunting throng,
  Who hate thy holy name.

5 Calm me, my God, and keep me calm,
  Soft resting on thy breast;
Soothe me with holy hymn and psalm,
  And bid my spirit rest.

415 Oh for a Closer Walk with God.

1 Oh for a closer walk with God!
  A calm and heavenly frame!
A light to shine upon the road
  That leads me to the Lamb.

2 Return! O holy Dove, return,
  Sweet messenger of rest;
I hate the sins that made thee mourn,
  And drove thee from my breast.

3 The dearest idol I have known,
  Whate'er that idol be,
Help me to tear it from thy throne,
  And worship only thee.

4 So shall my walk be close with God,
  Calm and serene my frame;
So purer light shall mark the road
  That leads me to the Lamb.

416 How Blest the Man.

1 How blest the man whose sins the Lord
  Has pardoned in his grace,
All whose transgressions are removed,
  And covered from his face.

2 How blest the man to whom the Lord
  Imputeth not his sin;
And in whose spirit is no guile,
  Nor fraud is found therein.

3 Surely, when floods and waters great
  Do swell up to the brim,
They shall not overwhelm his soul,
  Nor once come near to him.

Lebanon. S. M. D.

417 *I was a Wandering Sheep.*

1 I was a wandering sheep,
  I did not love the fold,
I did not love my Shepherd's voice,
  I would not be controlled;
I was a wayward child,
  I did not love my home,
I did not love my Father's voice,
  I loved afar to roam.

2 The Shepherd sought his sheep,
  The Father sought his child;
They followed me o'er vale and hill,
  O'er deserts waste and wild;
They found me nigh to death,
  Famished, and faint, and lone;
They bound me with the bands of love,
  They saved the wandering one.

3 Jesus my Shepherd is,
  'Twas he that loved my soul,
'Twas he that washed me in his blood,
  'Twas he that made me whole;
'Twas he that sought the lost,
  That found the wandering sheep,
'Twas he that brought me to the fold—
  'Tis he that still doth keep.

418 *Jesus, my Strength, my Hope!*

1 Jesus, my strength, my hope!
  On thee I cast my care;
With humble confidence look up,
  And know thou hear'st my prayer:
Give me on thee to wait,
  Till I can all things do;
On thee,—almighty to create,
  Almighty to renew.

2 I rest upon thy word;
  The promise is for me;
My succor and salvation, Lord,
  Shall surely come from thee;
But let me still abide,
  Nor from my hope remove,
Till thou my patient spirit guide
  Into thy perfect love.

3 I want a sober mind,
  A self-renouncing will,
That tramples down and casts behind
  The baits of pleasing ill;
A soul inured to pain,
  To hardship, grief, and loss;
Bold to take up, firm to sustain,
  The consecrated cross.

4 I want a godly fear,
  A quick discerning eye,
That looks to thee when sin is near,
  And sees the tempter fly;
A spirit still prepared,
  And armed with jealous care;
Forever standing on its guard,
  And watching unto prayer.

419 **Forever with the Lord.**

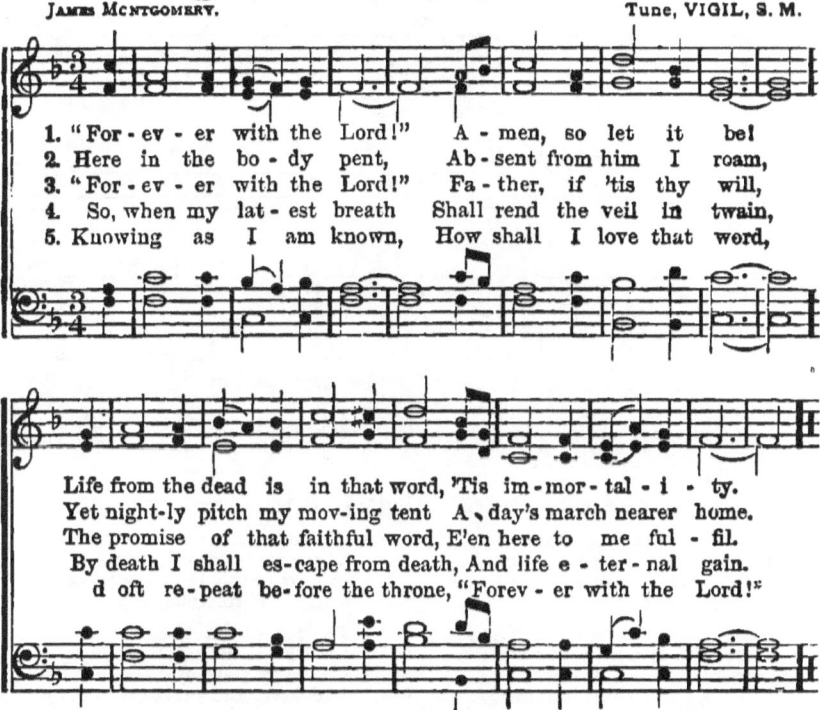

1. "For-ev-er with the Lord!" A-men, so let it be! Life from the dead is in that word, 'Tis im-mor-tal-i-ty.
2. Here in the bo-dy pent, Ab-sent from him I roam, Yet night-ly pitch my mov-ing tent A day's march nearer home.
3. "For-ev-er with the Lord!" Fa-ther, if 'tis thy will, The promise of that faithful word, E'en here to me ful-fil.
4. So, when my lat-est breath Shall rend the veil in twain, By death I shall es-cape from death, And life e-ter-nal gain.
5. Knowing as I am known, How shall I love that word, d oft re-peat be-fore the throne, "Forev-er with the Lord!"

420 **Oh, Bless the Lord, My Soul.**

1 Oh, bless the Lord, my soul,
 Let all within me join,
And aid my tongue to bless his name,
 Whose favors are divine.

2 Oh, bless the Lord, my soul,
 Nor let his mercies lie
Forgotten in unthankfulness,
 And without praises die.

3 'Tis he forgives thy sins,
 'Tis he relieves thy pain,
'Tis he that heals thy sicknesses,
 And makes thee young again.

4 He crowns thy life with love,
 When ransomed from the grave;
He that redeemed my soul from hell
 Hath sovereign power to save.

421 **Father, a Weary Heart.**
Tune, Lebanon.

1 Father a weary heart,
 Hath come to thee for peace;
The world hath not the healing art
 To bid its troubles cease;
It brings before thy throne
 Its weight of woe and care;
Do thou accept its pleading tone —
 The contrite sinner's prayer.

2 Father—it hath rebelled,
 Hath wandered from thy path,
Nor heeded when the thunder swelled
 The tempest of thy wrath;
But now, a bruised thing,
 Neglected, pale, and bare,
Lo, at thy footstool it doth bring
 The contrite sinner's prayer.

3 Father, it bends before
 Thy throne among the blest;
Peace to the wretched heart restore,
 Give to the weary rest:
Through Christ's atonement given,
 It trusteth yet to share
The glorious heritage of heaven,
 By lowly, contrite prayer.

St. Thomas. S. M.

422 My Soul, Repeat His Praise.

1 My soul, repeat his praise,
   Whose mercies are so great;
Whose anger is so slow to rise,
   So ready to abate.

2 High as the heavens are raised
   Above the ground we tread,
So far the riches of his grace
   Our highest thoughts exceed.

3 His power subdues our sins,
   And his forgiving love,
Far as the east is from the west,
   Doth all our guilt remove.

4 The pity of the Lord,
   To those who fear his name,
Is such as tender parents feel;
   He knows our feeble frame.

423 Jesus, Who Knows Full Well.

1 Jesus, who knows full well
   The heart of every saint,
Invites us all our griefs to tell,
   To pray and never faint.

2 He bows his gracious ear,
   We never plead in vain:
Yet we must wait till he appear,
   And pray, and pray again.

3 Though unbelief suggest,
   Why should we longer wait?
He bids us never give him rest,
   But be importunate.

4 Jesus the Lord will hear
   His chosen, when they cry;
Yes, though he may awhile forbear,
   He'll help them from on high.

424 Welcome, Sweet Day of Rest.

1 Welcome, sweet day of rest,
   That saw the Lord arise,
Welcome to this reviving breast,
   And these rejoicing eyes.

2 The King himself comes near,
   And feasts his saints to-day;
Here we may sit, and see him here,
   And love, and praise, and pray.

3 One day amidst the place
   Where my dear God hath been,
Is sweeter than ten thousand days
   Of pleasurable sin.

3 My willing soul would stay
   In such a frame as this,
And sit and sing herself away
   To everlasting bliss.

425 Come, Holy Spirit, Come.

1 Come, Holy Spirit, come,
   Let thy bright beams arise;
Dispel the darkness from our minds,
   And open thou our eyes.

2 Revive our drooping faith,
   Our doubts and fears remove,
And kindle in our breasts the flame
   Of never-dying love.

3 'Tis thine to cleanse the heart,
   To sanctify the soul,
To pour fresh life on every part,
   And new create the whole.

4 Dwell, therefore, in our hearts,
   Our minds from bondage free;
Then shall we know, and praise, and love
   The Father, Son and Thee.

426. Not all the Blood of Beasts.

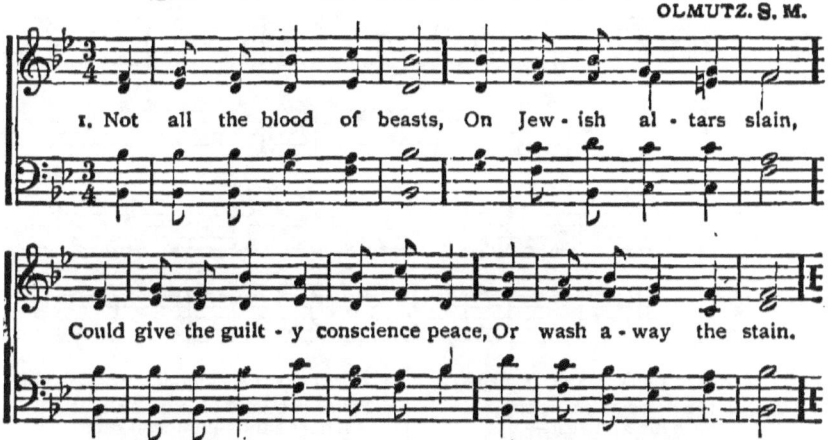

OLMUTZ. S. M.

1. Not all the blood of beasts, On Jewish altars slain,
Could give the guilty conscience peace, Or wash away the stain.

2 But Christ, the heavenly Lamb,
Takes all our sins away;
A sacrifice of nobler name,
And richer blood than they.

3 My faith would lay her hand
On that dear head of thine,
While, like a penitent, I stand,
And there confess my sin.

4 My soul looks back to see
The burdens thou didst bear,
When hanging on the accursed tree,
And hopes her guilt was there.

5 Believing, we rejoice
To see the curse remove;
We bless the Lamb, with cheerful voice,
And sing his bleeding love.

Laban. S. M.

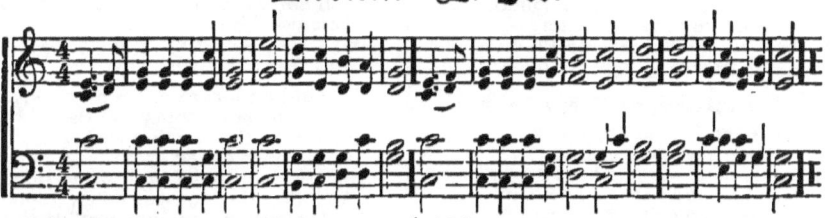

427 Come, We that Love the Lord.

1 Come, we that love the Lord,
And let our joys be known;
Join in a song with sweet accord,
And thus surround the throne.

2 The men of grace have found
Glory begun below;
Celestial fruits on earthly ground
From faith and hope may grow.

3 The hill of Sion yields
A thousand sacred sweets,
Before we reach the heavenly fields,
Or walk the golden streets.

4 Then let our songs abound,
And every tear be dry;
We're marching through Immanuel's ground
To fairer worlds on high.

428 My Soul, be on Thy Guard.

1 My soul, be on thy guard,
Ten thousand foes arise,
And hosts of sin are pressing hard
To draw thee from the skies.

2 Oh, watch, and fight, and pray,
The battle ne'er give o'er,
Renew it boldly every day,
And help divine implore.

3 Ne'er think the victory won,
Nor once at ease sit down;
Thine arduous work will not be done
Till thou hast got the crown.

4 Fight on, my soul, till death
Shall bring thee to thy God:
He'll take thee, at thy parting breath,
Up to his blest abode.

Varina. C. M. D.

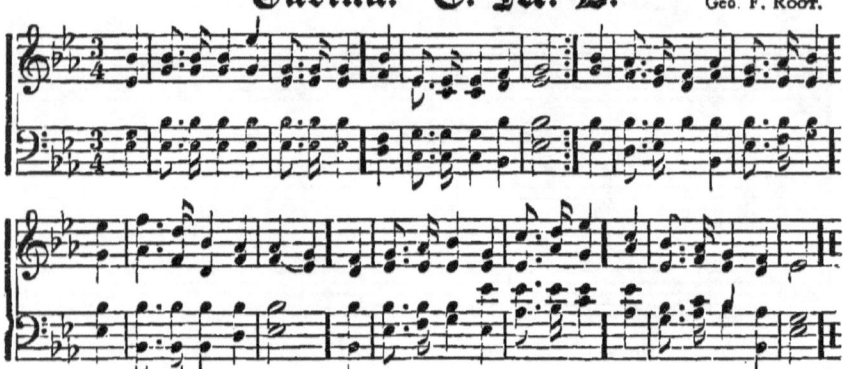

429 I Heard the Voice of Jesus say.

1 I heard the voice of Jesus say,
  Come unto me and rest,—
Lay down, thou weary one, lay down
  Thy head upon my breast:
I came to Jesus as I was,
  Weary, and worn, and sad:
I found in him a resting place,
  And he has made me glad.

2 I heard the voice of Jesus say,
  I am this dark world's light,—
Look unto me, thy morn shall rise,
  And all thy day be bright:
I looked to Jesus, and I found
  In him my Star, my Sun;
And in that light of life I'll walk,
  Till traveling days are done.

430 Jerusalem, my Happy Home.

1 Jerusalem, my happy home,
  Name ever dear to me,
When shall my labors have an end,
  In joy, and peace, and thee?
Oh, when, thou city of my God!
  Shall I thy courts ascend?
Where congregations ne'er break up,
  And Sabbaths have no end.

2 There happier bowers than Eden's
  Nor sin nor sorrow know;   [bloom,
Blest seats! thro' rude and stormy scenes
  I onward press to you.
Why should I shrink at pain and woe,
  Or feel at death dismay?
I've Canaan's goodly land in view,
  And realms of endless day.

3 Apostles, martyrs, prophets, there
  Around my Saviour stand;
And soon my friends in Christ below
  Will join the glorious band.
Jerusalem, my happy home,
  My soul still pants for thee;
Then shall my labors have an end,
  When I thy joys shall see.

431 There is a Land of Pure Delight.

1 There is a land of pure delight,
  Where saints immortal reign;
Infinite day excludes the night,
  And pleasures banish pain.
There everlasting spring abides,
  And never-withering flowers;
Death, like a narrow sea, divides
  This heavenly land from ours.

2 Sweet fields beyond the swelling flood
  Stand dressed in living green;
So to the Jews old Canaan stood,
  While Jordan rolled between.
But timorous mortals start and shrink
  To cross this narrow sea;
And linger, shivering on the brink,
  And fear to launch away.

3 Oh, could we make our doubts remove,
  Those gloomy doubts that rise,
And see the Canaan that we love
  With unbeclouded eyes:
Could we but climb where Moses stood,
  And view the landscape o'er, [flood,
Not Jordan's stream, nor death's cold
  Should fright us from the shore.

432 Whilst Thee I seek.

1 Whilst thee I seek, protecting Power!
  Be my vain wishes stilled,
And may this consecrated hour
  With better hopes be filled.
Thy love the power of thought bestowed,
  To thee my thoughts would soar:
Thy mercy o'er my life has flowed,
  That mercy I adore.

2 In each event of life, how clear
  Thy ruling hand I see;
Each blessing to my soul most dear,
  Because conferred by thee.
In every joy that crowns my days,
  In every pain I bear,
My heart shall find delight in praise,
  Or seek relief in prayer.

Alida. C. M. Double.
D. B. Thompson.

433 How happy every child.

1 How happy every child of grace,
 Who knows his sins forgiven!
"This earth," he cries, "is not my place,
 I seek my place in heaven,—
A country far from mortal sight;
 Yet O, by faith I see
The land of rest, the saints' delight,
 The heaven prepared for me."

2 O what a blessed hope is ours!
 While here on earth we stay,
We more than taste the heavenly
 And antedate that day;   [powers,
We feel the resurrection near,
 Our life in Christ concealed,
And with his glorious presence here
 Our earthen vessels filled.

3 O would he more of heaven bestow,
 And let the vessels break,
And let our ransomed spirits go
 To grasp the God we seek;
In rapturous awe on him to gaze,
 Who bought the sight for me;
And shout and wonder at his grace
 Through all eternity!

435 Sweet Hour of Prayer.

1 ‖: Sweet hour of prayer,:‖
That calls me from a world of care,
And bids me at my Father's throne
Make all my wants and wishes known:
In seasons of distress and grief
My soul has often found relief,
And oft escaped the tempter's snare,
By thy return, sweet hour of prayer.

2 ‖: Sweet hour of prayer,:‖
Thy wings shall my petition bear
To him whose truth and faithfulness
Engage the waiting soul to bless:
And since he bids me seek his face,
Believe his word, and trust his grace,
I'll cast on him my ev'ry care,
And wait for thee, sweet hour of prayer.

3 ‖: Sweet hour of prayer,:‖
May I thy consolation share;
Till, from Mount Pisgah's lofty height,
I view my home, and take my flight:
This robe of flesh I'll drop, and rise
To seize the everlasting prize;
And shout, while passing thro' the air,
Farewell farewell, sweet hour of prayer.

434 Work, for the night is coming.

1 Work, for the night is coming,
 Work through the morning hours;
Work, while the dew is sparkling,
 Work 'mid springing flowers;
Work, when the day grows brighter,
 Work in the glowing sun;
Work, for the night is coming,
 When man's work is done.

2 Work, for the night is coming,
 Work through the sunny noon;
Fill brightest hours with labor,
 Rest comes sure and soon,
Give every flying minute
 Something to keep in store:
Work, for the night is coming,
 When man works no more.

3 Work, for the night is coming,
 Under the sunset skies;
While their bright tints are glowing,
 Work, for daylight flies.
Work till the last beam fadeth,
 Fadeth to shine no more;
Work while the night is darkening,
 When man's work is o'er.

Woodstock. C. M.

436   I Love to Steal Awhile Away.

1 I love to steal awhile away
  From every cumbering care,
And spend the hours of setting day
  In humble, grateful prayer.

2 I love in solitude to shed
  The penitential tear,
And all his promises to plead,
  Where none but God can hear.

3 I love to think on mercies past,
  And future good implore,
And all my cares and sorrows cast
  On him whom I adore.

4 I love by faith to take a view
  Of brighter scenes in heaven;
The prospect does my strength renew
  While here by tempests driven.

5 Thus, when life's toilsome day is o'er,
  May its departing ray
Be calm as this impressive hour,
  And lead to endless day.

437   See Israel's Gentle Shepherd.

1 See Israel's gentle Shepherd stand
  With all-engaging charms!
Hark, how he calls the tender lambs,
  And folds them in his arms!

2 "Permit them to approach," he cries,
  "Nor scorn their humble name,
For 'twas to bless such souls as these
  The Lord of angels came."

3 We bring them, Lord, in thankful hands,
  And yield them up to thee;
Joyful that we ourselves are thine,—
  Thine let our offspring be,

---

438   **Father! I Know.**

Tune, SPOHR. C. M. 6 lines.

1. Father! I know that all my life   Is portioned out for me;
2. I ask thee for a thoughtful love, Through constant watching wise,
3. I ask thee for the daily strength, To none that ask denied,
4. And if some things I do not ask   Among my blessings be,

Father! I Know.—CONCLUDED.

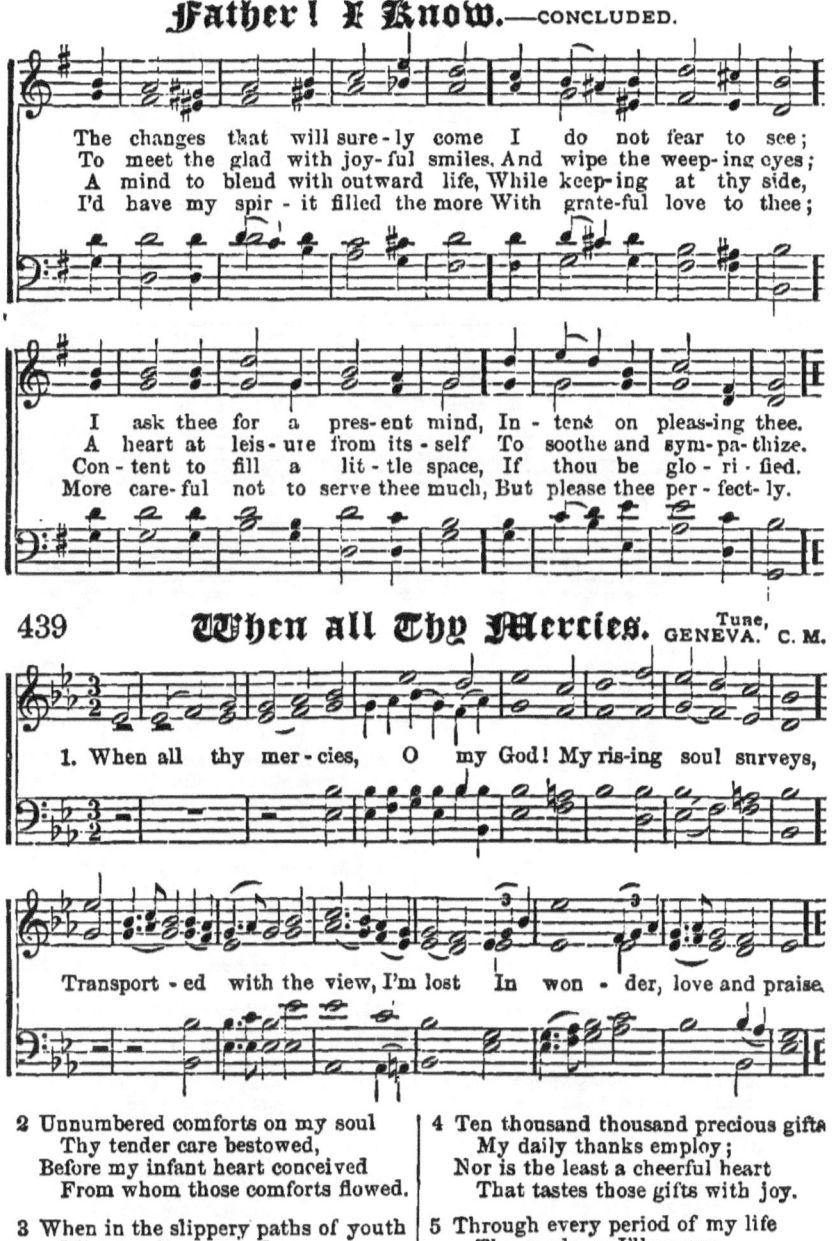

The changes that will sure-ly come I do not fear to see;
To meet the glad with joy-ful smiles, And wipe the weep-ing eyes;
A mind to blend with outward life, While keep-ing at thy side,
I'd have my spir-it filled the more With grate-ful love to thee;

I ask thee for a pres-ent mind, In-tent on pleas-ing thee.
A heart at leis-ure from its-self To soothe and sym-pa-thize.
Con-tent to fill a lit-tle space, If thou be glo-ri-fied.
More care-ful not to serve thee much, But please thee per-fect-ly.

439. When all Thy Mercies. GENEVA. Tune, C. M.

1. When all thy mer-cies, O my God! My ris-ing soul surveys,
Transport-ed with the view, I'm lost In won-der, love and praise.

2 Unnumbered comforts on my soul
   Thy tender care bestowed,
Before my infant heart conceived
   From whom those comforts flowed.

3 When in the slippery paths of youth
   With heedless steps I ran,
Thine arm, unseen, conveyed me safe,
   And led me up to man.

4 Ten thousand thousand precious gifts
   My daily thanks employ;
Nor is the least a cheerful heart
   That tastes those gifts with joy.

5 Through every period of my life
   Thy goodness I'll pursue,
And after death in distant worlds
   The glorious theme renew.

440 My Times are in Thy Hand.

W. F. Lloyd
Tune, SELVIN. S. M.

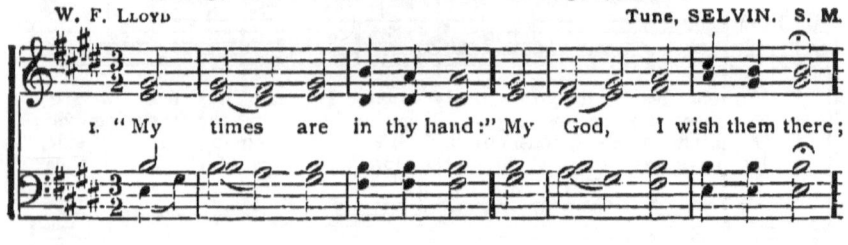

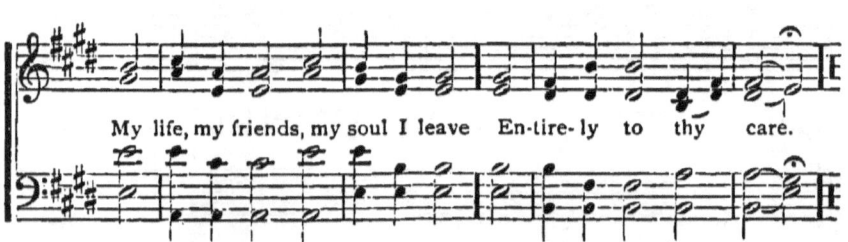

2 "My times are in thy hand,"
Whatever they may be;
Pleasing or painful, dark or bright,
As best may seem to thee.

3 "My times are in thy hand;"
Why should I doubt or fear?
My father's hand will never cause
His child a needless tear.

4 "My times are in thy hand,"
Jesus, the crucified!
The hand my cruel sins had pierced
Is now my guard and guide.

5 "My times are in thy hand;"
I'll always trust in thee;
And, after death, at thy right hand
I shall forever be.

---

441 O Lord, Thy Perfect Word

1 O Lord, thy perfect word
Directs our steps aright,
Nor can all other books afford
Such profit and delight.

2 Celestial beams it sheds,
To cheer this vale below:
To distant lands its glory spreads,
And streams of mercy flow.

3 True wisdom it imparts,
Commands our hope and fear;
Oh, may we hide it in our hearts,
And feel its influence there.

442 Not what I feel or do.

1 Not what I feel or do
Can give me peace with God;
Not all my prayers, and sighs, and tears,
Can bear my awful load.

2 Thy work alone, O Christ,
Can ease this weight of sin,
Thy blood alone, O Lamb of God,
Can give me peace within.

3 'Tis Christ who saveth me;
And freely pardon gives;
I love because he loveth me,
I live because he lives.

Dennis. S. M.

443 Blest be the Tie that Binds.

1 Blest be the tie that binds
  Our hearts in Christian love;
  The fellowship of kindred minds
  Is like to that above.

2 Before our Father's throne
  We pour our ardent prayers;
  Our fears, our hopes, our aims are one,
  Our comforts and our cares.

3 We share our mutual woes,
  Our mutual burdens bear;
  And often for each other flows
  The sympathizing tear.

4 When we asunder part,
  It gives us inward pain;
  But we shall still be joined in heart,
  And hope to meet again.

444 How Gentle God's Commands!

1 How gentle God's commands!
  How kind his precepts are!
  Come, cast your burdens on the Lord,
  And trust his constant care.

2 His bounty will provide,
  His saints securely dwell;
  That hand which bears creation up,
  Shall guard his children well.

3 Why should this anxious load
  Press down your weary mind?
  Oh, seek your heavenly Father's throne,
  And peace and comfort find!

4 His goodness stands approved,
  Unchanged from day to day;
  I'll drop my burden at his feet,
  And bear a song away.

445 A few more Years shall roll.

1 A few more years shall roll,
  A few more seasons come,
  And we shall be with those that rest,
  Asleep within the tomb.

2 A few more storms shall beat
  On this wild, rocky shore,
  And we shall be where tempests cease,
  And surges swell no more.

3 A few more struggles here,
  A few more partings o'er,
  A few more toils, a few more tears,
  And we shall weep no more.

4 A few more Sabbaths here
  Shall cheer us on our way;
  And we shall reach the endless rest,
  Th' eternal Sabbath day.

446 Did Christ o'er Sinners weep.

1 Did Christ o'er sinners weep,
  And shall our cheeks be dry?
  Let floods of penitential grief
  Burst forth from every eye.

2 A cloud of witnesses around
  Hold thee in full survey;
  Forget the steps already trod,
  And onward urge thy way.

3 'Tis God's all-animating voice
  That calls thee from on high;
  'Tis his own hand presents the price
  To thine aspiring eye

447. How Sweet the Name.

JOHN NEWTON.   Tune, DOWNS. C. M.

1. How sweet the name of Jesus sounds In a believer's ear!
It soothes his sorrows, heals his wounds, And drives away his fear.

2 It makes the wounded spirit whole,
   And calms the troubled breast;
'Tis manna to the hungry soul,
   And to the weary, rest.

3 Dear name! the rock on which I build,
   My shield and hiding-place;
My never-failing treasure, filled
   With boundless stores of grace!

4 Jesus, my Shepherd, Saviour, Friend,
   My Prophet, Priest, and King,
My Lord, my Life, my Way, my End,
   Accept the praise I bring!

5 I would thy boundless love proclaim
   With every fleeting breath;
So shall the music of thy name
   Refresh my soul in death.

448. O that the Lord would Guide.

1 O that the Lord would guide my way
   To keep his statutes still!
Oh that my God would grant me grace
   To know and do his will!

2 Oh, send thy Spirit down to write
   Thy law upon my heart;
Nor let my tongue indulge deceit,
   Nor act the liar's part.

3 Order my footsteps by thy word,
   And make my heart sincere:
Let sin have no dominion, Lord,
   But keep my conscience clear.

4 My soul hath gone too far astray,
   My feet too often slip;
Yet, since I've not forgot thy way,
   Restore thy wandering sheep.

5 Make me to walk in thy commands,
   'Tis a delightful road;
Nor let my head, or heart, or hands
   Offend against my God.

449. Plunged in a Gulf.

1 Plunged in a gulf of dark despair,
   We wretched sinners lay,
Without one cheerful beam of hope,
   Or spark of glimmering day.

2 With pitying eyes the Prince of grace
   Beheld our helpless grief;
He saw, and—oh, amazing love!—
   He ran to our relief.

3 Down from the shining seats above,
   With joyful haste he fled,
Entered the grave in mortal flesh,
   And dwelt among the dead.

4 Oh for this love let rocks and hills
   Their lasting silence break,
And all harmonious human tongues
   The Saviour's praises speak.

450. The Saviour Calls; let every Ear.

1 The Saviour calls; let every ear
   Attend the heavenly sound;
Ye doubting souls, dismiss your fear,
   Hope smiles reviving round.

2 For every thirsty, longing heart,
   Here streams of bounty flow,
And life, and health, and bliss impart
   To banish mortal woe.

3 Ye sinners, come, 'tis mercy's voice;
   The gracious call obey;
Mercy invites to heavenly joys,—
   And can you yet delay?

4 Dear Saviour, draw reluctant hearts;
   To thee let sinners fly,
And take the bliss that love imparts,
   And drink, and never die.

451. All for Jesus.

Mary D. James. *Arranged.*

1. All for Jesus! all for Je-sus! All my being's ransomed powers:
   All my thoughts, and words, and doings, All my days, and all my hours.
2. Let my hands perform his bidding, Let my feet run in his ways—
   Let my eyes see Jesus on-ly, Let my lips speak forth his praise,

All for Jesus! all for Je-sus! All my days, and all my hours; hours.
All for Jesus! all for Je-sus! Let my lips speak forth his praise; praise.

3 Since my eyes were fixed on Jesus,
I've lost sight of all besides;
So enchained my spirit's vision,
Looking at the Crucified.
‖: All for Jesus! all for Jesus!
Looking at the Crucified. :‖

4 Oh, what wonder! how amazing!
Jesus, glorious King of kings—
Deigns to call me his beloved,
Lets me rest beneath his wings.
‖: All for Jesus! all for Jesus!
Resting now beneath his wings! :‖

452. Sitting at the Feet of Jesus.

1 Sitting at the feet of Jesus,
Oh, what words I hear him say!
Happy place! so near, so precious!
May it find me there each day!
Sitting at the feet of Jesus,
I would look upon the past;
For his love has been so gracious,
It has won my heart at last.

2 Sitting at the feet of Jesus,
Where can mortal be more blest?
There I lay my sins and sorrows,
And, when weary, find sweet rest.
Sitting at the feet of Jesus,
There I love to weep and pray,
While I from his fulness gather
Grace and comfort every day.

3 Bless me, O my Saviour! bless me,
As I sit low at thy feet;
Oh! look down in love upon me;
Let me see thy face so sweet.
Give me, Lord, the mind of Jesus;
Make me holy as he is:
May I prove I've been with Jesus,
Who is all my righteousness!

453. While in Different Paths Dividing.

1 While in different paths dividing,
We our pilgrimage pursue,
May our Shepherd, safely guiding,
Keep his scattered flock in view!
May the bond of blest communion
Every distant soul embrace,
Till in everlasting union,
We attain our resting place.

2 Oh, 'tis sweet, each other aiding,
In companionship to move,
One pure flame each heart pervading,
One, our Lord, our faith, our love;
Sweet when each can bend, imploring
Solace for our brother's pain,
And, the stumbling foot restoring,
Cheer him to the race again.

3 We may part in tearful sadness,
Bearing forth the precious grain,
But we shall return with gladness,
Bringing harvest sheaves again.
Thus, though fond affection weepeth,
Faith exalts her cheering voice;
He that soweth, he that reapeth,
Soon together shall rejoice.

Rockingham. L. M.
Lowell Mason.

454 Of Him Who Did Salvation Bring.

1 Of him who did salvation bring,
   I could forever think and sing;
   Arise, ye needy,—he'll relieve;
   prise, ye guilty,—he'll forgive.

2 Ask but his grace, and lo, 'tis given;
   Ask, and he turns your hell to heaven:
   Though sin and sorrow wound my soul,
   Jesus, thy balm will make it whole.

3 To shame our sins he blushed in blood;
   He closed his eyes to show us God:
   Let all the world fall down and know
   That none but God such love can show.

4 'Tis thee I love, for thee alone
   I shed my tears and make my moan;
   Where'er I am, where'er I move,
   I meet the object of my love.

5 Insatiate to this spring I fly;
   I drink, and yet am ever dry:
   Ah! who against thy charms is proof?
   Ah! who that loves, can love enough?

455 So Let Our Lips and Lives Express.

1 So let our lips and lives express
   The holy gospel we profess;
   So let our works and virtues shine
   To prove the doctrine all divine.

2 Thus shall we best proclaim abroad
   The honors of our Saviour God,
   When his salvation reigns within,
   And grace subdues the power of sin.

3 Religion bears our spirits up,
   While we expect that blessed hope,
   The bright appearance of the Lord,
   And faith stands leaning on his word.

456 Another Six Day's Work is Done.

1 Another six days' work is done,
   Another sabbath is begun;
   Return, my soul, enjoy thy rest,
   Improve the day thy God hath blest.

2 Oh that our thoughts and thanks may rise
   As grateful incense to the skies,
   And draw from heaven that sweet repose,
   Which none but he that feels it knows.

3 This heavenly calm within the breast
   Is the dear pledge of glorious rest,
   Which for the church of God remains,
   The end of cares, the end of pains.

4 In holy duties let the day,
   In holy pleasures pass away;
   How sweet a Sabbath thus to spend,
   In hope of one that ne'er shall end!

457 Thine Earthly Sabbaths.

1 Thine earthly Sabbaths, Lord, we love,
   But there's a nobler rest above;
   To that our longing souls aspire,
   With ardent love and strong desire.

2 In thy blest kingdom we shall be
   From every mortal trouble free;
   No groans shall mingle with the songs
   Which warble from immortal tongues.

3 Oh, long expected day, begin,
   Dawn on this world of woe and sin;
   Fain would we leave this weary road,
   And sleep in death, and rest in God.

Doxology.

To God the Father, God the Son,
And God the Spirit, three in one,
Be honor, praise and glory given,
By all on earth and all in heaven.

458 I Lay My Sins on Jesus.

H. Bonar. D. D. Tune, ANGELUS. 7s, 6s.

1. I lay my sins on Jesus, The spotless lamb of God;
   He bears them all and frees us From the accursed load.
   I bring my guilt to Jesus, To wash my crimson stains
   White in his blood most precious, Till not a stain remains.

2 I lay my wants on Jesus;
   All fulness dwells in him;
   He healeth my diseases;
   He doth my soul redeem.
  I lay my griefs on Jesus,
   My burdens and my cares;
   He from them all releases,
   He all my sorrows shares.

3 I rest my soul on Jesus,
   This weary soul of mine;
   His right hand me embraces,
   I on his breast recline.
  I love the name of Jesus,
   Immanuel, Christ the Lord;
   Like fragrance on the breezes,
   His name abroad is poured.

4 I long to be like Jesus,
   Meek, loving, lowly, mild;
   I long to be like Jesus,
   The Father's holy child.
  I long to be with Jesus
   Amid the heavenly throng,
   To sing with saints his praises,
   And learn the angels' song.

459 I Could Not do Without Thee.

1 I could not do without thee,
   O Saviour of the Lost!
   Whose precious blood redeemed me
   At such tremendous cost.
  My righteousness, my pardon,
   Thy precious blood must be
   My only hope and comfort,
   My glory and my plea.

2 I could not do without thee,
   I cannot stand alone;
   I have no strength or goodness
   No wisdom of my own;
   But thou, beloved Saviour,
   Art all in all to me;
   And weakness will be power,
   If leaning hard on thee.

2 I could not do without thee,
   For oh! the way is long,
   And I am often weary,
   And sigh replaces song.
   How could I do without thee?
   I do not know the way;
   Thou knowest and thou leadest,
   And wilt not let me stray.

Shall we Meet?

H. L. Hastings.   Elisha S. Rice.

1. Shall we meet beyond the riv-er, Where the surg-es cease to roll?
2. Shall we meet in that blest harbor, When our storm-y voyage is o'er?

Where in all the bright for-ev-er, Sor-row ne'er shall press the soul?
Shall we meet and cast the anchor By the bright ce-les-tial shore?

D.S. Shall we meet be-yond the riv-er, Where the surg-es cease to roll?

CHORUS.

Shall we meet, shall we meet, Shall we meet be-yond the riv-er?

3 Shall we meet in yonder city,
   Where the towers of crystal shine?
Where the walls are all of jasper,
   Built by workmanship divine?

4 Where the music of the ransomed
   Rolls its harmony around,
And creation swells the chorus
   With its sweet melodious sound?

5 Shall we meet there many a loved one,
   That was torn from our embrace?
Shall we listen to their voices,
   And behold them face to face?

6 Shall we meet with Christ our Saviour,
   When he comes to claim his own?
Shall we know his blessed favor,
   And sit down upon his throne?

461 Awake, My Soul.

MEDLEY.   Tune, LOVING-KINDNESS. L.M

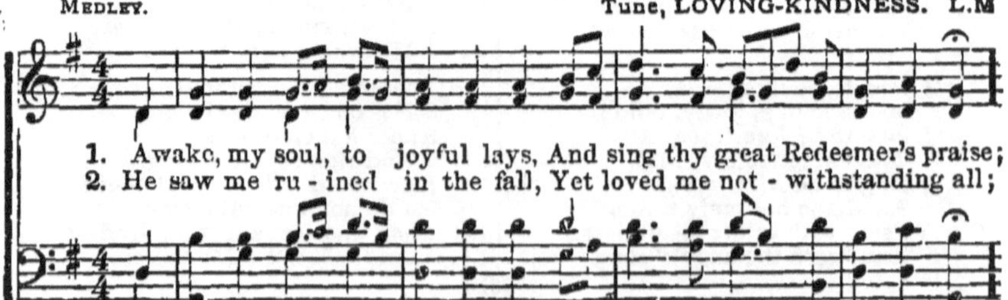

1. Awake, my soul, to joyful lays, And sing thy great Redeemer's praise;
2. He saw me ru-ined in the fall, Yet loved me not-withstanding all;

3 Though num'rous hosts of mighty foes,
Though earth and hell my way oppose,
He safely leads my soul along,
His loving-kindness, oh, how strong!

4 When trouble, like a gloomy cloud,
Has gathered thick, and thundered loud,
He near my soul has always stood,
His loving-kindness, oh, how good!

462 My Faith Looks Up to Thee.

RAY PALMER.   L. MASON.

1 My faith looks up to thee,
Thou Lamb of Calvary,
 Saviour divine!
Now hear me while I pray;
Take all my guilt away;
Oh, let me from this day
 Be wholly thine!

2 May thy rich grace impart
Strength to my fainting heart,
 My zeal inspire!
As thou hast died for me,
Oh, may my love to thee
Pure, warm, amd changeless be—
 A living fire!

3 While life's dark maze I tread,
And griefs around me spread,
 Be thou my guide;
Bid darkness turn to day,
Wipe sorrow's tears away,
Nor let me ever stray
 From thee aside.

4 When ends life's transient dream,
When death's cold sullen stream
 Shall o'er me roll,
Blest Saviour! then, in love,
Fear and distrust remove;
Oh, bear me safe above—
 A ransomed soul!

Orders of Worship

For the Sabbath-school.

These are the Orders of Worship used since 1860 in the Bethany School of Philadelphia; many of them have been greatly blessed.

No. 1.

Superintendent.—Worthy is the Lamb that was slain to receive power, and riches, and wisdom, and strength, and honor, and glory, and blessing.—Rev. v. 12.

Scholars and Teachers.—Him hath God exalted with his right hand to be a Prince and a Saviour, for to give repentance to Israel and forgiveness of sins.—Acts v. 31.

Associate Superintendent.—Let us therefore come boldly unto the throne of grace, that we may obtain mercy, and find grace to help in time of need. Heb. iv. 16.

Silent Prayer.

Superintendent.—Blessed is he whose transgression is forgiven, whose sin is covered.—Psalm xxxii. 1.

Scholars and Teachers.—Blessed is the man unto whom the Lord imputeth not iniquity.—Psalm xxxii. 2

Chant. (All).—1. Lord, thou hast been our dwelling place in | all gene- | ra- tions. ‖ Before the mountains were brought forth, or ever thou hadst formed the earth and the world, even from ever- | lasting to everlasting | Thou art | God.

Creed. (All).

Superintendent.—The Catechism question of the day.

Scholars and Teachers.—The Catechism answer of the day.

All.—Hymn. page 44.

Scripture of the day. (Alternate or otherwise as directed).

Invocation Hymn. No. 324.

Prayer.—Scholars and Teachers repeating.

Hymn. page 15.

Lesson Study.

One Bell.—Giving notice that lessons must close in five minutes.

Two Bells.—Attention—Silence.

Hymns and Notices.

Superintendent's Lesson.

Hymns.

Superintendent.—Grace be to you, and peace from God our Father and from the Lord Jesus Christ.—Galatians i. 3.

Scholars and Teachers.—Who gave himself for our sins: that he might deliver us from this present evil world, according to the will of God and our Father.—Galatians i. 4.

Superintendent.—To him be glory, both now and forever.—2 Peter iii. 18.

All.—Amen.

Last Song.
Hallelujah, thine the glory,
Hallelujah, Amen!
Hallelujah, thine the glory,
Revive us again.

The Lord's Prayer.

School Dismissed.—Singing.

No. 2.

Organ.—Ten minutes before school opens.

Singing: No. 274.
Holy, Holy, Holy! Lord God Almighty!
Early in the morning our song shall rise to thee;
Holy, Holy, Holy! Merciful and Mighty!
God in Three Persons, blessed Trinity!

Superintendent.—Know ye that the Lord he is God; it is he that hath made us, and not we ourselves; we are his people and the sheep of his pasture.

Associate Superintendent.—The Lord is merciful and gracious, slow to anger, and plenteous in mercy.

Officers and Teachers.—God commendeth his love toward us in that, while we were yet sinners, Christ died for us.

Silent prayer.

Superintendent.—He that spared not his own Son, but delivered him up for us all, how shall he not with him also freely give us all things?

School.—God so loved the world, that he gave his only begotten Son, that whosoever believeth in him should not perish, but have everlasting life.

(*To be said responsively.*)

Males.—So teach us to number our days, that we may apply our hearts unto wisdom.

Females.—The fear of the Lord is the beginning of wisdom.

Males.—Thy word is a lamp unto my feet.

Females.—And a light unto my path.

Males.—Order my steps in thy word.

Females—And let not any iniquity have dominion over me.

Bible Class.—Blessed are they that keep his testimonies, and that seek him with the whole heart.

Superintentent.—Blessed are they which do hunger and thirst after righteousness; for they shall be filled.

(*The school will rise.*)

The Apostles' Creed or Ten Commandments.—(Immediately preceding Hymns.)

Choir.—It is a good thing to give thanks unto the Lord, and to sing praises unto thy name, O Most High.

Scripture of the Day.

Invocation. *Hursley, 276.*
Come, gracious Spirit, Heavenly Dove,
With light and comfort from above,
Be thou our guardian, thou our guide,
O'er every thought and step preside.

Prayer.—Ending with Chant, Our Father.

Singing. Page 106.

Missionary Offerings.—During which Organ plays. Then shall be read suitable passages of Scripture.

Catechism.

Notices.

Secrataries.—Whatsoever thy hand findeth to do, do it with thy might; for there is no work, nor device, nor knowledge, nor wisdom, in the grave wither thou goest.

Study.

Golden Text.

Review.

Distribution of Papers, etc.

Singing.

Superintendent.—Here have we no continuing city.

Scholars.—But we seek one to come.

Superintendent.—Blessed are the pure in heart.

Scholars.—For they shall see God.

Superintendent.—Fear not, little flock; for it is your Father's good pleasure to give you the Kingdom.

(*Perfect silence for one minute before any one stirs.*)

No. 3.

Organ.—10 minutes.

First Bell.—Preparation.

Second Bell.—Perfect silence.

Hymn: *America, 252.*
Father, to thee I come,
Owning how weak I am;
Grant thy sustaining arm;
Lead me, I pray.

Silent prayer.

Superintendent.—Have respect, therefore, to the prayer of thy servant, and to his supplication, O Lord, my God. 2 Chron. vi. 19.

School.—Amen.

Superintendent.—That thine eyes may be open upon this house day and night, upon the place whereof thou hast said that thou wouldest put thy name there. 2 Chron. vi. 20.

School.—Amen.

Associate Superintendent.—But will God in very deed dwell with men on the earth? 2 Chron. vi. 18.

Pastor.—Behold the tabernacle of God is with men, and he will dwell with them. Rev. xxi. 3.

Boys.—For thus saith the high and lofty One that inhabiteth eternity, whose name *is* Holy; I dwell in the high and holy *place*. Isa. lvii. 15.

Girls.—With him also *that is* of a contrite and humble spirit. Isa. lvii. 15.

Boys.—If we confess our sins, He is faithful and just to forgive us our sins, and to cleanse us from all unrighteousness. 1 John i. 9.

Girls.—All we like sheep have gone astray; we have turned every one to his own way, and the Lord has laid on him the iniquity of us all. Isa. liii. 6.

Bible Class.—The Lord is merciful and gracious, slow to anger, and plenteous in mercy. Psalm ciii. 1.

Associate Superintendent.—I will sing of mercy and judgement; unto thee, O Lord, will I sing. Psalm ci. 8.

Lord's Prayer.—Chant. No. 348.

Creed.
Catechism.
Golden Text.
Hymn. No. 452.
Superintendent.—And Ezra opened the book in the sight of all the people, and when he opened it all the people stood up. Neh. viii. 5.
Holding up Bibles.
Scripture Lesson.
Invocation. *Sicily, 321.*
  Boys.—Father, let thy benediction,
    Gently falling as the dew,
  Girls.—And thy ever-gracious presence,
    Bless us all this service thro',
    May we ever
    Keep the end of life in view.
Prayer.
Hymn. page 124.
Missionary Offerings.—During which suitable portions of Scripture shall be read—the organ playing softly.
Notices.—Teachers marking roll.
Lesson Study.
Review.
Hymns.
Secretary's time for Distribution.
Superintendent.—In all thy ways acknowledge him, and he shall direct thy paths. Prov. iii. 6.
Scholars.—I will lift up mine eyes unto the hills, from whence cometh my help. Psalm cxxi. 1.
Silent Prayer.—No one stirring for a full minute until the organ plays.

No. 4.

Questions to the Soul! Asked by the Holy Bible. Answers of the Holy Bible.

Anthem. "Onward," (Page 242).
Superintendent, Scripture Question—If God be for us, who can be against us? Rom. viii. 31.
Answer, All.—There shall not any man be able to stand before thee all the days of thy life: As I was with Moses, so I will be with thee; I will not fail thee, nor forsake thee. Joshua i. 5.
Hymn. "Nearer to thee," (Page 65).
Superintendent, Question.—Will God in very deed dwell with men on the earth? 2 Chron. vi. 18.
Boys, Answer.—For thus saith the high and lofty One that inhabiteth eternity, whose name is holy: I dwell in the high and holy place, with him also that is of a contrite and humble spirit. Isa. lvii. 15.
Hymn. "The Lord shall comfort Zion," (Page 245).
Superintendent, Scripture asks.—On whom dost thou trust? Isa. xxxvi. 5.
Girls, Scripture offers for Answer.—The Lord also will be a refuge for the oppressed; a refuge in times of trouble. And they that know thy name will put their trust in thee; for thou, Lord, hast not forsaken them that seek thee. Psalm ix. 9, 10.
Girls. "Art thou in darkness?" (Page 189).
Associate Superintendent, Scripture asks. And who is he that will harm you, if ye be followers of that which is good? 1 Peter iii. 13.
Boys, Answer.—Because thou hast made the Lord, which is my refuge, even the Most High, thy habitation: there shall no evil befall thee, neither shall any plague come nigh thy dwelling. Psalm xci. 9, 10.
Superintendent, Scripture Question.—What must I do to be saved? Acts xvi. 31.
Scripture Answers. "Come unto me, the Saviour said," (Page 48).
Superintendent, Scripture Question.—What saith the Scripture? Rom. iv. 3.
Answer with Golden Text of the Day.
Who like to bring their Bibles, show up!
Give the place of the day's Lesson and the Title.
Hymn. "O heavenly Father, thou hast told," (Page 207).
Read Scriptures in Concert.

(*School rising at tap of bell.*)

Sing. "There is a green hill far away," (Page 240).
Prayer.
Worship in Giving.
Question.—What amount was given last Sabbath, and what for?
Answer, by Treasurer.
Question.—What is the object of to-day's collection?
Answer, by Secretary.
Lesson Study.
Review.
Hymns.
Silent Prayer.

No. 5.

The Scripture Verses embrace the whole of Psalm cxi.

Invocation. *Ellesdie, 267.*

Through thy all atoning merit,
In thy holy name alone,
Weak and helpless, yet believing,
Lord, we come before thy throne.

CHO.—Let thy blessing rest upon us,
Like the early morning dew;
From the wells of thy salvation
May we draw and drink anew.

Silent Prayer.

Hear the prayers that now are rising
On the wings of faith to thee;
Feed our souls that now are hungry
With the bread of life so free.—CHO.

Supt.—Praise ye the Lord. I will praise the Lord with my whole heart, in the assembly of the upright, and in the congregation.

Hymn. "Come, O my soul." (Page 39).

Associate Supt.—The works of the Lord are great, sought out of all them that have pleasure therein.

Boys.—His work is honorable and glorious; and his righteousness endureth forever.

Girls.—He hath made his wonderful works to be remembered: the Lord is gracious and full of compassion.

Bible Class.—He hath given meat unto them that fear him: he will ever be mindful of his covenant.

School.—He hath showed his people the power of his works, that he may give them the heritage of the heathen.

Hymn.—"Stepping in the light," p. 23.

Supt.—The works of his hand are verity and judgement: all his commandments are sure.

Bible Class.—They stand fast forever and ever, and are done in truth and uprightness.

Supt.—He sent redemption unto his people: he hath commanded his covenant for ever: holy and reverend is his name.

School.—The fear of the Lord is the beginning of wisdom: a good understanding have all they that do his commandments: his praise endureth forever.

Hymn. "Awake, awake, O heart of mine." (Page 98).

Supt.—What is the reason we are careful about the Sabbath day?

Girls Answer.—God said, Ye shall keep my Sabbaths, and reverence my sanctuary: I am the Lord. Lev. xxvi. 2.

Supt.—Why do we think so much of the Bible?

All Answer.—All Scripture is given by inspiration of God, and is profitable for doctrine, for reproof, for correction, for instruction in righteousness. 2 Tim. iii. 16.

Supt.—What is the object of this Sunday-school?

Answer, by the Secretary.—To teach the word of God, to bring souls to Christ, to watch over them and build them up in Christian character.

Infant School Hymn.—"More about Jesus would I know." (Page 180).

Supt.—What do we believe upon the Temperance question?

All Answer.—That the only safe ground for ourselves and the best example for our neighbor is total abstinence.

Hymn. Whatsoever burden," (Page 61).

How many attended church this morning?

How many Bibles can the Scholars and Teachers show?

What is title of to-day's lesson?

What chapter and verse will we read it in?

Say the Golden Text.

Hymn. "Up and onward," (Page 130).

Reading of Scriptures.

Hymn.—"Let Him in," page 148.

Short Prayer by Superintendent.

Treasurer states amount of last Sabbath's collection and what given for.

Secretary states object of to-day's collection.

Notices for the week. Music playing softly.

No. 6.

The Keyword is "REMEMBER."

First Signal.—Indicating that everybody must be ready in five minutes for opening of School.

Instrumental Music.

Bell No. 2.—Silence. No walking or talking.

ORDERS OF WORSHIP.

Opening Invocation.—"Hark! hark! my soul!" (Page 19)."
Silent Prayer.
Supt.—*Remember* the word which Moses the servant of the Lord commanded you. Josh i. 13.
Scholars.—*Remember* now thy Creator in the days of thy youth, while the evil days come not, nor the years draw nigh, when thou shalt say, I have no pleasure in them. Eccles. xii. 1.
Choral.—"Blessed be the Fountain of blood." (Page 36).
Supt.—But, beloved, *Remember* ye the words which were spoken before of the apostles of our Lord Jesus Christ. Jude i. 17.
Girls.—*Remember* how he spake unto you when he was yet in Galilee, saying, The Son of man must be delivered into the hands of sinful men, and be crucified, and the third day rise again. Luke xxiv. 6, 7.
Boys.—*Remember* that Jesus Christ of the seed of David was raised from the dead according to my gospel.
Refrain.—"Low in the grave he lay." (Page 164).
Pastor.—*Remember*, that by the space of three years I ceased not to warn every one night and day with tears. Acts xx. 31.
Associate Supt.—*Remember* them which have the rule over you, who have spoken unto you the word of God: whose faith follow, considering the end of their conversation. Heb. xiii. 7.
Teachers.—Son, Remember. Luke xvi. 25.
School.—Remember Lot's wife. Luke xvii. 32.
Infant Room Song—"Only Remembered." (Page 235).
Bible Inspection by Superintendent.
Give title of the day's Lesson study.
State book, chapter, verse.
Recite together Golden Text.
Rise and Sing.—"We shall know." (Page 172).
Scripture Lesson Read.
Apostles' Creed.
The Lord's Prayer. (No. 348).
Supt.—*Remember* the words of the Lord Jesus, how he said, It is more blessed to give than to receive. Acts xx. 35.
Associate Supt. and School Ask.—What was amount of last Sabbath's collection, and what was it for?
Answer, by Treasurer.
Teachers.—What is the object of to-day's collection?
Answer by Secretary.
Choir sings while Classes gather the offering. "I'll live for him." (No. 263).
Doors open during singing.
Notices.
Pastor.—State chief idea of the day's lesson.
All fold hands, and remain seated, leaning forward as an act of worship, while the Superintendent prays.
Hymns.—If time allows.
Class Studies.
Closing Worship.—Hymns.
Review by either Pastor or one of the Superintendents.
Secretaries' distributions.
Last Bell.—All rise, engaging in prayer for one minute.
Choir sings while School retires.

No. 7.

Cornet Signal Call.—School will open in five minutes.—Be ready.
Five Minutes Musical Recital.
First Bell.—Perfect silence, no walking, no talking, no changing seats, no chair moving.
Silent Prayer.
Anthem.—No. 1. in "Anthems and Voluntaries."

All.
Praise the Lord our God, praise the Lord our God,
He that is,
He that was,
And is to come;
Praise his holy name, praise his holy name,
Praise his holy name who giveth us eternal life:

Girls—Infant Room.
His be the honor, and majesty, and glory;
His be the honor, and majesty, and glory,

Girls.
Worship and adore him, worship and adore him,
Worship and adore him, now and evermore:

All.
Worship and adore him, worship and adore him,
Worship and adore him, now and evesmore :
Praise him, praise him, glory to God;
Praise him, praise him, glory to God, praise him,
praise him.

Supt.—Wherewithal shall a young man cleanse his way? Psalm cxix. 9.

ORDERS OF WORSHIP.

School.—By taking heed thereto according to THY WORD. Psalm cxix. 9.
Pastor.—THY WORD have I hid in mine heart, that I might not sin against thee. Psalm cxix. 11.
Associate Supt.—So shall I have wherewith to answer him that reproacheth me—for I trust in THY WORD. Psalm cxix. 43.
School.—I thought on my ways and turned my feet unto THY TESTIMONIES. Psalm cxix. 59.
Hymn. "Jesus, lover of my soul." (Page 386).
Bible Showing.
State the title of the lesson of the day.
Give book, chapter, verse.
Say in concert the Golden Text.
While each one is finding chapter and verses, sing page 94, 'Anthems and Voluntaries.'

Girls.
Let not your heart be troubled,
All.
Let not your heart be troubled,
Girls.
Ye believe in God, believe also in me,
All.
Ye believe in God, believe also in me.
Boys.
In my Father's house are many mansions ;
Girls.
Are many mansions, are many mansions :
Choir.
If it were not so, I would have told you.
All.
I go to prepare a place for you,
Girls.
And if I go and prepare a place for you,
All.
I will come again, I will come again,
Girls.
And receive you unto myself
Boys.
That where I am,
Girls.
There ye may be also,
Boys.
That where I am,
Girls.
There ye may be also.
All.
That where I am, that where I am,
There ye may be also.
And whither I go ye know,
Girls.
And the way ye know.
All.
And whither I go ye know,
Girls.
And the way ye know,
All.
And the way, the way ye know.

Choristers.
Thomas saith unto him, Lord, we know not whither thou goest;
And how can we know the way?
Choir.
Jesus saith unto him,
All.
I am the way, the truth, and the life,
I am the way, the truth, and the life,
I am the way, the truth, and the life,
The way, the truth, the life:
No man cometh unto the Father,
No man cometh unto the Father, but by me but by me, but by me.

Reading Scriptures.
Scripture Response. (Page 114).
Creed.
The Lord's Prayer. Chant, (No. 348).
Treasurer states amount of last Sabbath's collection?
Secretary states object of to-day's collection.
Worship in Giving.—Scripture encouragements by the Superintendent or Pastor.
Notices for the Week.—Music playing softly
Hymn. "Jesus, I come to thee." (Page 25).
Short Prayer by Supt.
Hymn. If time allows.
Class Studies.
Closing Worship.—Hymns.
Review by either Pastor or one of the Superintendents.
Secretaries' distributions.
Last Bell.—All rise, engaging in prayer for one minute.
Choir sings while School retires.

No. 8.

Cornet Signal Call.—School will open in five minutes.—Be ready.
Five Minutes Musical Recital.
Second Bell.—Perfect silence, no walking, no talking, no changing seats, no chair moving.
Silent Prayer.
Hymn. "I will sing when morning cometh." (Page 24).
Supt.—How amiable are thy tabernacles O Lord of hosts! Psalm lxxxiv. 1.
Pastor.—My soul longeth, yea, even fainteth for the courts of the Lord: my heart and my flesh crieth out for the living God. Psalm lxxxiv. 3.

ORDERS OF WORSHIP.

Bible Class.—Yea, the sparrow hath found a house, and the swallow a nest for herself, where she may lay her young, even thine altars, O Lord of hosts, my King, and my God.

Hymn. "O give thanks." (Page 28).

Supt.—Blessed are they that dwell in thy house; they will be still praising thee.

Scholars.—Blessed is the man whose strength is in thee: in whose heart are the ways of them. Ps. lxxxiv. 5.

Associate Supt.—Who passing through the Valley of Baca make it a well; the rain also filleth the pools.

Bible Class.—They go from strength to strength, every one of them in Zion appeareth before God. Ps lxxxiv. 7.

Hymn. "I've been to the field with the reapers." (Page 185).

Associate Supt.—O Lord God of hosts, hear my prayer; give ear, O God of Jacob. Selah. Psalm lxxxiv. 8.

Bible Class.—Behold, O God, our shield, and look upon the face of thine anointed. Psalm lxxxiv. 9

Door Keepers.—For a day in thy courts is better than a thousand. I had rather be a doorkeeper in the house of my God, than to dwell in the tents of wickedness. Psalm lxxxiv. 10.

Teacher of Bible Class.—For the Lord God is a sun and a shield: the Lord will give grace and glory: no good thing will he withhold from them that walk uprightly. Psalm lxxxiv. 11.

Scholars.—O Lord of hosts, blessed is the man that trusteth in thee.

Infant School Hymn "Leading souls to Jesus." (Page 162).

The Apostles' Creed.

The Lord's Prayer. (No. 348).

Echo Song by Quartet. "Who is this that waiteth." (Page 140). Last verse and chorus by School.

Bible Showing.

State the Title of the Lesson of the day.

Give book, chapter, verse.

Say in concert the Golden Text.

While each one is finding chapter and verses, sing "In thy book where glory bright," page 21.

Scriptures read.

Scripture Response. (Page 114).

Worship by Offerings.

Supt.—Blessed is he that considereth the poor; the Lord will deliver him in time of trouble. Psalm xli. 1.

Associate Supt. leads the School, who asks the following:—The Treasurer will please report the amount of the collection of last Sabbath, and what it was for?

The Treasurer reports promptly.

The Secretary States—The object of today's collection is——

Notices.

Pastor.—State chief idea of the day's lesson.

All fold hands, and remain seated, leaning forward as an act of worship, while the Superintendent prays.

Hymn. If time allows.

Class Studies.

Closing Worship.—Hymns.

Review by either Pastor or one of the Superintendents.

Secretaries' distributions.

Last Bell.—All rise, engaging in prayer for one minute.

No. 9.

Opening Anthem. — "The Earth is the Lord's." page 236.

Supt.—I was glad when they said unto me, Let us go into the house of the Lord.

Chant—The Lord's Prayer. No. 348.

Repeat The Apostles' Creed.

How many Bibles can we show?

Title of Lesson.

Golden Text.

Where is the Lesson found?

Hymn. "Onward and upward," page 74

Read Scripture for the day's study.

Invocation Song. Tune 385.

    Jesus, thou art all compassion,
    Pure, unbounded love thou art;
    Visit us with thy salvation,
    Enter every trembling heart.

Prayer.

Hymn.—"His yoke is easy," page 27.

Missionary Offering, while organ plays softly, and the superintendent reads suitable portions of Scripture.

Notices of the day and week, rolls marked.

Class Studies.

Review by Pastor or Superintendents.

Hymns.

Secretaries' Distribution.

Bell calls all to rise for parting salutations.

ORDERS OF WORSHIP.

No. 10.
The JOY Order of Worship.

Second Bell.—Perfect silence, no one to move.

Hymn—"I will bless the Lord." p. 138.

Supt. Break forth into JOY, sing together, ye waste places of Jerusalem: for the Lord hath comforted his people, he hath redeemed Jerusalem. Is. 52: 9.

Hymn. "Sing on," page 76.

Supt.— . . Therefore will I offer in his tabernacle sacrifices of JOY; I will sing, yea, I will sing praises unto the Lord. Ps. 27: 6.

School.—He shall pray unto God, and he will be favorable unto him: and he shall see his face with JOY: for he will render unto man his righteousness. Job 33: 26.

Pastor. For ye shall go out with JOY, and be led forth with peace: the mountains and the hills shall break forth before you into singing, and all the trees of the field shall clap their hands. Isa. 55: 12.

School.—And the angel said unto them, Fear not; for, behold, I bring you good tidings of great JOY, which shall be to all people. Lu. 2: 10.

Associate Supt.—Thy word was unto me the JOY and rejoicing of mine heart.

Infant Room Song.

Supt.—And these things write we unto you, that your JOY may be full.

Boys.—Hitherto have ye asked nothing in my name: ask, and ye shall receive, that your JOY may be full.

Girls.—Looking unto Jesus, the author and finisher of our faith; who, for the JOY that was set before him, endured the cross, despising the shame, and is set down at the right hand of the throne of God. Heb. 12: 2.

Associate Supt.—But the fruit of the Spirit is love, JOY, peace, longsuffering, gentleness, goodness, faith, meekness, temperance: against such there is no law. Gal. 5: 22, 23.

How many Bibles can we show?

Title of Lesson.

Golden Text.

Where is the Lesson found?

Pastor.—State chief idea of the day's lesson.

Hymn. "With our colors waving," p. 11.

Read Scripture for the day's study.

Silent Prayer for one minute

Hymn. "Casting your care." p. 105.

Repeat The Apostles' Creed.

Chant—The Lord's Prayer. No. 348.

Supt.—Give and it shall be given unto you; good measure, pressed down and shaken together, and running over, shall men give into your bosom. For with the same measure ye mete withal, it shall be measured to you again. Lu. 6: 38.

Associate Supt. and School ask—What was the amount of last Sabbath's collection, and what was it for.

The Treasurer reports promptly.

The Secretary States—The object of to-day's collection is——

Choir sings while Classes gather the offering.

Notices.

Hymn. "By the grace of God." p 196.

All fold hands, and remain seated, leaning forward as an act of worship, while the Superintendent prays.

Hymn. If time allows.

Class Studies.

Closing Worship.—Hymns.

Review by either Pastor or one of the Superintendents.

Secretaries' distributions.

Last Bell.—All rise, engaging in prayer for one minute.

Choir sings while school retires.

No. 11.

Cornet Signal Call.—School will open in five minutes.

Second tap of bell exactly on the minute of school opening time.

Hymn. "O could I speak." No 366.

Supt.—What shall we say of God's care of us during the past week?

Sing.—"Light in our darkness." page 43

Supt.—Is the Christian life a happy life?

Sing.—"Since I have been." Page 79.

Supt.—What is the cause of the Christian's happiness?

Sing.—"Treasures in heaven." Page 204.

Supt.—What can you say for your Saviour?

Sing—"Trusting in Jesus," page 10.

Infant Room Hymn, selected.

ORDERS OF WORSHIP.

Supt.—What is it to become a Christian?
Sing—"Trusting Jesus." page 45.
Who have brought their Bibles?
Where is the Day's Lesson?
What is its Title?
Who can tell the Golden Text?
What do we believe? Apostles' Creed.
Read the Scriptures.
Hymn. "The Firm Foundation" p. 359.
Prayer.
Worship in Giving.
What was last Sabbath's Collection for, and the Amount?
What is the object of to-day's Collection?
Notices of the day and week, rolls marked.
Class Studies.
Review by Pastor or Superintendents.
Hymns and Parting Prayer.
Good-byes.

No. 12.
HOW TO BE HAPPY.

Opening Anthem.—From "The Joyful Sound," 138. If preferred use instead "He Comes," page 154.

All.
Awake, awake, with cheerful heart and voice,
  To Zion's God our sweetest anthem raise;
Awake, awake, let heav'n and earth rejoice,
  And shout aloud in tuneful strain
    Jehovah's praise.

Girls.
He crowns the year with mercy,
  He fills our cup with joy,
His love is everlasting,
  Let praise our tongues employ;
He cheers the path before us,
  And makes it bright with flowers.

Primary Department.
He is watching kindly o'er us,
  Bending low our song to hear;
And we know with ev'ry moment
  Guardian angels hover near.

All.
Joyful, joyful, glorify his name.
  Now in his temple grateful homage pay;
Hail him, hail him, join the loud acclaim,
  Sing hallelujah, worship him to-day.
Shout, shout aloud, come with one accord,
  Sing hallelujah, praise ye the Lord.

Supt.—HAPPY is that people whose God is the Lord. Ps. 144: 15.
School.—HAPPY is he that hath the God of Jacob for his help, whose hope is in the Lord his God. Ps. 146: 5.
Hymn.   *Tune Henley.*
Come unto me when shadows darkly gather,
  When the sad heart is weary and distressed,
Seeking for comfort from your heavenly Father;
  Come unto me, and I will give you rest.

Large are the mansions in thy Father's dwelling,
  Glad are the homes that sorrows never dim,
Sweet are the harps in holy music swelling,
  Soft are the tones which raise the heavenly hymn
There, like an Eden blossoming in gladness,
  Bloom the fair flowers the earth too rudely pressed;
Come unto me, all ye who droop in sadness,
  Come unto me, and I will give you rest.

Boys.—HAPPY is the man that findeth wisdom, and the man that getteth understanding. Prov. 3: 13.
Girls.—And HAPPY is every one that retaineth her. Prov. 3: 18.
Hymn—"Saviour, comfort me," page 65.
Associate Supt.—Whoso trusteth in the Lord HAPPY is he. Prov. 16: 20.
Hymn.—"Softly and tenderly," page 200.
Supt.—He that keepeth the law HAPPY is he. Prov. 29: 18
Hymn.—"The Altered Motto." page 255.
Bible Classes.—HAPPY is the man that feareth always: but he that hardeneth his heart shall fall into mischief.
Infant Room Hymn, selected.
Hymn. "The Saviour with Me." p. 121.
Distance Song. page 102.
Bibles—Hold them up.
Title of Lesson.
Golden Text.
Where is the Lesson found?
Hymn. "The Summer land," page 118.
Read Scripture for the day's study.
Pastor. If ye know these things, HAPPY are ye if ye do them. Jn 13: 17.
Chant—The Lord's Prayer. No. 348.
Associate Supt. and School ask—What was the amount of last Sabbath's collection, and what was it for.
The Treasurer reports promptly.
The Secretary States—The object of to-day's collection is——
Notices.
Class Studies.

No. 13.
THE COMMANDMENTS.

Cornet Signal Call.—School will open in five minutes.
Second Bell.—Perfect silence, no one to move.
Invocation—"Great is the Lord," p. 202.
Silent Prayer for one minute
Sing "Beautiful day," page 18.
Supt.—Know therefore this day, and consider it in thine heart, that the Lord

ORDERS OF WORSHIP.

he is God in heaven above, and upon the earth beneath; there is none else. Deut. 4: 39.

Associate Supt.—And Moses called all Israel, and said unto them, Hear, O Israel, the statutes and judgments which I speak in your ears this day, that ye may learn them, and keep, and do them. Deut. 5: 1.

The Ten Commandments.—page 249.

Pastor.—Ye shall walk in all the ways which the Lord your God hath commanded you, that ye may live, and that it may be well with you, and that ye may prolong your days in the land which ye shall possess.

Teacher.—Ye have said, It is vain to serve God; and what profit is it that we have kept his ordinance, and that we have walked .. before the Lord of hosts? Mal. 3: 14.

Girls.—And they shall be mine, saith the Lord of hosts, in that day when I make up my jewels, and I will spare them, as a man spareth his own son that serveth him. Mal. 3: 17.

Boys.—Then shall ye .. discern between the righteous and the wicked, between him that serveth God and him that serveth him not. Mal. 3: 18.

Primary Dept.—"Little ones," page 183.

Repeat The Apostles' Creed.

Chant.—The Lord's Prayer. No. 348.

Supt.—Wherewithal shall a young man cleanse his way?

Scholars.—By taking heed thereto according to thy word. Ps. 119: 9.

Bibles—Hold them up.

Title of Lesson.

Teachers give Golden Text of the day.

Where is the Lesson found?

Hymn. "Light after darkness," p 135.

As the last verse is being sung, at tap of bell school will rise, and with books open be ready to read the Scriptures, and when last verse is read, close books, and hold them in hands, and sing:—(page 241)

Glory be to the Father, glory be to the Son, glory be to the Holy Ghost.
Girls.
As it was in the beginning, is now, and ever shall be,
All.
World without end Amen, amen.

Sentence Prayer, following Superintendent.

The worship of making offerings to the Lord, and verses of exhortation.

Choir.—"Cast thy bread." page 31.

Notices for the coming week.

Hymn. If time allows.

Class Studies.

Review by Pastor or Superintendents.

Hymns and Parting Prayer.

No. 14.

The Key word is HOLD.

Cornet Signal Call.—School will open in five minutes.

Second Bell.—Perfect silence, no one to move.

Hymn.—"I will praise him," page 206.

Supt.—HOLD FAST the form of sound words, which thou hast heard of me, in faith and love which is in Christ Jesus. 2 Tim. 1: 13.

Associate Supt.—Prove all things; HOLD FAST that which is good. 1 Th. 1: 13.

School.—Seeing then we have a great high priest, that is passed into the heavens, Jesus the Son of God, let us HOLD FAST our profession. He. 4.

Hymn. "God bless our," page 53.

Supt.—HOLD thou me up, and I shall be safe; and I shall have respect unto thy statutes continually. Ps. 119: 117.

Boys.—The righteous also shall hold on his way, and he that hath clean hands shall be stronger and stronger.

Girls.—HOLD UP my goings in thy paths, that my footsteps slip not. Ps. 17: 5.

Boys.—Even there shall thy hand lead me, and thy right hand shall HOLD me. Ps. 139: 10.

Pastor.—For I the Lord thy God WILL HOLD thy right hand, saying unto thee, Fear not, I will help thee.

Associate Supt.—Remember, therefore, how thou hast received and heard, and HOLD FAST, and repent. If, therefore, thou shalt not watch, I will come on thee as a thief, and thou shalt not know what hour I shall come upon thee. Rev. 3: 3.

Hymn.—"All the day, in sweet," p. 220.

Prayer. Led by Superintendent.

(Everybody in a reverent attitude, seated with folded hands, closed eyes, and bowing before the Heavenly Father.—Particular attention to this very earnestly desired.)

ORDERS OF WORSHIP.

Worship in Giving.
☞ At sound of bell scholars will ask,
What was last Sabbath's Collection for, and the Amount?
Answer by the Treasurer.
What is the object of to-day's Collection?
Answer by the Secretary.

School.—I the Lord have called thee in righteousness, and will HOLD thine hand, and will keep thee, and give thee for a covenant of the people, for a light of the Gentiles. Isa. 42: 6.

Bible Class.—Yea, he shall be holden up; for God is able to make him stand.

Young Men's Bible Class.—Let us hold fast the profession of our faith without wavering; for he is faithful that promised. Heb. 10: 23.

School.—Behold, I come quickly; HOLD that fast which thou hast, that no man take thy crown. Rev. 3: 11.

Infant Room Song.
The Apostles' Creed.
The Lord's Prayer. No. 348.
Who have brought their Bibles?
Title of the Day's Lesson.
Pastor.—State chief idea of the day's lesson.
Who can tell the Golden Text?
Book, Chapter, Verses for the day.
Hymn.—"Trust and obey." page 117.
All will rise at beginning of last chorus, be ready to read.
Read Scripture for the day's study.
Silent Prayer for one minute.
Resume seats when bell rings.
Notices of the day and week, rolls marked.
Hymn. Selected.
Class Studies.
Closing Hymns.
Birthday Texts.
Questions and Answers, verbal or written, and laid on desk).
Hymn. Selected.
Review by either Pastor or one of the Superintendents.
Secretaries' distributions.
Last Bell.—All rise, engaging in prayer for one minute.
Choir sings while school retires.

No. 15.

This order includes all of the 34th Psalm. Almost any one can commit to memory these beautiful verses, and can have a psalm in his heart.

Opening Anthem.— From "*The Banner Anthem Book*," page 16. Or, if preferred, a hymn in this book.
Girls.
Know ye that the Lord he is God, he is God: It is he that hath made us, and not we ourselves: We are his people, and the sheep of his pasture.
Quartet.
Enter into his gates with thanksgiving, And into his courts with praise.
All.
Know ye that the Lord he is God, he is God: It is he that hath made us, and not we ourselves: We are his people, and the sheep of his pasture. Amen, amen.

Supt.—I will bless the Lord at all times his praise shall continually be in my mouth.

1st Associate Supt.—My soul shall make her boast in the Lord: the humble shall hear thereof, and be glad.

2nd Associate Supt.—O magnify the Lord with me, and let us exalt his name together.

3d Associate Supt.—I sought the Lord, and he heard me, and delivered me from all my fears.

4th Associate Supt.—They looked unto him, and were lightened; and their faces were not ashamed.

Boys.—This poor man cried, and the Lord heard him, and saved him out of all his troubles. The angel of the Lord encampeth round about them that fear him, and delivereth them.

Girls.—O taste and see that the Lord is good: blessed is the man that trusteth in him. O fear the Lord, ye his saints; for there is no want to them that fear him.

Bible Class.—The young lions do lack, and suffer hunger: but they that seek the Lord shall not want any good thing.

Supt.—Come, ye children, hearken unto me: I will teach you the fear of the Lord. What man is he that desireth life, and loveth many days, that he may see good.

Girls.—Keep thy tongue from evil, and thy lips from speaking guile.

Boys.—Depart from evil, and do good; seek peace, and pursue it.

Secretary.—The eyes of the Lord are upon the righteous, and his ears are open unto their cry.

Bible Class.—The face of the Lord is against them that do evil, to cut off the remembrance of them from the earth.

ORDERS OF WORSHIP.

Pastor.—The righteous cry, and the Lord heareth, and delivereth them out of all their troubles.

School.—The Lord is nigh unto them that are of a broken heart; and saveth such as be of a contrite spirit. Many are the afflictions of the righteous: but the Lord delivereth him out of them all. He keepeth all his bones: not one of them is broken. Evil shall slay the wicked: and they that hate the righteous shall be desolate. Psa. 34: 18–21.

Supt.—The Lord redeemeth the soul of his servants: and none of them that trust in him shall be desolate.

Anthem. "*Banner Anthem Book,*" *page 35.*
Girls.   Boys.   All.
How holy, how holy, how holy is this place!
All.
Lord, I have loved the place of thine abode.
Girls.
Lord, I have loved the place of thine abode,
All.
And the temple where thy glory dwelleth.
Primary Department.
Lord, I have loved the place of thine abode,
All.   Primary Dept.
Have loved the place, Have loved the place of
All.   [thine abode.
And the temple where thy glory dwelleth.
Girls.   All.
Thy glory dwelleth.   Amen, amen, amen.

Bibles—Hold them up.
Where is the Lesson found?
Title of Lesson.
Golden Text.
Anthem. "*Banner Anthem Book,*" *page 18.*
Girls.
Teach me, O Lord, the way of thy statutes,
Boys.   Girls.
Teach me, O Lord, Teach me, O Lord, the way
                   of thy statutes; and I shall
Boys.   keep it unto the end.
Unto the end.   *Girls.*
                   Give me understanding,
All.   and I shall keep thy law;
Yea, I shall observe it with my whole heart.
Amen, amen, amen.

Read from Bibles the Lesson of the day.
Invocation Hymn. *Girls only.* "In the hour of trial." Page 133.
Prayer.
Worship in giving.
What was last Sabbath's Collection for, and the amount? Answer by treasurer.
What is the object of to-day's Collection? Answered by the secretary.
Notices for the coming week.
Class Studies.

Review by Pastor or Superintendent.
Hymns and Parting Prayer.

No. 16.

"*THESE SAYINGS OF MINE.*"

Opening Anthem. "*Anthems and Voluntaries,*" *page 52.*
All.
I was glad when they said unto me,
Let us go up to the house of the Lord.
Infant School.
Our feet shall stand within thy gates,
Choir.   All.   Girls.
O Jerusalem, O Jerusalem, Our feet shall stand
Choir.   Girls.   within thy gates,
O Jerusalem, O Jerusalem. *Alto and Tenor.*
              Pray for the peace of Jerusalem.
Girls.   All.
They shall prosper   That love thee.
Boys.   Girls.   Choir.
‖: Peace be within thy walls, :‖
All.
Peace be within thy walls, and prosperity within
thy palaces.   *Choir.   All.*
                Amen,   amen,

Silent Prayer at tap of bell—one minute.

Supt.—My son, attend to my words, incline thine ear unto my SAYINGS.

School.—Whosoever heareth these sayings of mine, and DOETH THEM, I will liken him unto a wise man, which built his house upon a rock. And the rain descended, and the floods came, and the winds blew, and beat upon that house; and it fell not, for it was founded upon a rock.

Supt.—And every one that heareth these sayings of mine, and DOETH THEM NOT, shall be likened unto a foolish man, which built his house upon the sand. And the rain descended, and the floods came, and the winds blew, and beat upon that house; and it fell: and great was the fall of it.

Boys.—And it came to pass when Jesus had ended THESE SAYINGS the people were astonished at his doctrine.

Girls.—For he taught them as one having authority, and not as the scribes.

Pastor.—But while they wondered every one at all things which Jesus did, he said unto his disciples, Let THESE SAYINGS sink down into your ears.

School.—Jesus answered and said unto him, If a man love me, he will keep my words; and my Father will love him, and we will come unto him, and make our abode with him. He that loveth me not keepeth not my SAYINGS. John 14: 23, 24.

Primary Dept.— This is a faithful saying and worthy of all acceptation that Christ Jesus came into the world to save sinners. 1 Tim. 1: 15.

Infant Room Song

Associate Supt.—These sayings are faithful and true: and the Lord God of the holy prophets sent his angel to shew unto his servants the things which must shortly be done. Rev. 22

Bible Class.—Behold, I come quickly, blessed is he that keepeth the SAYINGS of the prophecy of this book.

Supt.— Blessed are they that do his commandments, that they may have right to the tree of life, and may enter in through the gates into the city. Rev. 22: 14.

School rise and all sing, "What shall separate us?" page 88.

The Apostles' Creed.

The Lord's Prayer. No. 348.

Supt.—Whatsoever things were written aforetime were written for our learning, that WE, through patience and comfort of the Scriptures, might have hope. Rom. 20: 1.

Who have brought their Bibles?

Title of Day's Lesson. Golden Text.

Book, Chapter, Verses for the day.

Hymn.—"Tell me the story." Page 51.

Read the Scriptures.

Doxology. (page 241)

Sentence Prayer, led by Superintendent.

Collection—verses of exhortation read.

Notices of the day and week, rolls marked.

Hymn. "The child of a King," page 72.

Class Studies.

Closing Exercises as in Order No. 14.

No. 17.

Opening Hymn. "Bless the Lord," p. 56.

Silent Prayer for one minute.

Supt. — Hearken unto me, ye that know righteousness, the people in whose heart is my law; fear ye not the reproach of men, neither be ye afraid of their revilings. Isa. 51: 7.

Associate Supt. — Ye are my witnesses, saith the Lord, and my servant whom I have chosen; Fear ye not, neither be afraid. Isa. 43: 10; 44: 8.

School.—O bless our God, ye people, and make the voice of his praise to be heard. Psa. 66: 8.

All Sing "Praise ye the Lord," page 232.

Supt.—I have set watchmen upon thy walls, O Jerusalem, which shall never hold their peace day nor night; ye that make mention of the Lord, keep not silence. Isa. 62: 6.

School. — Go through, go through the gates; prepare ye the way of the people; cast up, cast up the highway; lift up a standard for the people.

Boys.—And as ye go, preach, saying, The kingdom of heaven is at hand.

Girls.—Preach the word; be instant in season, out of season; reprove, rebuke, exhort, with all longsuffering and doctrine. 2 Tim. 4: 2.

Associate Supt. And fear not them which kill the body, but are not able to kill the soul. . . Whosoever shall confess me before men, him will I confess also before my Father which is in heaven. Mat. 10: 28, 32.

Hymn. "He will hide me," page 132.

Supt.—Say to them that are of a fearful heart, Be strong, fear not; behold, your God will come with vengeance, even God with a recompense; he will come and save you. Isa. 35: 4.

Bible Class.—There shall not any man be able to stand before thee all the days of thy life; as I was with Moses, so I will be with thee. I will not fail thee nor forsake thee. Josh. 1: 5.

Infant Room Song.

Repeat The Apostles' Creed.

Hymn. Selected.

How many Bibles can we show?

Where is the Lesson found?

Golden Text.

Supt.—Behold, I have longed after thy precepts; quicken me in thy righteousness. Psa. 119: 40.

School.—So shall I keep thy law continually, for ever and ever.

Rise and Sing *Bera, 302.*
   The heavens declare thy glory, Lord;
   In every star thy wisdom shines,
   But when our eyes behold thy word,
   We read thy name in fairer lines.

Read Scripture for the day's study.

Sentence Prayer, led by Superintendent, closing with The Lord's Prayer, 343.

Worship in Giving.

Notices for the week.

Hymn. Selected.

Class Studies.

Closing Exercises as in Order No. 14.

INDEX.

Titles in CAPITALS; Metrical Tunes in *Italic*; First lines in Roman.

First line / Title	HYMN
Abide with me, fast falls the even-	254
A BLESSING IN PRAYER,	91
Abundant salvation thro' Jesus I.	205
According to thy gracious word,	368
A charge to keep I have,	334
A Christian band from far and	108
A few more years shall roll,	445
A HANDFUL OF LEAVES,	190
Alas! and did my Saviour bleed,	22, 370
Alida, C. M. D.	433
A little talk with Jesus.	68
All for Jesus! all for Jesus!	451
All hail the power of Jesus'	345
All the day in sweet communion,	220
Along the River of Time we glide	120
ALWAYS ABOUNDING,	159
America,	252
Am I a soldier of the cross,	396
Amsterdam, 7s, 6s, D.	342
Angels above are singing,	71
Angelus, 7s, 6s,	458
ANNIVERSARY SONG OF PRAISE,,	201
Another six day's work is done,	456
Antioch, C. M.	346
Anywhere with Jesus,	67
Approach, my soul, the mercy	407
ARE YOU READY?.	59
Ariel,	366
Arlington, C. M.	394
Art thou in darkness?	189
Art thou weary, art thou	233
ASKING.	207
Asleep in Jesus! blessed	302
As pants the hart,	285
As the twilight shadows fall,	373
AT THE CROSS,	22
AT THE DOOR.	226
At the sounding of the trumpet	222
Avon, C. M.	368
Awake, awake; O heart of mine	98
Awake, awake, our festive day is.	97
Awake! awake! O Zion lift thy.	154
Awake, awake! the Master.	96
Awake, my soul, in joyful lays,	461
Awake, my soul, stretch every	295
Balerma, C. M.	398
BATTLING FOR THE LORD,	63
Beautiful day, lovely thy light,	18
BEAUTIFUL HOME,	128
BEAUTIFUL ROBES,	156
Be earnest, my brother, in word	159
Before Jehovah's awful throne	279
Begone, unbelief, my Saviour	357
Behold a stranger at the door,	49
BEHOLD THE FIELDS ARE WHITE,.	110
Beneath Moriah's rocky side,	397
Bera, L. M.	302
BEULAH LAND,	178
Beyond the smiling and the.	260
Blessed assurance, Jesus is mine!	147
Blessed be the fountain,	36
Blessed Bible! how I love it!	186
BLESS THE LORD, MY SOUL,	56
Blest are the pure in heart,	338
Blest be the tie that binds,	443
Blow ye the trumpet, blow;	281
Boyleston, S. M.	330
BRINGING IN THE SHEAVES,	89
Brother, you've come to the Lord,	131
By cool Siloam's shady rill,	408
By faith the Lamb of God I see,	296
BY GRACE I WILL,	155
BY THE GRACE OF GOD WE'LL	196
CALLING, GENTLY CALLING,	211
Calm me, my God,	414
CALVARY,	165
CASTING YOUR CARE UPON HIM,	105
Cast thy bread upon the waters,	31
CAST THY BURDEN ON THE LORD,	149
Child of God, be not discouraged,	105
Children of the heavenly King,	361
CHRIST AROSE,	164
CHRISTIAN ENDEAVOR SONG,	182
CHRIST IS ALL,	152
Christmas, C. M.	295
Church of God, whose conquering	124
CHURCH RALLYING SONG,	96
COME,	224
Come, every pious heart,	282
Come hither, all ye weary souls,	313
Come, Holy Spirit, calm my mind	292
Come, Holy Spirit, come, let thy.	425
Come, Holy Spirit, come, with en-	331
Come home! come home! you are	103
Come, humble sinner, in whose	371
Come, my Redeemer, come and	317
Come, my soul, thy suit prepare,	360
Come, oh, come with me where	192
Come, O my soul, in sacred lays,	284
Come, O my soul, my every pow-	89
Come, said Jesus' sacred voice,	372
Come, thou fount of every blessing	318
Come unto me, the Saviour said,	48
Come, we that love the Lord,	427
Come with all thy sorrow,	298
Come, ye sinners, poor and needy,	64
Come, ye that love the Saviour's.	389
COMING HOME,	136
Conquering now and to conquer,	6
CONSECRATION.	107
Coronation, C. M.	344
CROWN HIM,	203

347

Dark are the waters before me,	177
Delay not, delay not, O sinner,	358
Dennis, S. M.	443
Depth of mercy, can there be	375
Did Christ o'er sinners weep?	446
Dorrnance, C. M.	385
Down at the cross where my Sav-.	99
Down life's dark vale we wander,	35
Downs, C. M.	447
Do you hear that gentle whisper,	181
Do you know what makes us hap-	111
DRAW ME TO THEE,	44
Dundee, C. M.	401
EDEN SHORE,	219
Ellesdie, 8s, 7s, D.	267
Eltham, 7s, 6s, D.	341
ENTIRE CONSECRATION,	69
Eternity, where,	101
Evan, C. M.	413
Ere another Sabbath close,	379
EVEN ME,	87
Ewing, 7s, 6s,	346
Fade, fade, each earthly joy,	262
Fading away like the dew of the	235
FAITHFUL UNTO DEATH,	130
Far away my steps have wandered	37
Father all holy,	1
Father, a weary heart	421
Father! I know that all	438
Father, whate'er of earthly bliss.	256
Federal street, L. M.	311
For Christ and the church,	80
Forest, L. M.	287
Forever with the Lord,	419
Frederick, 11s,	316
From every stormy wind that	304
From Greenland's icy mountains,	300
GATHERING HOME,	66
Geneva, C. M.	439
Gentle Jesus, meek and mild,	374
Gently, Lord, oh, gently lead us,	268
Gifts we bring to our King,	33
GIVE ME JESUS,	58
Give me the wings of faith to rise	297
Glory be to the Father, and to the	261
Glory be to the Father, glory be to	241
GLORY TO HIS NAME,	99
Glory to Jesus who died on the	143
Go and tell Jesus, O desolate	193
God be with thee, God be with,	231
God be with you till we meet a-	151
God bless our Sabbath School,	53
God calling yet! shall I not hear	212
God has blessd us without meas-.	201
God loved the world so tenderly,	42
GOD'S HOLY CHURCH SHALL TRI-.	134
Go, labor on,	294
Goshen,	356
Grace! 'tis a charming sound	336
Gracious Spirit, love divine,	376
Great is the Lord, the Prince of	128
Great is the Lord, who ruleth,	202
Guide me, O thou great Jehovah!	380
Hail! glorious company to Zion's	114
Hail to the Lord's Anointed,	301
Hamburg, L. M.	290
Hark! hark! my soul,	19
Hark, my soul, it is the Lord,	362
Hark! the herald angels sing,	299
Hark, the song of holy rapture,	92
Hasten, Lord, the glorious time	341
Hasten, sinner, to be wise,	377
Hear the footsteps of Jesus,	80
HEAVEN IS MY HOME,	309
HE COMES,	154
HE IS CALLING,	239
HE LOVED ME SO,	296
HEM OF HIS GARMENT,	223
Hendon, 7s,	360
Here in thy name we are gathered	14
HE'S MIGHTY TO SAVE,	13
HE WILL GATHER THE WHEAT,	176
HE WILL HIDE ME.	132
HE WILL HIDE THEE,	16
HIM THAT COMETH UNTO ME,	70
HIS CHILD I WANT TO BE,	141
HIS YOKE IS EASY,	27
Holy Ghost, with light divine,	378
Holy, holy, holy,	274
Holy Spirit, faithful guide,	197
HOME AT LAST,	92
HOME OF THE SOUL,	122
Horton,	372
How blest the man whose	416
How blest the righteous,	286
How do thy mercies close me	311
How firm a foundation,	359
How gentle God's commands!	444
How happy every child of grace,	433
How happy is the youth who hears	398
How oft, alas! this wretched heart	402
How sweet and awful is the place	401
How sweet is the Sabbath, the m.	356
How sweet the name of Jesus	447
Hursley, L. M.	276
I am coming to the cross,	271
I am passing down the valley,	7
I bring my sins to thee,	171
I could not do without thee,	459
I entered once a home of care,	152
I gave my life for thee,	73
I have a song, I love to sing,	79
I have read of a beautiful city,	194
I heard the voice of Jesus say,	429
I lay my sins on Jesus,	458
I'LL LIVE FOR HIM,	263

I love thy kingdom, Lord,	335
I love to steal awhile away,	436
I love to tell the story,	86
I'm but a stranger here,	309
I must have the Saviour with me,	121
In a world so full of weeping,	218
In darkness I wandered till Jesus	144
In some way or other, the Lord	253
In the Christian's home in glory,	227
In the cross of Christ I glory,	405
In the dark and cloudy day,	95
In the hour of darkness,	138
In the hush of early morning,	34
In the midnight silent watches,	211
IN THE MORNING,	20
In the murmur of the breeze,	159
In the shadow of his wings,	17
In thy book where glory bright,	21
In this sinful world I'm walking,	26
In vain, in high and holy lays,	113
I SHALL BE SATISFIED,	9
IS MY NAME WRITTEN THERE?	93
IT FILLS MY HEART WITH JOY,	145
I thirst, thou wounded Lamb,	289
IT IS WELL WITH MY SOUL,	163
I've a message from the Lord,	4
I've been to the field with the	185
I've reached the land of corn and	178
I waited for the Lord, my God,	411
I was a wandering sheep,	417
I will bless the Lord,	138
I will praise him, I will praise	206
I will sing of my Redeemer,	174
I will sing when morning cometh,	24
I will sing you a song of that	122
I would not live alway,	316
Jerusalem, my happy home,	430
Jerusalem, the golden,	349
Jesus, and shall it ever be,	312
Jesus, engrave it on my heart	278
Jesus, I come to thee,	25
Jesus, I love thy charming name,	369
Jesus, I my cross have taken,	267
JESUS IS MINE,	262
Jesus is the light, the way,	169
Jesus is waiting his grace to be-	18
Jesus is waiting to welcome the	5
Jesus, lover of my soul!	386
Jesus, my strength, my hope!	418
JESUS SAVES,	116
Jesus, Saviour, pilot me,	127
Jesus shall reign where'er the sun	305
Jesus! the name high over all,	344
Jesus, the very thought of thee	413
Jesus, thou art the sinner's friend	400
Jesus when he left the sky,	183
Jesus, who knows full well,	423
Jewett. 6s,	273
JOYFULLY SING,	217
JOYFUL PRAISE,	38
JOY IN HEAVEN,	137
Joy to the world, the Lord is come	347
Just as I am, without one plea,	291
Keep thy faith steady, my brother	153
Laban, S. M.	427
Land ahead! its fruits are	234
Leading souls to Jesus who are	162
LEAD ME, SAVIOUR,	15
LEANING ON JESUS,	168
Lebanon, S. M. D.	417
Lenox, H. M.	281
LET HIM IN,	148
Let us ask the precious Saviour,	85
Let us endeavor to speak for the	182
Let us gather up the sunbeams,	213
LET YOUR LIGHT SHINE,	181
Lift the voice in holy song,	188
Light after darkness, gain after	135
Light in our darkness, hope,	43
Like an army we are marching.	40
LITTLE FRIENDS OF JESUS,	111
Little children of Jesus,	90
LITTLE ONES LIKE ME,	188
Little voices, happy voices,	175
Living for Jesus, living for Jesus,	126
LOOK AND LIVE,	4
Look up, behold the fields are	110
Look, ye saints, the sight is glori-	203
Lord, dismiss us with thy blessing	321
Lord God, the Holy Ghost,	330
Lord, I am thine, entirely thine,	288
Lord, I care not for riches neither.	93
Lord, I hear of showers of bless-.	87
Lord, teach us how to pray,	333
Lo! 'round the throne a glorious.	306
Lo! the day of rest declineth,	320
Lo! the stone is rolled away,	364
Love divine, all love excelling,	350
Loving kindness, L. M.	461
Low in the grave he lay,	164
Luther, S. M.	335
Luton, L. M.	284
Maitland, C. M.	173
MAKING MELODY,	24
Make room for Jesus,	139
MARCHING ON,	11
March steadily onward to the bat-	230
Master, the tempest is raging!	228
May the grace of Christ, our	323, 383
MEET ME THERE,	60
Mendebras, 7s, 6s,	325
Meribah, C. P. M.	315
'Mid scenes of confusion and crea-	47
Missionary chant, L. M.	294
MIZPAH,	95
More about Jesus, would I know,	180

More like Jesus,	57	O Lord, thy perfect word	441
Must Jesus bear the cross alone,	173	O love divine, how sweet thou	366
My body, soul and spir t,	107	On Calv'ry's brow my Saviour	165
My country, 'tis of thee,	252	One more day its twilight brings,	142
My faith looks up to thee,	462	One sweetly solemn thought.	250
My Father is rich in houses and	72	One there is above all others,	384
My gracious Lord! I own thy	314	Only a beam of sunshine,	84
My hope is built on nothing less,	355	Only believe,	146
My Jesus, as thou wilt,	273	Only Jesus, blessed Jesus,	112
My Jesus, I love thee,	352	Only remembered,	235
My life, my love, I give to thee,	263	On Jordan's stormy banks I stand	283
My Redeemer,	174	On the sweet Eden shore,	219
My Saviour stands waiting,	226	On the happy, golden shore,	60
My Shepherd,	82	On the mountain's top appearing.	382
My soul, be on thy guard,	428	Onward,	242
My soul in sad exile was out on	160	Onward still, and upward,	74
My soul, repeat his praise,	422	O praise his name,	210
My times are in thy hand,	440	O that my load of sin were gone,	287
Naomi, C. M.	256	O the bitter shame and sorrow,	255
Nature's praise,	158	O thou God of my salvation,	125
Nearer home,	250	O thou to whose all-search'ng	280
Nearer, my God, to thee,	310	Our Father which art in heaven,	348
Nearer to thee,	65	Our Sunday-school,	109
Nettleton,	318	Out on the cold, cold mountain,	438
Not all the blood of beasts,	426	Out on the midnight deep,	44
Not half has ever been told,	194	Over the ocean wave,	109
Not what I feel or do,	442	Over the tide,	177
Now be the gospel banner	326	Park street, L. M.	306
Now the day is over,	225	Passing homeward, O how gladly	102
Now to the Lord a noble song,	307	People of the living God,	388
O bless the Lord, our souls and	52	Peterborough, C. M.	411
O could I speak the matchless	367	Pleyel's hymn, 7s,	376
O day of rest and gladness,	325	Plunged in a gulf of dark despair	449
Of him, who did salvation bring,	454	Portuguese hymn,	359
O for a closer walk with God,	415	Praise and magnify our King,	202
O for a heart to praise my God,	399	Praise him for his glory,	56
O for a thousand tongues to sing.	346	Praise the Lord,	188
Of thy love, some gracious token,	410	Praise the Lord, the Rock of Ages	210
O give thanks unto the Lord,	28	Praise ye the Lord! joyfully.	232
O God, our help in ages past,	403	Praise ye the Lord, the hope of	47
O happy day that fixed my choice	272	Praise the Saviour; O ye people,	199
Oh, bless the Lord, my soul, let	420	Prayer is the key,	157
Oh, come with hearts rejoicing,	208	Press on, press on, ye workers, be	134
Oh! do not let the word depart,	191	Press onward,	167
O heavenly Father, thou hast told	207	Rathbun, 8s, 7s,	405
Oh, I often sit and ponder,	8	Remember me,	400
Oh, that the Lord would guide	448	Rest by and by,	185
Oh, the song of the soul shall not.	54	Rest in Jesus,	298
Oh, to be like him, tender and	221	Rest for the weary,	227
Oh, to be over yonder!	94	Revive thy work, O Lord, thy	198
Oh, to have the mind of Jesus,	46	Revive us again,	269
Oh, we are young soldiers for Je-	166	Rise, my soul, and stretch thy	342
Oh, where are the reapers that	184	Rockingham, L. M.	454
Oh, why should we wrestle with	146	Rock of Ages, cleft for me,	275
Oh, word of words the sweetest;	224	Safely through another week,	340
O land of rest, for thee I sigh,	257	Safe within the vail,	234
Old hundred, L. M.	279	Saved to the uttermost: I am the.	150
Olmutz, L. M.	426	St. Thomas, S. M.	422

Salvation! O the joyful sound,	392	The everlasting song,	39
Saviour, comfort me!.	95	The firm foundation,	359
Saviour, lead me, lest I stray,	15	The fountain of blessing,	205
Saviour, like a shepherd lead us,	266	The future,	8
Saviour, pilot me,	127	The golden key,.	157
Saviour! visit thy plantation,	322	The great Physician now is here,	75
Scatter seeds of kindness,	213	The haven of rest,	160
Scripture response,	114	The land just across the riv-.	173
See Israel's gentle Shepherd stand,	437	The lights of home,	62
Seeking, calling, knocking,	5	The Lord bless thee,	351
Selvin, S. M.	440	The Lord Jehovah unto all,	404
Shall we meet beyond the river,	460	The Lord is my Shepherd, my	82
Should the summons quickly fly-.	59	The Lord shall comfort Zion,	245
Showers of blessing,.	14	The Lord's my Shepherd, I'll not.	27
Sicily, 8s, 7s,	321	The Lord's prayer,	348
Siloam, C. M.	407	The Lord will provide,	253
Simply trusting every day, trusting	45	The mind of Jesus,	46
Since I have been redeemed,	79	The morning light is breaking,	327
Sing on, ye joyful pilgrims, nor	76	The new name,	129
Sing the dear name softly,	112	The new song,	170
Sing them over again to me,.	81	The prodigal child,	108
Sing unto God, our hope and our	214	There are songs of joy that I love	170
Sing with a tuneful heart, sing	217	There comes to my heart,	12
Sitting at the feet of Jesus,	452	There is a fountain filled with	29
Smyrna,.	265	There is a green hill far away,	240
Softly and tenderly Jesus is calling	200	There is a happy land,	258
Softly fades the twilight ray	209	There is a home eternal,	128
So let our lips and lives express,	455	There is joy, there is joy,	137
Soon may the last, glad song arise	308	There is a land of pure delight,	431
Sowing in the morning, sowing	89	There is an hour of peaceful rest,	412
Spohr, 6s, C. M..	438	There is rest, sweet rest, at the	91
Stand up, and bless the Lord,	337	There's a crown in heaven for the.	204
Stand up, stand up for Jesus,	328	There's a stranger at the door,	148
Steadily marching on,	232	There's a wideness in God's mercy	239
Steersman, steersman, the chan..	62	The Saviour calls, let every ear,	450
Stepping in the light,	23	The Saviour is my all in all,.	50
Steps are before me, dear Saviour,	57	The Saviour with me.	121
Stockwell, 8s, 7s..	353	The song of the soul,	54
Stonefield, L. M..	280	The stranger at the door,	49
Sun of my soul, thou Saviour dear	276	The summer land	118
Sweet home,	251	The ten commandments,	249
Sweet hour of prayer,	435	The tranquil hours steal by,.	406
Sweet is the work, my God, my,	277	The waiting guest,	140
Sweet peace; the gift of God's	12	The whole wide world for Jesus,.	100
Sweet the moments, rich in bless-.	385	The wonderful name,	32
Take the world but give me Jesus	58	Thine earthly Sabbaths, Lord, I	457
Take my life and let it be..	69	This I did for thee,	73
Tarry with me, O my Saviour,	354	This is the day the Lord hath	395
Tell me the story of Jesus,	51	Though your sins be as scarlet,	161
That gentle whisper,	181	Thou shalt not have,—so saith the	249
The altered motto,	255	Thou wilt defend us,	43
The beautiful light,	169	Through all the changing scenes,.	394
The child of a King,.	72	Through the gates of pearl and	196
The children to Jesus may come,	141	Thy Saviour calls! oh, come and	70
The clear light of heaven,	144	Thy word have I hid in my heart	114
The day is past and gone,	332	Time is winging us away,	343
The earth is the Lord's, and the	236	Title clear,	259
The endeavor band,.	108	To-day God is telling a wonderful	55

To-day the Saviour calls,	195	What sinners value I resign,	303
To Father, Son, and Holy Ghost,	393	What! sitting at ease when there's	190
To God, the Father, Son,	339	Whatsoever burden presses on thy	61
Toil on, teachers, toil on boldly	265	What will you do with the King	106
Toplady, 7s,	275	When all thy mercies, O my God,	439
To the summer land of glory	118	When doubt and conflict weigh	65
To us a child of hope is born,	391	When his salvation bringing,	329
TREASURES IN HEAVEN,	204	When I can read my title clear,	259
TRUST AND OBEY,	117	When I shall wake in that	9
Trusting in Jesus,	10	When I survey the wondrous cross	293
TRUSTING JESUS, THAT IS ALL,	45	When Jesus called the little ones,	145
Trying to walk in the steps of the.	23	WHEN JESUS COMES,	35
'Twas a night of long ago	119	When Jesus shall gather the na-	176
Up and away, like the dew of the.	235	When my Saviour I shall see,	216
Up and onward, Christian soldier,	130	When peace, like a river, attendeth	163
Up for Jesus! up and onward!	78	When the mists have rolled in	172
Up to the bountiful Giver of Life,	66	When the morning breaks in	38
VALE OF BEULAH,	7	When the storms of life are.	132
Varina, C. M. D.	429	When the worn spirit wants repose	409
Vespers, 8s, 7s,	320	When thou, my righteous Judge,	315
VICTORY THROUGH GRACE,	6	When we walk with the Lord,	117
Vigil, S. M.	419	Where we oft have met in glad-	381
Wait, my soul, upon the Lord,	365	While in different paths,	453
Wake from thy drowsy sleep, yon-	187	While Jesus whispers to you,	270
WALKING AT HIS SIDE,	26	While life prolongs its precious	290
Ward, L. M.	285	While the years are rolling on,	218
Watchman, tell us of the night,	387	Whilst I seek, protecting	432
Weak and weary, poor and sinful,	223	Who is this that waiteth, waiteth.	140
We are looking away from the	167	Why art thou fearful,	16
WE ARE MORE THAN CONQUERORS	88	Why do you wait, dear brother,	104
We are pilgrims looking home,	20	WHY NOT TO-NIGHT?	191
Weary pilgrim on life's pathway,	149	Will you go to Jesus now, dear	155
Weary with walking alone, long	168	Will you meet me in the morning,	179
Webb, 7s, 6s,	327	*Wilmot, 8s, 7s,*	384
We have come to worship Jesus,	324	Wilt thou be made whole?	80
We have heard a joyful sound,	116	With our colors waving bright.	11
We have wandered far away, from	136	WONDERFUL LOVE OF JESUS,	113
Welcome, sweet day of rest,	424	WONDERFUL STORY OF LOVE,	55
Welcome, welcome, dear Redeem-	319	WONDERFUL WORDS OF LIFE,	81
WE'LL WORK TILL JESUS COMES,	257	*Woodland, C. M..*	412
We praise thee, O God!	269	*Woodstock. C. M.*	436
We shall have a new name,	129	WORDS OF JESUS,	48
WE SHALL KNOW,	172	Work, for the night is coming,	434
We shall walk with him in white,	156	Worthy to be praised is God, my	41
We've listed in a holy war,	63	Yes, for me, for me he careth,	353
What a friend we have in Jesus,	264	Yield not to temptation,	363
WHAT A GATHERING THAT WILL	222	YOUNG SOLDIERS FOR JESUS,	166
What did the angels say! hymn-	32	*Zebulon, C. M.*	317
What glory gilds the sacred page!	390	*Zerah, C. M..*	389
What shall separate us from the	88	*Zion, 8s, 7s, 4s,*	380

www.ingramcontent.com/pod-product-compliance
Lightning Source LLC
Chambersburg PA
CBHW032353230426
43672CB00007B/691